THE PRELUDE TO THE REFORMATION

RICHARD FOX, BISHOP OF WINCHESTER

Frontispiece

STUDIES IN CHURCH HISTORY

THE PRELUDE TO THE REFORMATION

A STUDY OF ENGLISH CHURCH LIFE FROM THE AGE OF WYCLIFFE TO THE BREACH WITH ROME

BY

R. S. ARROWSMITH, M.A.

RECTOR OF SEALE, SURREY

WITH TWO PORTRAITS

LONDON
SOCIETY FOR PROMOTING
CHRISTIAN KNOWLEDGE
NEW YORK AND TORONTO: THE MACMILLAN CO.
1923

Printed in Great Britain.

PREFACE

In the following pages an attempt is made to give, from reliable contemporary documents, some account of English Church life in the century and a half which preceded the breach with Rome. My treatment of the period lays no claim to being in any way adequate or exhaustive. Exigencies of space have precluded any treatment of the Friars, or of the survival and influence of Lollardy, or of the relation between the Renaissance and the Reformation. Each of these subjects demands (and deserves) a separate monograph. The present work is simply a sketch of certain aspects of Church life, and in no sense a formal history. What is termed the Reformation was no sudden Movement forced upon the Church by an obscure student in Germany, or by an autocratic sovereign in England, but was the result of causes which had long been at work, and which made reformation, in some form or another and sooner or later, inevitable. The Movement can, therefore, only be understood by reference to the events which long preceded it, and to the life, work and general conditions—intellectual, social, political and religious—of the Church in the 15th and first quarter of the 16th centuries.

During the last few years much new light has been thrown upon Church life during this period by the publication of a number of episcopal registers, more particularly the splendid series of those of the Bishops of Hereford, edited by Canon Bannister; and by the recent publication of the very full and illuminating episcopal *Visitations* of certain religious houses in the diocese of Lincoln in the first half of the 15th century. These *Visitations*, edited by Mr. Hamilton

Thompson, form the most valuable material yet discovered for giving us a knowledge of the internal life of the houses to which they relate. Similar visitations are not known to have survived, so that it is not likely that much further light of a similar nature can in future be thrown upon the internal conditions of the religious houses.

It may, perhaps, be objected that in the following pages the less attractive side of Church life has been emphasised at the expense of the brighter and happier. The criticism is just. There are, however, several books (easily accessible), such as the writings of Cardinal Gasquet, which deal with this latter aspect of Church life; and it would have been superfluous to repeat what has been so well done by abler writers. It must also be remembered that the period dealt with is a period of *decline*, when the Church was suffering from spiritual apathy, ecclesiastical abuses, and the depressing atmosphere of a difficult time. As Bishop Stubbs says in the chapter which closes his great work: "The most enthusiastic admirer of medieval life must grant that all that was good and great in it was languishing even to death. The sun of the Plantagenets went down in clouds and thick darkness; the coming of the Tudors gave as yet no promise of light." "The attenuated life of the later Middle Age is in thorough discrepancy with the grand conceptions of the earlier times." "Literature has reached the lowest depths of dulness: religion, so far as its chief results are traceable, has sunk, on the one hand into a dogma fenced about with walls which its defenders cannot pass either inward or outward, on the other hand into a mere war-cry of the cause of destruction."[1]

We cannot expect to find the Church at its best in an age like that. Nor do we; and the evidence must be fairly faced. Yet in forming conclusions it must not be forgotten that institutions (like individuals) may legitimately claim to be judged at their best rather than at their worst, by

[1] *Constit. Hist.*, III, pp. 632, 634.

their virtues quite as much as by their faults, by their positive achievements more than by their deficiencies and failures. The history of the Christian Church is a history of vicissitudes and a strange and perplexing blend of ages of spiritual languor and decadence with ages of faith and revival. The 15th century is only an episode in Church history, which must be surveyed as a whole; for there is always the danger, in dealing with a period of decline, of placing undue emphasis upon the dark side. The object of the following pages is certainly not to bring a general indictment against the later medieval Church, its clergy and institutions, but rather to show from reliable contemporary evidence the conditions which prevailed in the English Church in a difficult and depressing period, as well as to indicate the pressing need of radical reform in so many departments of Church life. It might not have been difficult, by undue emphasis on darker aspects, to frame an indictment, more particularly from the Visitation documents (to which readers are referred in order that they may form their own conclusions) relating to certain religious houses. But I have had no wish either to frame an indictment or to compose a panegyric, but rather to write of things as they are, remembering the warning:—

> Nothing extenuate
> Nor set down aught in malice.

I can only trust that the evidence has been fairly given, and that no prejudiced or unjustifiable conclusions have been drawn. That I have succeeded in this aim, I am not (I hope) so foolish as to suppose.

Though I neither wish nor ask for a more lenient judgment on that account, yet it is obvious that a country parson, living far from books and libraries, distracted (too) from study by parochial duties, has neither the opportunity nor the leisure to deal so thoroughly or so accurately with a difficult subject as professional students who live in the midst of public libraries and intellectual life. This will account for (though not excuse) many defects in the following pages.

In conclusion, I should like to express my sincere thanks to Mr. G. G. Coulton of Cambridge for his kindness in lending me books and referring me to authorities; and to Mr. Hamilton Thompson for allowing me to quote from his Introduction to the *Lincoln Visitations*, and for the trouble which he so readily and kindly took in reading the proofs of Chapter VII, as well as for his invaluable advice. Neither of these scholars is responsible for any of the opinions expressed or for any of the conclusions drawn in the book.

To the late Canon Vaughan (a personal friend), whose recent death is so great a loss to the diocese of Winchester, I am indebted for invaluable help with the unpublished register of Bishop Fox.

R. S. A.

November, 1922.

CONTENTS

ILLUSTRATIONS

ABBREVIATIONS

USED IN THE NOTES

Arch.	= *Archæologia.*
Coll.	= *Collectanea Anglo-Premonstratensia,* 3 vols. (Camden Soc.), ed. by Cardinal Gasquet. [Visitations by Bishop Redman of the Premonstratensian Houses in England, in the last quarter of the 15th century.]
Concilia.	= *Concilia Magnæ Britanniæ et Hiberniæ,* 446–1717, 4 vols., ed. David Wilkins, 1737.
Coulton, Social Life.	= *Social Life in Britain from the Conquest to the Reformation,* by G. G. Coulton.
D.N.B.	= *Dictionary of National Biography.*
Deanesley.	= *The Lollard Bible,* by Miss Deanesley.
Dugdale.	= *Monasticon,* 3 vols., 1655–73, by David Dugdale.
E.E.T.S.	= *Early English Text Society.*
Educ. Charters.	= *Educational Charters,* ed. by A. F. Leach.
Gascoigne.	= *The Dictionary of Theology,* by Dr. Thomas Gascoigne, ed. Thorold Rogers.
Gasquet, Monasteries.	= *Henry VIII and the English Monasteries,* by Cardinal Gasquet.
Gee and Hardy.	= *Documents Illustrative of English Church History,* ed. by Gee and Hardy.
Italian Relation.	= *A Relation of the Island of England,* c. 1500, by an Italian (Camden Soc.).
L.V.	= *Visitations of Religious Houses in the Diocese of Lincoln,* from the Registers of Flemyng, Gray and Alnwick, ed. by A. Hamilton Thompson.

Leadam, Select Cases. = *Select Cases before the Star Chamber*, 1477–1509, ed. I. S. Leadam.

L. and P. = Letters and Papers, Foreign and Domestic, of the reign of Henry VIII, ed. Brewer. (Rolls Series.)

Liber Albus. = *The Liber Albus of Worcester Cathedral Priory*, ed. Canon Wilson.

Lupton. = *Life of Dean Colet*, by J. H. Lupton.

N.V. = *Visitations of the Diocese of Norwich*, 1492–1532, ed. Jessopp.

P.L. = *Paston Letters*, ed. Gairdner.

Rashdall. = *Universities of Europe in the Middle Ages*, by H. Rashdall.

Reg. = *Register*.

Savine. = *English Monasteries on the Eve of the Reformation* (Oxford Studies in Social and Legal History), by Prof. Savine.

Sur. Soc. = *Surtees Society*.

V.C.H. = *Victoria County Histories*.

Valor Eccles. = *Valor Ecclesiasticus*, c. 1534, ed. Caley, 6 vols., 1810–34.

Watson, Gr. Sch. = *The English Grammar Schools to* 1660, by Foster Watson.

Yorks Arch. = *Yorkshire Archæological Journal*.

THE PRELUDE TO THE REFORMATION

CHAPTER I

THE LATER MEDIEVAL BISHOP

IN thinking of the medieval bishop we must dismiss from our minds modern conceptions of a bishop and his work. A bishop of the Church of England to-day spends a large part of his time in the train or the episcopal motor, rushing from one engagement to another; devotes hours daily to an enormous correspondence, for the post and the telegraph put him in touch with the most distant parts of his diocese; is engaged during half the year upon an arduous confirmation tour; and (such are our modern requirements) has to attend an endless succession of meetings, both secular and religious, where he is expected to speak at a moment's notice upon the most diverse subjects.

Contrast between the medieval and the modern bishop.

The life and work of a medieval bishop were quite different. In one respect, however, the conditions were similar; for, like many of his successors to-day, the medieval bishop had to rule over a diocese which covered so wide an area as to be practically unworkable. At the close of the fifteenth century there were twenty-one dioceses in England and Wales, many of which were enormous in size.[1] The diocese of Exeter included the two large

Large medieval dioceses.

[1] Canterbury, London, Winchester, Bangor, Bath and Wells, Chichester, Ely, Exeter, Hereford, Lichfield and Coventry, Lincoln, Llandaff, Norwich, Rochester, St. Asaph, St. David's, Salisbury, Worcester, York, Durham, Carlisle. Sodor and Man was not united to

counties of Devonshire and Cornwall; the diocese of Winchester the counties of Surrey and Hampshire, together with the Isle of Wight and the Channel Islands;[1] the diocese of York the whole of Yorkshire, together with the county of Nottingham; the diocese of Lichfield the counties of Staffordshire, Cheshire, Lancashire, Shropshire, Warwick, and Derby; while the diocese of Lincoln stretched from the Humber to the Thames, and included, besides the county of Lincoln, which is itself the third largest in England, the counties of Leicester, Northampton, Rutland, Huntingdon, Bedford, Buckingham, Oxford, and part of Herts. Bishops complain to-day that they find it difficult to visit all their parishes because of the size of their dioceses, but what must it have been in the Middle Ages, in a great diocese like York or Lincoln, at a time when there were no railways or motors or even coaches, and when, owing to the bad state of the roads, the wide stretches of forest, moor, and fen, and the presence of highwaymen and outlaws, travelling was not only slow and difficult, but highly dangerous as well? In 1362 Archbishop Islip was riding on horseback in Kent, paying a visit to his diocese. The roads were so bad that his horse stuck fast in the deep mud; the Archbishop was thrown and was drenched to the skin; as a result, he caught a chill which proved fatal.[2]

Difficulty of travel in the Middle Ages.

No bishop in the Middle Ages could possibly have visited all the parishes under his charge, even if he had resided constantly in the diocese, and had spent his whole time in attending to his episcopal duties. But it sometimes happened that a medieval bishop never set foot inside his diocese at all.[3] Some were

Bishops were often non-resident.

the Province of York until 1542. Henry VIII created the following new dioceses in 1541–2: Bristol, Gloucester, Peterborough, Oxford, Chester, and Westminster, the latter of which was suppressed a few years later. See a very useful map of the dioceses in the time of Henry VIII in *Dict. Eng. Ch. Hist.*

[1] The Channel Islands were transferred from the spiritual jurisdiction of the Bishop of Coutances to that of the Bishop of Winchester in the year 1500 by a Bull of Alexander VI.

[2] Denton, *England in 15th Cent.*, p. 179. For bad state of 15th-cent. roads see Bennett, *The Pastons and their England*, c. X.

[3] Thomas Polton, Bp. of Chichester 1422–6, never visited his diocese, *Reg. Polton*, p. ii.

foreigners and lived abroad.[1] Silvester de Gigleis, Bishop of Worcester (1499–21), Wolsey's great friend and ally, lived at the papal court; Cardinal Campeggio was Bishop of Salisbury (1525–35), but was absent from his diocese, chiefly in Italy, the whole time; Dr. Robert Sherborne, Bishop of Chichester, was for a long period Henry VIII's agent at Rome to further the King's wishes in the matter of preferments in the English Church; Cardinal Bainbrigge, Archbishop of York (1508–14), lived and died at Rome. Many other bishops who had perhaps less excuse for non-residence write that they are far too much occupied with other matters to give personal attention to the affairs of their dioceses.[2]

A typical 15th-century bishop.

What precisely these other matters were we are not always informed; but the vague expression would serve as a general excuse; while the truth of the matter often was that the average medieval bishop preferred to spend the greater part of his time in London to doing his duty in his diocese. Take a typical bishop of the 15th century, Nicholas Bubwith, Bishop of Bath and Wells (1407–24). His itinerary has been preserved,[3] and we find that in 1410 he left his diocese for London on January 28th, and remained there during February, March, April, May and June. During these months he was certainly not idle, for he was genuinely engaged in State affairs; but in July it suddenly occurred to him, just when the King was trying to borrow money from his "faithful servants" (the Bishop had already lent him 500 marks), that he had better make some return, in the shape of the performance of episcopal duties, for his many thousands a year. So he went down to his diocese and made a short stay, first at Wells and then at Woolsey; but the diocese was remote, the country clergy were dull, stupid and often refractory, the work was irksome and distasteful, the expense of hospitality was great, affairs of State were pressing, and (weighing up all these considerations) the good bishop, thinking at the beginning of August

[1] The following foreigners held English Sees in the reign of the first two Tudors: John and Silvester Gigleis, J. de Medici, J. de Ghinucci (all Worcester), Adrian de Castello (B. and W.), Campeggio (Sarum); for It. Bps. of Worcester, Creighton, *Hist. Essays*.

[2] e.g. *Reg. Lacy*, p. 571; *Reg. Mylling*, p. ii.

[3] *Reg. Bubwith*, pp. xl–xliii.

that he had now performed sufficient episcopal functions to justify his existence, decided to return to town. He found it very much pleasanter, especially in winter, to live in his delightful London house, beautifully situated as it was by the banks of the Thames, in the centre of political and social life, surrounded by friends, enjoying all the luxuries of the Capital, than to travel about in a remote country district, amid dull country people and continually bothered with the worries and details of episcopal administration. He decided, therefore, that duty (duty and pleasure happily coinciding) called him to remain in London for the winter, and did not permit him to return to his diocese until the following year.

But though love of London life and disinclination for banishment to remote country regions may account for much neglect and non-residence, the chief cause, undoubtedly, of the absence of prelates from their dioceses was that many of them were engaged in affairs of State, and had no time for their ecclesiastical duties. John Stanbury remained in his diocese about a month after his enthronement in 1453, and during the next ten years only paid very occasional visits, being in constant attendance at the court of Henry VI. Flemyng and Gray, Bishops of Lincoln in the early part of the 15th century, were frequently out of England, engaged in the business of the State. These are only a few instances out of many which prove how impossible it was for statesmen-ecclesiastics to attend to their spiritual duties. As Fox put it, they could not "on account of much business touching our lord the King and the condition and defence of the Universal Church and the realm of England continually reside in their dioceses."[1] In fact, many of them were statesmen by profession and ecclesiastics only in name. The King paid his ministers by appointing them to great posts in the Church, and it was clearly understood that they were to devote their whole time to secular pursuits.[2] They were chief ministers of the Crown, like Beaufort and Wolsey;

Many bishops too much occupied with State duties to attend to their dioceses.

[1] *Reg. Fox* (B. and W.), p. 1. See also *Reg. Mayew*, p. 230; *Reg. Bubwith*, p. 185; *Reg. Stanbury*, p. iii.

[2] It would almost seem that their State duties were regarded as more important than their ecclesiastical, for Bishop Mayew had to get a special licence to absent himself from Parliament, *Reg. Mayew*, p. 208.

or lord chancellors, like Morton and Warham; or ambassadors, like Fox, engaged in delicate foreign negotiations which often took them out of England. Highly indeed were they rewarded for their services to the King. The Secretary of Henry VIII, Thomas Ruthall, became Bishop of Durham; the Master of the Rolls, Cuthbert Tunstall, was given the Bishopric of London; Warham became Primate; Wolsey united in himself all possible ecclesiastical preferments; while Fox, the Lord Treasurer, a good man and no unscrupulous self-seeker, did not lack for earthly reward. In quick succession he received the wealthy and important Bishoprics of Exeter (1487–92), Bath and Wells (1492–94), Durham (1494–1501), and Winchester, the latter of which he held until his death in 1528. These were the rewards not of service to the Church, but of service to the King and the State. Is it any wonder that prelates who were ambassadors, ministers of the Crown, lord chancellors, or even courtiers, had but little leisure or inclination to visit their remote dioceses? Archbishop Kempe, who died in 1452, was Archbishop of York for twenty-eight years; but during the whole of that time he was, with the exception of a few days' visit once in ten or a dozen years, absent from his diocese, residing chiefly in London.[1] In the following century there was another Archbishop of York, Cardinal Wolsey, who until his fall never went near his diocese. Fox was a bishop for forty-one years; but of these forty-one by far the larger portion were spent outside his diocese in the performance of secular duties. While Bishop of Exeter (1487–92) he never once set foot inside his diocese; and it was only towards the close of his long episcopate at Winchester, when he was old and blind and feeble, that he made any attempt to attend seriously to his diocesan duties. In 1522, on retiring from State affairs, he wrote to Wolsey:

Splendid ecclesiastical reward for State duties.

Instances of non-residence.

Kempe.

Wolsey.

Fox.

[1] Gascoigne, p. 37, says he was never in the city of York; but Gascoigne's prejudices have led him into error. Kempe was in York in 1440, when he held a visitation of the Cathedral Chapter. He was lord chancellor for many years, and on account of his absorption in State affairs Eugenius IV dispensed him from personal visitations. His diocese was well managed by capable officials. See *Visitations of the Diocese and Province of York,* Sur. Soc., cxxvii, pp. 201–90.

"Truly, my singular good lord, since the King's grace licensed me to remain in my Church, and thereabouts upon my care wherein I have been almost by the space of thirty years so negligent that of the four several Cathedral Churches that I have successively held there be two, Exeter and Wells, that I have never seen; and innumerable souls whereof I have never seen the bodies. . . . I have determined and betwixt God and me utterly renounced the meddling with worldly matters, thinking if I did continual penance for it all the days of my life, though I should live twenty years longer than I may do, I could not yet make sufficient recompense therefore."[1]

Diocesan administration in the bishop's absence.

At the same time it must be admitted that the administration of the diocese suffered much less than might have been expected from the absence of its chief. By the 15th century episcopal functions had become completely stereotyped; there was little of that personal touch between bishop and clergy which counts for so much; the greater part of the work was purely official, and so numerous and so highly organised were the officials of a medieval prelate that, even under the least satisfactory bishops, the routine work of the diocese still went on. During their absence the administration was placed in the hands of a Vicar-General, or Vicars-General, officials of the Bishop to whom he entrusted his *potestas jurisdictionis*, which included large powers of oversight and often of patronage.[2] They also employed the services of assistant bishops, who were entrusted with the diocesan's *potestas ordinis*, and performed certain other episcopal functions, but who were (apparently) placed under the direction of the Vicars-General and could only act with their authority and under their instruction. As a rule, they went where their services were required, and took some outlandish title such as that of the Suffragan of Bishop Lacy of Exeter, Bishop Richard Catensis, or the Suffragan of Bishop Bubwith, who was known by the somewhat uncompromising title of the Bishop of Innis-Scattery.[3]

[1] *L. and P.*, iii, 2207.

[2] The Bp. of Hereford, in 1429, appointed the Bp. of Norwich to act for him in presenting to vacant benefices during his absence abroad, *Reg. Spofford*, p. 117.

[3] See *Reg. Bubwith*, pp. 185, 374; *Reg. Lacy*, p. 571; *Reg. Spofford*,

Bishops like Fox, in spite of their absorption in affairs of State, took an interest in their dioceses, and did their best (apart from personal residence) to maintain order, discipline and sound doctrine. The Vicars-General had stringent injunctions to punish scandals and correct immorality both among the clergy and the laity, and archdeacons were frequently warned to remedy abuses. In 1508 Fox issued a very solemn monition to the Archdeacon of Winchester to visit his parishes; find out whether the eucharistic chrism and oil were kept under lock and key; make strict inquiries about ornaments, books, fabrics, dilapidations; and scrutinise the teaching given by the clergy, whether it was regular, efficient and orthodox.[1] But performance of duty by proxy is not a very conscientious method of earning one's income, nor did it tend to the influence or popularity of the episcopal Order.

Great wealth and power of the medieval bishop.

Between the medieval bishop and his clergy there was a great gulf fixed. To begin with, the bishop was not only a spiritual lord and the head of the diocese: he was a peer of the realm and a great territorial magnate as well. His wealth, his palaces, his manors, his patronage, his power, his position in the nation were splendid indeed. The Bishop of Durham ruled as a prince in the north, with his own court, his own army, his own mint, his own legal authority. His income amounted to about £34,000 a year; and he owned, beside several manors and houses, the three great castles of Durham, Norham and Auckland, as well as Durham Place in the Strand. The Bishopric of Winchester was even wealthier, being, indeed, the wealthiest See in England. Bishop Fox enjoyed an income of about £50,000 a year.[2] He owned

p. 26. For commissions from the Vicars-General to Suffragans see *Reg. Fox* (B. and W.), p. 1; *Reg. Mayew*, pp. 230–2. For the appointment and duties of a Suffragan see *Reg. Bothe*, p. 16.

[1] *Reg. Fox* (Winton), ii, f. 97.

[2] For episcopal incomes from the *Valor Ecclesiasticus* (1535) see *Appendix*. The figures given above represent approximately the value of the English sovereign in 1913, on the eve of the Great War. The income of the See of Winchester for 1522, after deducting necessary outgoings, is given by Fox as £3691 11s. 11d. (*Reg. Fox*, V, f. 94). The *Valor* returns it as £3880, which Leach regards as equal to £75,000 (*Hist. Win. Coll.*, pp. 59, 241). The value of the Bishopric in 1850 was £28,000. For Wykeham's income and houses see his *Reg.*, II,

sixteen manors, ten in and six outside the diocese, as well as Farnham Castle, the palaces of Wolvesey and Bishop's Waltham, and Winchester House in London. He was richer than the Archbishop of Canterbury; for, as he once gently reminded Warham at a time when the relations between them were somewhat strained, "If Canterbury had the higher rack, Winchester had the deeper manger." Nor were less important bishoprics far behind in power and wealth. The Bishop of Exeter had an income of £18,800, enjoyed a large amount of patronage, and was possessed of fourteen houses, among which were the palace at Exeter, various parks and manors, and Exeter House, a very charming riverside residence in the Strand. The Bishop of Bath and Wells had an even greater position and received an even more princely income. In 1405 it was returned at a figure equalling £20,000; and for residences there were the palace at Wells, eight manor houses in Somersetshire, a favourite place at Dogmersfield in Hampshire and Bath House in the Strand.[1] However kindly or fatherly bishops might wish to be, it was inevitable that between great territorial magnates like these and the lower clergy, many of whom were on the verge of destitution, there was, as between Dives and Lazarus, a great gulf fixed. The "lower" clergy had, in fact, come to look upon bishops not as fathers in God or as spiritual leaders, but rather as great absentee landlords, whose chief business was the exaction of taxes, fees and fines; as masters appointed to maintain discipline and punish offenders; as great rulers to be feared and obeyed, rather than trusted or loved.[2]

p. ix. The great wealth of bishops may be gauged by the fact that for the subsidy of 1523 the assessment on Magdalen and New Colleges, the two richest in Oxford, was £333 6s. 8d. each; while the charge on Warham was £1000; on Fox £2000; on Wolsey £4000, Fowler, *Hist.*, *C.C.C.*, p. 19.

[1] *Reg. Fox* (ed. Batten), pp. 14, 26. It should be added that manors in various parts of his diocese were necessary to a bishop. He required them as resting-places when visiting the diocese, and as centres where local clergy might come to see him.

[2] The Bishops had great power and could, if the clergy proved refractory, call in the secular arm to enforce their pains and penalties. See *Reg. Mylling*, p. 56; *Reg. Bubwith*, pp. 66–7. In 1524 Bothe of Hereford placed the church of Garway under an interdict because the parishioners refused to pay procurations and slighted his authority *Reg. Bothe*, p. 151.

But if the medieval bishop had great wealth, he had also great expenses and great responsibilities. He had to maintain a large staff of servants and dependents; travelling in great state with a large retinue was very expensive; and the upkeep of his houses, manors, palaces and parks must have run away with a large part of his income. Hospitality, too, of which he was expected to be very profuse to all comers, was a heavy drain upon his purse; while he was constantly being called upon to pay out large sums in subsidies, procurations, and grants both to the Pope and to the King. The expenses of great magnates like the Bishop of Durham, who was a prince as well as a prelate, were extremely heavy. Ruthall, writing to Wolsey in 1513, explains that the heavy demands constantly made upon his income prevent him from building, and adds: "I brought hither with me eight tunne of wine, and our Lord be thanked I have not two tunne left at this hour, and this is fair utterance in two months, and shame it is to say how many beeves and muttons have been spent in my house, besides other fresh meats, wheat, malt, fish and such baggage; on my faith you would marvel if my pastures had not been somewhat stocked beforehand, for 300 persons some day is but a small number, and of these days I have many, besides sixty or eighty beggars at the gate; and this is the way to keep a man poor."[1] It was indeed. Still, even if one has to spend a large proportion of it in profuse hospitality, it is not altogether a hardship to have at one's disposal a great princely income; and in any case, at least one is not reduced to the miserable seven marks, which was the miserable pittance of a miserable vicar.

The medieval bishop had great expenses and responsibilities.

The Bishop of Durham.

What class of men rose to the episcopate in the later medieval English Church? A glance at the list is interesting. Some of them bear aristocratic names, and we find among them a Neville, Arundel, Scroope, Bourchier, Peveril, Beauchamp, Lacy, Marmaduke Lumley, Woodville, Courtenay, Beaufort, Stafford, Clifford. But the Church was not un-

[1] Batten, *Reg. Fox*, p. 35. Neville's installation feast as Archbp. of York in 1464 was of astounding extravagance. At the table of the great E. of Warwick the flesh of six entire oxen was sometimes consumed at a single meal. For the expenses and regal state of a great nobleman see *The Earl of Northumberland's* (b. 1477) *Household Book*,

democratic, and side by side with the élite are the names of many who rose by their own ability, without the recommendation of birth or wealth or influence.[1] Three famous prelates sprang from the lower middle class—Wykeham, Chichele and Fox. Quite ordinary names appear in the episcopal lists—Hill, Young, Sampson, Wells, Green, Bell, Brown and Smith. Some of the bishops, like Beaufort and Courtenay, obtained bishoprics no doubt by right of their aristocratic birth ; some, like Mylling of Hereford (1474–92), who came from Westminster, where he was abbot, had been monks ; Mayhew of Hereford (1504–16) had had a distinguished career at the University of Oxford, having been President of Magdalen for many years, and was sixty-five on his appointment to Hereford ; but a considerable percentage gained their bishoprics solely as a reward for secular work in the service of the King.[2] Of the bishops from 1380–1530 the large majority were quite undistinguished, and rendered no conspicuous service either to the State or to the Church, either to literature or to learning.

The 15th-century bishop not highly regarded.

If we are to judge by contemporary evidence (which is by no means always unprejudiced), the episcopal Order was not, at any rate in the 15th century, held in very high esteem. Gower at the beginning of the century bitterly attacks the bishops for their greed and love of wealth. They seek the mitre "non ut prosint, sed ut præsint," not to do good, but to get goods. In 1414 the University of Oxford used some very plain speaking about the prelates of the age. It stated that they were unworthy of their responsibilities ; called them blind leaders of the blind ; and added that they possessed not the virtue of truth, but the vice of avarice, the root of all evil.[3]

[1] In 1392 the writer of *Piers Plowman's Crede* complains that every cobbler's son and every beggar's brat can become bishops :—

> Now mot ich soutere hys sone seten to schole
> And ich a beggeres brol on the book lerne,
> And worth to (become) a writere and with a lorde dwelle
> So if that beggares brol a bychop shal worthen,
> Among the peres of the lond prese to sytten.

[2] Spofford (1422–48) and Boulers (1451–3) had been monks ; Stanbury (1453–74) was a White Friar.

[3] Non virtute, moribus, et scientia, satis indigni qui ad præfata onera impudenter se ingerunt et admissi coeci coecos ducunt . . quibus

In the middle of the century Dr. Gascoigne (possibly in revenge for not being made a bishop himself) is vehement in his attacks on the bishops. There was William Booth (he tells us), the Bishop of Lichfield, quite an illiterate man, of dubious character, who had never taken a degree, who had been but a common lawyer and who had been thrust into the See by a papal Provision which he had obtained from Nicholas V. There was Archbishop Stafford (1443–52), the Lord Chancellor, who was reputed to be the least respected churchman of the day. There was George Neville, the boy bishop, who was appointed Bishop of Exeter when he was under twenty-one, but was allowed by the Pope to enjoy the temporalities of his See on condition that his consecration was postponed until he was twenty-seven. There was a more scandalous case still. In 1452 De la Bere, Bishop of St. David's, refused to allow his clergy to put away their mistresses, because if they did so he would lose the fines which were payable for episcopal permission to keep mistresses. He had been thrust into the bishopric by Pope Nicholas V.[1] The bishops of the middle of the 15th century were as a class (so Gascoigne informs us) held in general dislike and contempt, on account of their evil example, their greed, their failure to preach, to reside, to show the hospitality that was expected of them. They were, he says, ignorant and illiterate, bent merely on accumulating wealth. Nearly everyone was heard crying, "Down with the bishops, who grow rich, who wish to be called lords and served on bended knee, who ride about with so many and fine horses, and will do nothing by way of preaching to save men's souls." This was common talk with clergy and laity alike.[2] Gascoigne is, of course, prejudiced,

Gascoigne on bishops.

non est veritas sed cupiditas radix omnium vitiorum, *Concilia*, III, p. 360.

[1] Gascoigne, pp. 16, 35, 52. "Gower (in *Misour de l'Omme*, lines 20149–60) speaks of *deans* drawing revenue from harlots." Taylor, *Thought and Expression in 16th Cent.*, II, 48, footnote ; *ibid.* II, 37–49, for Gascoigne and Pecocke.

[2] Gascoigne, pp. 41, 43. An amusing instance of episcopal pride is recorded in the *Register of Beauchamp*, p. 6. The Bishop placed the churches of All Saints and St. Peter's, Hereford, under an interdict, because they did not ring the bells on his arrival. However, "*ad humilem supplicationem*" of the vicars of these parishes the interdict was graciously removed. In 1522 Bothe of Hereford enjoined penance

and he naturally makes the worst of the bishops; but this charge certainly cannot be brought against Reginald Pecocke, Bishop of Chichester (1450–59), the great defender of his Order; yet even *he* is compelled to admit the decadence of the 15th-century bishop, for he says: "If the bishops were learned and good men, no evil would arise from their wealth, but now children, vicious men of court and ignorant men of high birth are often promoted. Let only good men and well proved men in virtues be taken into priesthood and prelacy. The cause of the evil to the Church is because virtuous men and well proved men in learning and living be not chosen and taken into prelacy."[1] And the charge of avarice is supported by another 15th-century prelate. Bishop Alnwick of Lincoln in his will of 1445 provides against the not uncommon practice of bishops claiming money from their predecessors for alleged dilapidations. "Also," he writes, "seeing that cruel greed so greatly fills the hearts even of priests of the Lord and, which is more to be wondered at and lamented, the hearts of those who are raised aloft upon the pinnacle of the episcopate, that they care not with what pains they may refresh, albeit they do not quench, the thirst of their avarice," they exact from the estate of their predecessors money in "so immoderate and excessive a quantity" that the last wills of the deceased cannot be fulfilled.[2]

Pecocke's views.

Nor were matters apparently very much better in the first quarter of the 16th century. Colet in his famous sermon of 1512 lashes out unsparingly against the bishops of the day, and brings the same charges against the Order as had been brought by the writers of the 15th century. "Benefices were not conferred upon worthy persons; promotion did not go by merit; boys instead of old men, fools instead of wise men, wicked instead of good men, reign and rule." Many of the bishops were still engaged in worldly and secular pursuits to the neglect of their spiritual duties. They were wealthy and spent their

The Eve of the Reformation.

upon certain clergy of the neighbourhood of Leominster, because they had been so impertinent as to lower the dignity of the episcopate by receiving the Abbot of Reading with the honours due only to the Bishop, *Reg. Bothe*, p. 135.

[1] *Repressor* (Ed. Babington), c. viii, p. 331.

[2] *L.V.*, II, p. xxviii.

wealth in magnificence, in pomp, in feasts, in banquets, in keeping hounds, in all manner of luxury. Many did not reside. "My lord of Bangor," the complaint was made to Cromwell in 1529, "has not been in his diocese these fourteen years, but has his bishopric to farm. He is indicted in divers places of his diocese for lack of visitation." Erasmus urges Fisher to take care of his health, which "in the penury of good bishops" is important for the Church. He tells us of a youth who was made a bishop though he was quite illiterate. More satirises a bishop of whom he says "had the choice been made out of a thousand, a worse or more stupid bishop could possibly be found." The Bishop of Ely, James Stanley (1506–15), was leading a very unedifying life; and Wolsey's character was by no means above reproach.[1] It was an age of unblushing self-seeking, and the clergy shared in the general scramble for the loaves and fishes. Wolsey's self-seeking was flagrant and notorious; but he was not the only offender—others were almost as bad. In 1522 Jerome Ghinucci writes to Wolsey, begging that he may be appointed to the Bishopric of Worcester, and modestly adds, "I know my qualities and the services I have rendered do not deserve it."[2] Such candour and modesty disarm all criticism; they met (as they deserved) with their due reward, and the good man was made Bishop of Worcester. But if a simple request was insufficient, it was possible and by no means unusual in that age to buy what one wanted and to take one's choice in the way of spiritual offices. Bishoprics could be purchased, and simony, though always denounced and sternly forbidden by the rules of the Church, was everywhere rampant. Even Gasquet admits that it was the besetting sin of the time.[3] Bishop Bubwith was said to have purchased the Bishopric of Bath and Wells in 1407 for 13,000 gold florins.[4] But if one was poor, or if one grudged so much money, there was a simpler, easier, cheaper and perhaps not

An age of unblushing self-seeking.

[1] *L. and P.*, IV, 623, 5533; Seebohm, *Oxford Reformers*, p. 227. See also *Concilia*, III, p. 717, for the statutes and ordinances in a Provincial Council of 1529, where bishops are urged to be in their cathedrals more, to visit their dioceses, inspect churches and monasteries, be more careful about ordinations, licences, abuses, etc. The injunctions show the slackness and low standard of duty which prevailed.

[2] *L. and P.*, III, 1410.

[3] *Eve of the Reformation*, p. 129.

[4] *Reg. Bubwith*, I, p. xxiii.

less moral way. So thought Dr. Robert Sherborne. In 1505 he obtained the Bishopric of St. David's; he was regularly and duly appointed (with the consent of the King) by a papal Provision; but he thought it advisable not to mention the fact that the said papal Provision was a clever forgery, and that the clever forger was none other than Dr. Robert Sherborne himself.[1]

Though it would be unwise to take too seriously the complaints and denunciations of satirists like Gower, or disappointed place-hunters like Gascoigne, yet there is sufficient evidence from contemporary records, and from men of high standing and repute such as Colet, Erasmus, and More, to justify the conclusion that some of the bishops in the 15th century and on the eve of the Reformation were tainted with the spirit of the age; that worldliness, ambition, and self-seeking were their besetting sins; and that they were often indifferent to the spiritual welfare of their flocks and blind to the needs of the Church and to the signs of the times. What else, indeed, could be expected when it is remembered that often the last requirements for the episcopal office were a saintly life, religious zeal, and spiritual fitness for the pastoral office?

Some notable exceptions.

And yet, in spite of general laxity and many notorious instances of failure, it would be unjust to involve the whole episcopal bench in one sweeping condemnation. Bishops who neglected their dioceses were not necessarily idle or worthless. Indeed, they were often industrious and capable servants of the State, who bore a high character and were the victims rather than the originators of a vicious system. The itineraries of many bishops have been preserved, and from them it is possible to form an estimate of episcopal activities. Bishop Redman, first of St. Asaph (1471–96), and afterwards of Exeter and Ely, the restorer of the cathedrals of his Sees, was a man of immense energy. For twenty-seven years he was the official Visitor of the English houses of the Premonstratensian canons, and the records of his visitations are evidence of his incessant activity. Even in the worst periods of the 15th century there were exceptions to the prevailing slackness. William Alnwick, Bishop of Lincoln (1436–50), was a man

[1] *D.N.B.* The forgery was discovered; but the forger was left unpunished and unmolested.

both of learning and of practical ability, who displayed great energy in his diocese and was most conscientious in his visitations. His itinerary proves how much time he spent in travelling about his immense diocese. "In a bad age he worthily maintained the traditions of the great Bishops of Lincoln."[1] Lacy of Exeter (1421–56) was a conscientious bishop. Spofford of Hereford (1422–48) rarely left his diocese, only going abroad twice during an episcopate of twenty-six years, and very rarely going to London. When he felt his health no longer equal to the performance of his duties, he at once resigned and returned to his former monastery of York. Reginald Pecocke of Chichester (1450–59), though accused of heresy, was admitted to be a man of piety and great learning. And on the eve of the Reformation there were many good prelates who seem to have escaped the notice of Colet, whose eagle eyes (like those of most reformers) were keener to note defects than merits. Both Mylling and Mayew of Hereford administered the diocese well and were genuinely anxious to put down abuses. Alcock of Ely was held in general esteem for his high character. Warham was a good man ; Fox, in spite of his absenteeism, was thoroughly sincere and pious ; Dr. William Smith, the founder of Brasenose College and Farnworth School, was always spoken of as the good Bishop of Lincoln ; Hugh Oldham, Bishop of Exeter, a benefactor of the colleges of Brasenose and Corpus Christi, who refounded and re-endowed Manchester Grammar School, was a prelate worthy of all praise ; while John Fisher, Bishop of Rochester, with all his credulity, narrowness and reactionary views, commanded universal esteem for his learning, piety and courage. If, as a later prelate once wittily remarked, the good are not so good as they think themselves, it is certainly true that very often the bad are not as bad as the good think them.[2]

[1] *L.V.*, II, pp. xiv–xliv. For Wykeham's itineraries see his *Register*, II, Appendix I.

[2] *Life of Creighton*, II, 502.

CHAPTER II

THE LATER MEDIEVAL CATHEDRAL AND COLLEGIATE CLERGY

BELOW the bishops were the cathedral and collegiate clergy. There were two classes of cathedrals before the Reformation. One class, such as Canterbury, Durham, Winchester, Norwich, Ely, and Worcester, were great Benedictine Abbey churches, conducted like other large religious houses. The bishop of the diocese, who was supposed to be chosen by the monks, was the abbot and the nominal head of the abbey; but as he seldom took any part in its practical government, the real head was the prior. The other class of cathedrals, of which the chief were St. Paul's, York, Lincoln, Salisbury, Exeter, Hereford, and Lichfield, were composed of secular canons and were ruled by a Dean and Chapter, as at the present day. These cathedrals had the privilege of choosing their own head, like the majority of Oxford and Cambridge colleges, and were corporate bodies.[1] The Bishop had the formal right of visitation, but beyond this had no real authority or power of interference.[2] The Chapter consisted of the chief dignitaries, the chancellor, precentor, treasurer and sub-dean; of a large number of prebendaries; as well as of the vicars-choral, poor clerks and a large staff of workmen to look after the fabric. Archdeacons were usually, but not necessarily, attached to the cathedral staff. They were in many cases foreigners, trained in the school of law at Bologna, for their functions were purely legal. Occasionally, however, they were sporting Englishmen of the well-known John Bull type, for we are told of

Medieval cathedrals.

Archdeacons.

[1] The Chapter elected and the Bishop confirmed the election. For the procedure of election see *Reg. Mayew*, p. 156; *Reg. Bubwith*, pp. 466–75.

[2] Chapters habitually resisted the episcopal right of visitation, Hereford, successfully. See *Reg. Bothe*, pp. iv. and 57.

an Archdeacon of Richmond who "once came to Bridlington Priory in the course of his visitation with 97 horses, 21 dogs, and 3 hawks." Their income was derived from fees, and so exorbitant were their demands that the question was seriously debated whether an archdeacon could be "saved." In 1416 the Bishop of Bath and Wells sent a very severe letter to the Archdeacon of Taunton, ordering him not to be exacting in his fees, nor to take procurations from churches not actually visited, and, above all, not to usurp the Bishop's authority.[1] Indeed, the medieval archdeacon was little more than a cute and not over scrupulous lawyer, and for this reason he often combined with his archdiaconal functions the office of papal tax-gatherer. He made, as a rule, a very large income.

Wealth of Cathedral Chapters.

The income of a Cathedral Chapter was derived from land, from appropriated tithes, and from benefices, which were attached to the various official posts. The Dean and principal dignitaries usually held several livings in plurality, while the prebends were endowed sometimes with manors, but more often with rich livings. Besides these sources of income there were the offerings which poured in from visitors, especially where the cathedral contained the shrine of some popular saint, or was, like St. Paul's, situated in a great city. Kings, nobles and wealthy visitors all brought their offerings which swelled the coffers of the Chapter.[2] The cathedral clergy were for the most part very wealthy. In the time of Henry VIII the Dean of Lincoln, who was also a prebendary, the Master of Tattershall College, and the rector of five benefices, received (in modern values) an income of about £6576; the chancellor pocketed £3468; the precentor £3024; the sub-dean £2928; while the treasurer had to be content with £2280.[3]

Duties of Cathedral Clergy.

Each dignitary had a special work which he was supposed to do. The prebendary on duty for the week was in charge of the cathedral, had to attend the numerous services (in itself a great strain), and incurred heavy financial responsibilities in the way of hospitality. At Lincoln the residentiary had to entertain at dinner every

[1] *Reg. Bubwith*, pp. 250–3.

[2] For these and similar offerings see Milman, *Latin Christianity*, Bk. XIV, c. i, pp. 22 f.

[3] Cutts, *The Parish Priest in the Middle Ages*, p. 348.

Sunday twenty-two ministers of the cathedral staff; and every day he had to breakfast two bellringers as well as dine the deacon, sub-deacon and the vicar-choral. On feast days the number was still larger. At Chichester in 1251 a canon, on coming into residence, had to pay twenty-five marks to the Chapter and twenty-five to the fabric fund, had to give a feast (convivium) to the whole cathedral staff, and had to dine daily, while in residence, the vicar of his stall, the doorkeeper, two sacrists and one chorister.[1] All these troubles could be avoided by the very simple expedient of non-residence. Is it any wonder that deans, canons and prebendaries preferred to draw their money at a safe distance from the scene of their responsibilities, expenses and worries?

Character of the Cathedral Clergy.

The condition of many of the cathedral Chapters was during the later Middle Ages often far from edifying. A large number of prebendaries were foreigners appointed by the Pope; while of the rest the majority were pluralists who held similar preferments elsewhere and, wishing to observe strict impartiality in their neglect of duty, made a point of rarely, if ever, coming near any of the cathedrals from which they drew their income.[2] Such being the case, it is scarcely surprising that there was not a very exalted sense of duty or discipline among those who did reside. At Exeter, we are informed, the canons, even so early as the 14th century, neglected their spiritual duties, devoted themselves to hunting and hawking, and became mere sporting parsons. Similar complaints were frequent elsewhere. At Lichfield canons came to the choir in all sorts of dresses; the celebration of the Mass was irregular and slovenly; vessels, ornaments and other cathedral property were mishandled or sold; the substitutes put in by absentees were unqualified, unspiritual, and unlettered; and Chapter meetings were often a mere farce, since so few took the trouble to attend. So great were the disorder and negligence that the Bishop

[1] *Southwell Visit.*, p. xliv.

[2] Many deans never went near their cathedrals. Walter Medford, Dean of Wells, 1413–23, never resided, although he had taken an oath either to reside or to pay £100 a year for the repair of the fabric. He did neither. *Reg. Bubwith*, I, p. 4. For non-residence and letting of their houses see *Reg. Trefnant*, pp. 145–6.

in 1428 had to interfere and draw up rules for the guidance of the Chapter.[1] In 1432 Bishop Gray made a formal visitation of the cathedral church of Lincoln. The bells were rung on his approach, and he was received in great state by the Dean and Chapter. But this outward splendour was no guarantee of inward health, for the Bishop, after an exhaustive inquiry, found very much to correct. The services in church were badly attended and irreverently conducted; the canons "chattered," to the offence of others; while the vicars-choral and other ministers roamed about "disorderly wise" in the nave, and the church was "spotted by their impertinences." The discipline was bad. The poor clerks of the church, instead of devoting themselves to learning and the performance of the duties of their office, "almost every day spend their time in drinking and other unseemliness," to the grave scandal of the Church. Indeed, haunting of taverns and unseemly revellings seem to have been usual among the greater part of the staff. The chantries were indifferently served; dilapidations not attended to; the salaries of vicars and others very irregularly paid; the vestments of the church neither mended nor cleaned; while the continued non-residence of the dean and the sub-dean was, by its evil example of slackness, detrimental to discipline, duty and religion.[2]

Lincoln.

At Hereford the state of things was at times very bad, being characterised by much irreverence and neglect of duty. In 1434 Bishop Spofford, horrified at the scandalous desecration of the cathedral precincts, sent a stern note to the Dean and Chapter, peremptorily ordering them to reform abuses within twenty days. A market, it appears, was openly held on the consecrated ground of the churchyard; unburied corpses, mauled and partially devoured by prowling animals, were lying about to the danger and scandal of the faithful; while the general aspect of the Close was more befitting a camp than a cathedral.[3] In 1462 there was a violent quarrel between the

Hereford.

[1] *Concilia,* III, 504, cf. 572.

[2] *L.V.*, I, liii, p. 128 *seq.* The Dean and Chapter refused to reform abuses and the Bishop took the law into his own hands.

[3] *Reg. Spofford,* p. 180; cf. *Reg. Bubwith,* p. 453, for animals desecrating the churchyard at Wells. For the med. service of the Reconciliation

citizens and the Chapter with reference to the election of a dean. The former had by violence and threats forced their own nominee upon the Chapter, and so high ran the dispute that the Bishop had to interfere and restore order.[1] At the beginning of the 16th century there were unseemly quarrels even in the cathedral itself; while the state of morals among certain of the Chapter was so scandalous that Bishop Mayew in 1512 sent a stern monition to the Dean and Chapter, ordering them to put an immediate end to irregularities, which were inflicting immense harm upon the honour and prestige of the Church and the priestly Order.[2]

York.

York from 1426–1531 had a long succession of non-resident archbishops, and under the spiritual leadership of men like Kempe, Neville, Booth, Bainbrigge and Wolsey it was scarcely to be expected that the Chapter would excel in devotion and Christian concord. Here, as elsewhere, the relations between the Chapter and the city were often very strained. In 1494 there was a dispute between them which waxed so violent as to attract the attention of the Crown, and Henry VII had to interfere. He appointed the Earl of Surrey and the Abbot of St. Mary's to compose the quarrel. "Wherefore," wrote the King to the disputants, "we charge you under the straitest wise to be conformable to such order and direction as you shall sett betwixt you in the premises, and in the mean season to observe and duely kepe our pease in dreding our high displeasure and the grevous punishment."[3]

St. Paul's.

At *St. Paul's* in the early part of the 16th century the state of things was deplorable. The nave of the church was used as a common market-place, where vendors plied their trade and idlers gossiped and lounged. The Chapter was a large and powerful body, comprising,

of a churchyard after desecration see Maskell, *Mon. Rit. Eccles. Angl.*, III, 307–17.

[1] *Reg. Stanbury*, pp. 71–83.

[2] *Reg. Mayew*, pp. 112, 141, 181, 228.

[3] Pollard, *Henry VII*, III, 201. The *Fabric Rolls of York Minster* (Sur. Soc.) throw light upon the life and character of the Chapter in the 14th and 15th centuries, esp. pp. 242–74. See also the Visitations of the Chapter by Bowet in 1416, and by Kempe in 1440, where we find among the *Detecta*, absenteeism, neglect, moral scandals, buying and selling in the Cathedral, serious dilapidations and references to the prohibitive cost of residence, *Sur. Soc.*, cxxvii, pp. 198, 238–41.

besides the treasurer, precentor, and chancellor, thirty canons, four archdeacons, twelve minor canons and a whole host of chantry priests. The members of the Chapter seem to have been corrupted by idleness and wealth, for Colet gives a very unfavourable account of them. "They cast aside their care for the church; they pursue their private gains; they convert the common property to their private use. In these unhappy and disordered times residence in the cathedral is nothing less than seeking one's own advantage, and (to speak more plainly) robbing the Church and enriching oneself."[1] So wrote Colet. No wonder he was unpopular! Nor did he make himself any less unpopular by his attempts at reform. He tried to alter the state of things which he found and drew up some new statutes; but he could not enforce them, and they remained a dead letter. The Bishop of London was his enemy, and tried to hinder him at every turn. Besides, the Chapter was too large and too powerful to be reformed against its will.

Collegiate Churches.

Nor (to judge from the evidence which has come down to us) was the condition of things any better in the great Collegiate Churches. Before the Norman Conquest colleges of secular canons, who lived in a community round a church, which served both as the collegiate chapel and as the parish church of the place, were very numerous. When, later on, monasticism became popular and monopolised the favour of the wealthy, the colleges became more or less neglected; but when, after the Black Death, the popularity of the monk began to wane, Collegiate Churches revived and magnificent colleges were endowed by wealthy patrons. Many of these new colleges were founded for some particular purpose, eleemosynary or educational. The Duke of Lancaster in the 14th century founded the great Hospital and New College in the Newarke, Leicester, with its hundred poor men and women, its dean, canons, and numerous staff of vicars, ministers and servants. Wykeham, Chichele and Henry VI founded for the education and maintenance of poor boys splendid colleges, the pioneers of the Public Schools, the later history of which has somewhat obscured the original collegiate ideal. At the Dissolution there were about two hundred Collegiate Churches, some of them, such as Southwell, Ripon, Beverley

[1] Lupton, pp. 129, 134.

and many others, being among the most magnificent in England; and of these the greater number were dissolved, their endowments confiscated, and their Grammar Schools, for the most part efficient educational agencies, either destroyed or re-established on a smaller scale with diminished endowments and impaired efficiency.

Condition of the Collegiate Churches.

When the veil is lifted and we catch glimpses, through entries in episcopal registers or by means of occasional Visitations which have survived, the picture presented is not always very attractive. There are accusations both against the Chapter and the lesser lights of slackness, idleness, non-residence, irreverence in the conduct of the services, drinking, immorality, violent quarrels—all evidence of general demoralisation.

Southwell.

At Southwell, in the diocese of York, the Archbishops' Visitations of the Chapter are lost, but there remain certain Visitations of the vicars-choral and clerks by members of the Chapter. "The oddest farrago of offences is presented to us in these visitations. Crimes of the darkest complexion are mixed up with the most trivial delinquencies. Leaving the church door open, sleeping at Matins, talking and laughing during service, spitting and blowing your nose in the choir, are jumbled up higgledy-piggledy with stabbing and fighting, stealing and adultery." The vicars-choral seem to have been, at the close of the 15th century, at any rate, a noisy, quarrelsome, and unruly lot. Daggers were drawn on the slightest provocation, and blood was shed even in the church itself; drunkenness and immorality were so usual as to excite little notice; while the ideals of the religious life were easily lost amid the engrossing pleasures and temptations of the world. One, with the not unfamiliar name of John Bull, made himself notorious for his irregularities. He seems to have done pretty much as he liked, and to have taken scant notice of visitations or warnings. He stayed away from the services whenever it suited his purpose; in fact, he was more often absent than present. Perhaps this was a good thing, for when he *did* take it into his head to come to a service, he either slept the whole time or sang so loud as to distract the choir. He was a particularly quarrelsome person, ever ready with a word and a blow. On one occasion, in 1478, he and a fellow vicar-choral got quarrelling violently (*instigante zizannio*) in the

Close. They kept striking at one another with daggers until the blood ran and serious injury had been inflicted. The Archbishop of York (Booth) chanced to be staying in Southwell at the time, and he was highly indignant at such unseemly behaviour almost in his very presence. But this was not the worst, for the Rev. John Bull was accused (and convicted) on several occasions of grave offences. These aroused (apparently) little moral indignation; his punishments were usually light, just a small fine or a few words or a hint not to offend *too* often; at any rate, his irregularities were no bar to his continuance in office and even to his advancement, for at the ripe age of sixty he became a (more or less) respectable churchwarden of Southwell Minster.[1]

The New College in Leicester.

In 1440 Bishop Alnwick of Lincoln made a visitation of the New College in Leicester. Similar complaints were made. The canons were not a satisfactory body of men. They rarely rose for matins, preferring to pay the fine (2d.) for non-attendance, one of them openly saying, "I know how much I shall lose; I had rather lose it than get up!" Great irreverence was shown at the services. Canons and vicars clanked about in great noisy wooden shoes; the vicars were constantly chattering and laughing, to the grievous hindrance of devout worship; the singing was far from what it should have been, one singing too fast, another too loud, a third having so unpleasant (*tam alta et aperta*) a voice that he was a perfect nuisance. These are, perhaps, trivial points not worth a stern moralist's while shaking his head over; but there is much worse in the background. Four of the canons were accused of misconduct and promiscuous living, and a fifth was defamed of a very bad crime. The college (at any rate, in the year 1440) was not in a satisfactory state.[2] It is not altogether sur prising, either here or in any other collegiate establishment of the 15th century. There were many dangers in the life of men vowed to celibacy, not secluded from the world, but

[1] Leach, *Southwell Visit.*, pp. lxxiv, lxxix–lxxxii, 38.

[2] I owe this account of the New College in the Newarke, Leicester, to the kindness of Mr. Hamilton Thompson, who very kindly lent me his notes on the history of the College. See also Fowler, *Chapter Acts of Ripon*, 1452–1506, p. vi; and *Memorials of Ripon*, 4 vols., esp. Vol. II. These throw great light upon the life and morals of the Chapter. For 13th and 14th cents., Leach, *Memorials of Beverley* (all Sur. Soc.).

forbidden healthy games and innocent recreations, with little stimulus to work, with little or nothing to occupy the mind.

Before passing final judgment against the Cathedrals and Collegiate Churches of the 15th century, it is as well to bear in mind that the cases mentioned above are more or less isolated and do not profess to give a continuous picture through a long series of years. It would be unwise to argue from the known to the unknown, and to assert that all collegiate establishments were in an equally bad condition. They may have been; on the other hand, they may not. Where evidence is lacking, there is an opportunity for Christian charity to step in.[1]

Pluralism.

The truth was that the upper ranks of the clergy were in many cases demoralised by two evils which were widely prevalent, which reached their climax on the eve of the Reformation, and which, like some insidious disease, were gradually sapping the vitality and destroying the spiritual influence of the Church. The first of these was the evil system of *pluralities*. It was an age of pluralism, shameless and unabashed. One of the most frequent charges brought against the medieval clergy by Chaucer, by the Lollards, by the writers of the 15th century and by Colet is the charge of greed. Large incomes, preferments, pluralities were the object of their ambition and pursuit. Benefice was often heaped upon benefice in the most shameless manner. Bishops frequently pushed their relations and loaded them with a multitude of valuable preferments. Nepotism was rife, and prelates took a business as well as a spiritual view of their privileges and patronage. A nephew of Archbishop Chichele was prebendary of St. Paul's at the early age of sixteen; at the age of twenty he was prebendary of the Cathedrals of St. Paul's and Lincoln, of the Collegiate Churches of Bedford, Crediton and Heylesbury, and held in addition the free chapels of Sheriton, Wilts, and Allerton, Yorks.[2] Influence (aided by other advantages) rarely failed to win a substantial (but earthly) reward. Men who had interest with patrons, or men who had enough

[1] See *Reg. Lacy* for frequent disorders at Bosham. There are several monographs upon particular Collegiate Churches, e.g. *The Collegiate Church of Ottery St. Mary*, by Canon Dalton (1917). See also an article upon Collegiate Churches in the *Church Quarterly* for Jan., 1921, by Canon Watson.

[2] *L.V.*, I, pp. xix, 187–8.

money to buy a papal Provision, held several valuable preferments at the same time. Richard Courtenay, Dean of Wells (1410–13), held in 1407 a prebend, canonries at Exeter, Lincoln, Wells, York, London, the precentorship of Chichester, the Archdeaconry of Northampton, and the Chancellorship of the University of Oxford. Edmund Chaterton, a Master in Chancery in the reign of Henry VII and chancellor to the Queen, was prebendary of Southwell, Ripon, Lincoln, St. Paul's, St. Stephen's, Westminster, and Salisbury; Warden of Sibthorpe College; rector of Calverton, Bucks; Dean of Barking; and Archdeacon at the same time of Chester, Salisbury and Totnes.[1] Nicholas Bubwith, Bishop of Bath and Wells (1407–24), was in the year 1403 in possession of benefices worth in modern values about £10,000 a year, and is described as holding the prebends of Driffield in Yorkshire, Ilton in Wells, Offeley in Lichfield, Charminster and Beere in Salisbury; prebends in London, Exeter, and Ripon; canonries in Salisbury and Chichester; and the archdeaconries of Exeter and Richmond. In addition to all this he was a royal chaplain, Keeper of the Rolls, and the King's Secretary.[2] Gascoigne tells us with deep disgust of a youth who had by licence and provision of the Pope twelve prebends, a rectory or two, and the valuable archdeaconry of Oxford. The youth was half-witted and knew neither Latin nor even his mother tongue, and was, in fact, quite incapable. He never resided in any of his benefices, but completely neglected them, and never once set foot in his archdeaconry. In another place he tells of a physician, probably Dr. Keymer, Dean of Salisbury and physician of Humphrey, Duke of Gloucester, who had two great deaneries, two great prebends and a valuable rectory, and only occasionally resided in but one of these.[3] William of Wykeham (1324–1404) was as notorious as a pluralist as he was famous as a bishop or as a founder of colleges. He was not ordained even an acolyte until he was thirty-eight years of age; and yet, before this event, he was royal chaplain, rector of several livings, Dean of St. Martin-le-Grand, and held valuable prebends at St. Paul's, Hereford, Salisbury, St. David's, Beverley, Brom-

Gascoigne's instances.

William of Wykeham.

[1] *Southwell Visit*, p. 146, note. [2] *Reg. Bubwith*, pp. xxi, xxii.
[3] Gascoigne, pp. 43, 195.

yard, and Wherwell. To these were added in the next five years prebends at Lincoln, York, Wells, Hastings, Dublin, and Bridgenorth, together with the lucrative archdeaconry of Lincoln. At the age of forty-three he became Lord Chancellor and Bishop of Winchester. After this the good Bishop's munificent generosity must have been a pleasure as well as a duty, and as easy as it was praiseworthy.

George Neville.

The natural advantages and high connections of George Neville (1433–76) were sufficient of themselves, without the aid of any striking ability, to assure his (earthly) career; but these natural advantages he had the good sense to improve by the very useful quality of plebeian pushfulness; so that on reaching his majority he succeeded in getting the University of Oxford to make him their Chancellor and in obtaining the archdeaconry of Northampton and prebends at Lincoln and Ripon. At the age of twenty-two he was appointed Bishop of Exeter, though the tender conscience of the Pope made him insist that, while the new Bishop was at perfect liberty to receive all the temporalities of the See, the performance of its spiritual duties should more decently be deferred until the leader and head of the clergy of the diocese of Exeter should have attained to years of greater discretion. This arrangement admirably suited the new Bishop and gave him leisure for further pushfulness, with the result that at twenty-three he obtained the rich Mastership of the hospital of St. Leonard in York; at twenty-seven he was made Lord Chancellor; and at thirty-one he was exalted to the dignity of the Archbishopric of York.

At the close of the 15th century Dr. Robert Sherborne was Dean of St. Paul's, but this valuable and important preferment was quite insufficient to satisfy his worldly aspirations, for he was at the same time rector of Alresford, Master of St. Cross, Master of Holy Trinity Hospital, Kingsthorpe, Archdeacon of Bucks, Hunts, and Taunton. Richard Pace, the diplomatist who succeeded Colet in the Deanery of St. Paul's, was another cleric who did not do so badly for himself out of the Church. At one and the same time he was Dean of St. Paul's, Salisbury, and Exeter, and Archdeacon of Dorset; held four prebends, two rectories, and two vicarages; and was, in addition, Reader of Greek at Cambridge.

But the scandal of pluralities reached its climax in Cardinal Wolsey, who in his earlier years held in plurality two rectories, two deaneries, and several prebendaries; who in rapid succession was appointed to the Bishoprics of Lincoln, Bath and Wells, Durham, and Winchester, some of which he held in plurality with the Archbishopric of York, and who at the time of his fall in 1530 was Archbishop of York, Bishop of Winchester, Abbot of St. Albans, and Lord Chancellor. In addition to his English preferments it should not be forgotten that he received from Francis I an annual pension of 12,000 livres in lieu of the Bishopric of Tournay; that he held the Bishopric of Badajoz in Spain with 5000 ducats a year, to which Charles V added another 2000; and that he made a large income from presents, from his fees as Chancellor, and from the bribes which were offered by importunate suitors for his favour and influence.[1] His great aim was the Papacy, and to achieve this ambition he spared no pains or expense. "For goodness sake," he wrote to Pace on the death of Leo X, "don't let the election be lost for a mere trifle like 100,000 ducats."[2] But Charles V played him false, and, in spite of frantic efforts and lavish promises, he was unsuccessful both on the death of Leo X and on that of Adrian VI, two years later. Wolsey had an illegitimate son, one Thomas Wynter, for whom, though a minor, he tried to get the valuable Bishopric of Durham. He wrote to the King, begging this great preferment for his "pore scoler" when he himself should "fortune to leave the same." This modest request did not meet with the success he expected; but his disappointment had compensations, for he managed to secure for the youth in his teens "a deanery (Wells), four archdeaconries (Norfolk, Suffolk, York, Richmond), five prebends, and the Chancellorship of Salisbury. For each of these preferments a complaisant Pope had to grant two dispensations, one on account of the youth's illegitimacy, the other on account of his minority."[3] Even Colet, who lashed

Wolsey.

[1] *L. and P.*, I, 5518; II, 4354; III, 709; IV, 3334, 3464, 4452. 15,000 ducats werehis New Year gifts, *Venetian Cal.*, II, 1287. For his presents from foreign States see *Milanese Cal.*, 804; *Venetian Cal.*, II, 1287; III, 13, 14, 35; *Spanish Cal.*, III, i. It is only fair to add that he required a large income for his State expenses.

[2] *L. and P.*, III, 1892.

[3] Pollard, *Cranmer*, p. 324.

so unsparingly the greed of churchmen, was himself a pluralist, though *his* pluralism was mild when compared with that of many of his contemporaries; yet he held before he was even ordained to the diaconate three valuable livings, and was, while Dean of St. Paul's, rector of Dennington, prebendary of York, Salisbury and St. Paul's, with the treasurership of Chichester thrown in.[1]

Colet.

But there was an even worse evil than pluralism. Simony was very prevalent among the clergy, and it had increased to such an extent that it threatened the spiritual life of the Church. Spiritual promotions were shamelessly hawked about in all the great cities of England, and the traffic in advowsons was a common and a lucrative trade. The system of "provisions" directly encouraged the evil; and livings, prebends, bishoprics were openly put up to auction in Rome and sold like cattle in the market-place to the highest bidder. Spiritual offices could be bought by the least desirable men, for money could always procure the coveted prize. The system of ecclesiastical patronage was reduced to the worst jobbery, and simony became the curse of the Church.

Simony.

The more conscientious bishops fought against the evil and tried to keep it within bounds. In 1508 Bishop Mayew held a long inquiry into the case of Hugh Grene, a man who, *per simoniacam pravitatem*, had obtained preferment in the cathedral church of Hereford. The inquiry was stringent; the Bishop was severe, and the delinquent thought it wise to send in his resignation before a decision was pronounced. Owing to its increase, Archbishop Warham in 1509, with the approval of the Synod of the Province, granted fresh powers to the bishops to deal with cases of simony in their dioceses; while

Vain attempts to check it.

[1] Lupton, pp. 119–20. A licence to hold more than one preferment *with cure of souls* could only be obtained from the Pope; but, in spite of the decree of the 4th Lateran Council forbidding pluralities and of much subsequent legislation, there was no difficulty in obtaining one. The Papacy made a large income out of the practice. For papal licences see *Reg. Fox* (Bath and Wells), pp. 40, 48, 71, 122; *Reg. Mayew*, p. 75; *Reg. Gray*, f. 65. In 1305 Clement V granted a dispensation to a boy of ten to hold two livings, and when he reached the age of fourteen to hold two more; *Liber Albus*, pp. 49–53. Clergy took a delight in obtaining papal dispensations and flaunting them in the face of Bishops. See *Reg. Bothe*, p. 176.

in 1529 the bishops, assembled in a provincial Council, passed several ordinances against the ecclesiastical abuses of the day, and among them a very strong article dealing with the evil of simony. Its prevalence among all Orders of the Church, both regular and secular, the ill odour into which it brought the Church, the evil it inflicted upon religion, was, they declared, known and apparent to everyone. Men not only bought vacant preferments, but bought them before they actually fell vacant. It was a curse, and stringent rules were made for checking the evil.[1] Not, however, to much purpose; for in 1538 Bishop Longland of Lincoln denounced it as still the curse of the day. The evil is rooted in human nature, and, in spite of rules, laws, and monitions, in spite of the harm which it inflicts upon the spiritual life of the Church, in spite of stringent oaths and disclaimers, simony, sometimes openly, more often under a thin disguise, has in all ages been found in the Church of God.

[1] *Reg. Mayew*, pp. 34–47, 107. *Concilia*, p. 721.

CHAPTER III

SOME TYPES OF THE LATER MEDIEVAL PARISH CLERGY

IN an age like the 15th century, when the general standard of Church life was low, it would be foolish to expect to find so high a standard of life and work among the parochial clergy as that which existed in happier days. It would, indeed, be surprising if, in view of the ecclesiastical conditions of the day, the parochial clergy could altogether escape the dangers which beset the working of the Church in that difficult time.

In the Middle Ages the clerical Order was far larger than it is to-day.[1] It was representative of all social classes, and comprised within its ranks a large number of men who, though they ranked as clergy and shared in the privileges of the clerical Order, were for all practical purposes simply laymen. Holy Orders were divided into two classes, major and minor; the former consisting of bishops, priests, deacons, and sub-deacons; the latter of exorcists, readers, and ostiarii (sextons). A candidate for Holy Orders must have been baptised and confirmed; he must at least be able to read and write; and he was supposed to have received instruction in the Christian faith.[2]

Qualifications for Ordination.

[1] The length of ordination lists was often very great. In 1417 there were ordained in the diocese of Bath and Wells, one of the smaller dioceses, 82 acolytes, 69 sub-deacons, 35 deacons and 28 priests, a large number in proportion to the population. *Reg. Bubwith*, pp. 518–27; cf. *Reg. Mayew*, pp. 264–8. In the *Ely Register of Arundell* (1374–88), ff. 115–36, the number of ordinands was large, many rectors being among the lower Orders. In Feb., 1379–80, Arundell ordained for the Bp. of London in St. Paul's 77 acolytes, 88 sub-deacons, 59 deacons and 48 priests. This was, perhaps, an exceptionally large number. During the 37 years' episcopate of Wykeham there were ordained 1334 acolytes, 1382 sub-deacons, 1360 deacons and 1273 priests. In 1381 the number of clergy on the Poll-tax records was over 29,000.

[2] At 7 a boy could receive the tonsure; 7–14, minor Orders; 18, sub-deacon; 21, deacon; 25, priest.

At one time great care seems to have been exercised in the admission of candidates to the higher orders of the ministry. In 1370 the Bishop of Exeter asks the Bishop of Winchester to ordain for him certain men from the Exeter diocese, and he speaks of them as having been "carefully examined and found suitable."[1] But in the following century great laxity, due doubtless to the dearth of suitable candidates, an effect of the devastation caused by the Black Death, prevailed about admitting men to Holy Orders. In 1414 the University of Oxford in its *Articles of Church Reform* drew attention to the state of things, and demanded a much stricter examination of ordinands. Matters were very bad during the period of the civil wars, but they seem to have improved somewhat with the accession of the Tudors. Bishop Mayew of Hereford in 1516 was very anxious about the qualifications of candidates, and issued a commission to his archdeacons to make careful inquiries about their lives and to submit them to a very real examination; while in 1529 Convocation (somewhat late in the day) passed a resolution that none should be ordained who were not of the right age and character.[2]

Preferments often given to men in Minor Orders.

It seems extraordinary to us, but such is the fact, that men could be appointed and instituted to valuable benefices before they were even in Deacons' Orders; but the ecclesiastical rule was that, while no one could be instituted to a benefice unless he were a clerk, yet he might be, and indeed often was, only in minor Orders. He was supposed to proceed to Priests' Orders within a year, but very often he made no attempt to do so. In the episcopal registers we find several instances of this custom. William Lynton was presented to the rectory of Spaxton, in the diocese of Bath and Wells, on the 23rd of May, 1493. He must have been in the lowest Orders, for he was not even ordained acolyte until four months after his institution. There is a more striking case

[1] *Reg. Wykeham*, I, 284. Candidates were supposed to be physically sound, but if they were not they could generally get a dispensation. For an instance see *Reg. Bothe*, I, 93.

[2] *Reg. Mayew*, p. 97; *Concilia*, III, 717. Men were not supposed to be ordained until they had reached the canonical age, but it was possible to get a dispensation to be ordained at an earlier age. In 1429 Clement VII granted a dispensation for Charles Carew, a boy of twelve and also illegitimate, to be ordained, *Reg. Wolsey* (Winton), f. 50.

still a century earlier. In September, 1378, Walter Philipe was instituted to the valuable rectory of Abbott's Ann in Hampshire, and immediately obtained a licence of non-residence in order to study. He was only in minor Orders at the time of his institution; for it was in 1379 that he was ordained a sub-deacon; and it was not until five years later that he was ordained a deacon. He never entered the priesthood, and yet all this time he was receiving the great tithes of a valuable benefice, in which he never resided, and in the church of which he was not even qualified to celebrate the principal sacrament.[1]

Rectories.

At the close of the 15th century there were, it has been calculated, about 8000 parishes in England, and as several of these had more than one priest attached to them we shall not be far wrong in stating that there were over 10,000 clergy engaged, or supposed to be engaged, in parochial duties. Benefices were of two kinds, rectories and vicarages, the former being the more valuable and the more important; for a rector received *all* the tithes and fees, while a vicar was reduced to the smaller tithes, and was often deprived of the fees and dues belonging to the benefice. Rectories then, as now, varied very much in value, some being quite poor, while others were very valuable; of these latter nearly all were held either by wealthy pluralists among the more highly placed clergy, or by corporate bodies as part of their endowment.

Vicarages.

The evil system of appropriations.

At one time all benefices were rectories, but in course of time there grew up what is known as the system of appropriations. Bishoprics, Chapters of cathedrals, collegiate bodies, hospitals, and monasteries were endowed with valuable rectories. In the palmy days of monasticism patrons used to present the advowsons in their gift to religious houses as part of their endowment, and a large number of the best livings thus came into possession of the monks, who became in perpetuity the rectors of the livings bestowed upon them.[2] As these

[1] *Reg. Fox* (Bath and Wells), p. 14; *Reg. Wykeham*, I, 100, 290; II, 301, 309. Cf. *Reg. Lacy*, pp. 483, 527; *Reg. Bubwith*, p. 94.

[2] Rectories were generally given to religious houses for special purposes, e.g. "ad infirmariam monachorum"; "in augmentacionem bonorum sacristiariæ," *Reg. Arundell* (Ely), f. 63 b. Appropriations are found so late as 1513, for in that year Bishop West of Ely sanctioned an appropriation to the nunnery of Denny, *Reg. West*, ff. 61–8.

rectories were often at a considerable distance from the monastery it became necessary to appoint a resident priest to take charge of the parish. Hence there arose the practice of the delegation of the rectorial duties to a priest, who, being the deputy of the rector, was termed a vicar.[1] The tithes were divided into two (very unequal) parts. The greater tithes were called the rectorial, and were taken by the monasteries as rectors ; the lesser, termed the vicarial, were given to the vicar.[2] At the dissolution of the monasteries the rectorial tithes passed to the Crown, and for the most part found their way into the pockets of laymen, where they still remain.

Wretched condition of vicars.

These vicars or deputies of religious houses, hospitals, and cathedral Chapters were for the most part miserably paid. The chronicler Walsingham tells us that their incomes were so small that many were forced to steal ;[3] while Gascoigne says that the vicar in some cases had scarcely the means of life, for the monks, not content with the great tithes, tried to get hold of the parson's fees as well.[4] In 1424 the Convocation of Canterbury declared that the lower clergy were so poor that it was impossible for them to contribute to the subsidy—many, indeed, of the parishes having been reduced to such extreme poverty that priests could not be found to fill them. The same complaint was made in 1440 by Archbishop Chichele, who stated that the clergy were so impoverished that they had not sufficient even for a bare existence (*etiam ut tenuem vitam ducant*).[5] The lists which have come down to us bear eloquent testimony to the poverty of the clergy. In the diocese of Exeter in 1425 the average vicarage was worth

[1] By 4 Henry IV, c. 12, the vicar had to be a secular.

[2] The episcopal registers contain many instances of appropriations, and apportionments of tithe, e.g. *Reg. Bubwith*, pp. 361–73 ; *Reg. Wykeham*, II, pp. 285–9 ; *Reg. Arundell*, f. 37 ; *Reg. Bothe*, p. 96. There are two very good instances of appropriations in the *Liber Albus*, Nos. 1304, 1313. These give the sources from which the vicar's income was derived and show the extreme trouble he must have had in collecting so many things from so many people at such different times of the year.

[3] Quoted by Trevelyan, *Age of Wycliffe*, p. 124.

[4] Gascoigne, pp. 106–15.

[5] *Concilia*, III, 428, 535, cf. *Reg. Stanbury*, p. 90. The vicar complained *de nimia exilitate porcionis vicariæ*.

eight to ten marks.[1] In the diocese of Bath and Wells in 1414 the average was six to twelve marks,[2] while in 1419 it was stated that many vicars only got seven marks a year, or forty shillings with victuals. The poverty increased as the century advanced, and as the purchasing power of the mark declined. In the diocese of Hereford in 1478 Bishop Mylling states that, whereas formerly churches had been sufficient to support the vicar, now many have come to such misery, poverty, and want that they are quite unable to support a priest (*etiam miserrime viventem*).[3] The bishops, who had little love for the monks and their ways, disliked the whole system of appropriations, and did their best to protect the clergy from the rapacity of the religious houses and to secure a living wage for vicars. In 1372 the Bishop of Winchester appointed a commission to ascertain the value of the appropriated church of Romsey, with a view to adjusting the vicar's portion. In 1403 the Archdeacon of Surrey received a mandate from the Bishop to admonish the Prior and Convent of Newark to augment the vicarage of Weybridge.[4] Even cathedral corporations were not above reproach and often sweated the vicars of parishes from which they received valuable rectorial tithes. In 1437 the Bishop wrote to the Dean and Chapter of Hereford that, as they had not augmented the stipend of their vicar at Upton, he would take the matter into his own hands and compel them to give the man a living wage. The church of Great Paxton, appropriated to the Dean and Chapter of Lincoln, was in 1437 so impoverished that no vicar could be got to serve it "except some drunkard or idler such as the present vicar."[5] In 1379 Archbishop Sudbury issued a mandate (grudgingly, however, for he put down the request for a living wage to "greed and gluttony"),

Attempts to relieve their poverty and protect their interests.

[1] There are one or two exceptions, e.g. the Vicarage of Barnstaple is worth 20 marks, *Reg. Lacy*, pp. 545–8. A mark was worth 13s. 4d.

[2] *Reg. Bubwith*, pp. 191, 384.

[3] *Reg. Mylling*, p. 40.

[4] *Reg. Wykeham*, II, 185, 359, 549. There are several other instances in the registers. During an episcopal investigation into the condition of the Abbey of Wigmore in 1424 it transpired that the abbey was in the habit of compelling nominees to their livings by a fine of money not to proceed against them for an augmentation of the vicarial stipend, *Reg. Spofford*, p. 65. Between the monk and friar the medieval parson's life was by no means unmitigated bliss.

[5] *Reg. Spofford*, p. 221 ; *L.V.*, I, p. 143 note.

stating that, whereas Archbishop Islip (1349–66) had given vicars six marks, *he* raised their portion to eight, or as an alternative, four marks with food. Chantry priests were to receive seven.[1] Chichele in 1440 issued a constitution to compel appropriators and rectors to give their vicars a wage which would be sufficient for the adequate performance of their vicarial duties, and which was in no case to be less than twelve marks.[2] The constitution was a dead letter; for when vicars complained drastic measures were soon taken to reduce them to silence. So flagrant became the evil that some bishops ordered the union of benefices to provide a living wage, or allowed the vicar to serve a chantry as well.[3] Sir Thomas Cumberland in the 15th century gave lands and tenements to different parishes in order to make up the loss which their vicars suffered from the greedy monks and their appropriations.[4] But it was all to no purpose.

Failure to remedy the evil.

Wealthy abbeys, hospitals, colleges, and pluralists proved too strong for the wretched vicar, who preferred to endure in silence the pangs of poverty rather than fall foul of wealthy bodies which could crush him to the earth. The abuse continued to flourish, all remedies proving totally inadequate to restrict it; and so late as 1528 we find Archbishop Warham complaining to Wolsey that the poverty of many of the clergy was so great that they could not pay their quota to the Loan. "As," he writes, "the chief benefices are appropriated to religious houses, the vicar's portion is so small that they can scarcely live."[5] We can well imagine that men like these, on the verge of destitution, receiving the smallest possible wage, did in return (such is human nature) the smallest possible amount of work.

Disastrous results of the poverty of the clergy.

Parishes were neglected. There was little preaching or teaching or baptising or visitation of the sick or relief of the poor. In 1414 the University of Oxford complained that monasteries and prelates, who already have enough, appropriate rectories, and that, in consequence, the spiritual work of the

[1] *Reg. Arundell*, f. 88.
[2] *Concilia*, III, 535.
[3] *Reg. Bubwith*, p. 378; *Reg. Mylling*, pp. 40, 63, 66, cf. Morton's injunction in 1486, *Concilia*, III, 619.
[4] Gascoigne, p. 149; *Reg. Alcock*, f. 29.
[5] *L. and P.*, IV, 4631. In 1530 the Bp. of Hereford went so far as to sequestrate a living because of its poverty, *Reg. Bothe*, p. 240.

parishes suffered grave harm.[1] Gascoigne speaks very bitterly of the evils brought on the Church by the system, and in 1529, on the very eve of the dissolution of the monasteries, Convocation drew attention to the harm which was being done by these appropriations. Many of the vicars were actually men of bad character. In 1390 the vicar of Abbott's Ann in Hampshire was guilty of homicide and had his living sequestered; another who was caught in adultery with one of his parishioners received milder treatment, for the bishop let him off.[2] Colet gives these clergy a very bad character. They were often, he says, "illiterate, without judgement, unfit, wicked men who sought nothing but sordid gain." It is not surprising. A Church (like any other institution) which treats its servants badly must expect to be badly served.

Chapels-of-ease and their chaplains.

Besides the rectors and vicars there was a large body of clergy who were designated by the general name of *chaplains*. Some of these served as deputies for absentee rectors; others were placed in charge of the many chapels which, under the nominal direction of the parish priest, served hamlets and outlying parts of the parish. These chapels and their relation to the parish church were a source of constant friction and were often the centre of opposition to the incumbent. Legally they were under his control, but it was not always easy to exercise authority over unwilling parishioners, who, moreover, sometimes had a genuine grievance. Residents in hamlets however remote had to be buried in the churchyard of the mother church; and in winter, when the days were short, the weather bad, and the roads almost impassable, this was a very real grievance. In 1424 the Earl of March asks the Bishop of Hereford that his tenants may bury their dead in their own hamlet owing to floods, bad roads, and other inconveniences. After careful inquiry, the Bishop consents.[3] There were, too, disputes about the services held in these chapels. In 1490 the Bishop of Hereford sent careful direc-

[1] "Unde gravis suboritur parochianorum desolatio, pauperum subducitur hospitalis recreatio et quod his deterius est cura negligitur animarum," *Concilia*, III, 360.

[2] *Reg. Wykeham*, II, 429; Gascoigne, p. 24.

[3] See *Reg. Spofford*, pp. 57–9; *Reg. Fordham*, f. 4; *Reg. Arundell*, f. 136; *Reg. Bothe*, I, 25; *Reg. Lacy*, p. 698.

tions to the rector of Eastham with reference to the services in the chapel of Hanley in his parish. A little later he intervenes in a violent dispute between the vicar of Goodrich and the hamlet of Huntsham about the celebration of mass, and to settle the matter he draws up a list of the services which were to be held until the chapel was made a parish church.[1]

Constant friction between chapels and the parish church.

Beside these causes of friction there was often much unpleasantness about the payment of the chaplain. Who was responsible for his stipend? The inhabitants of the chapelry of Weston in the parish of Ross were much pleased with their chapel, their chaplain and their services, and everything ran quite smoothly until the time came for the chaplain to receive his salary, and then matters became less genial. "The vicar must pay him," said the people. "The people are responsible," said the vicar. The matter was referred to the Bishop, who bluntly (and wisely) said that, if the parishioners of Weston wanted a chaplain of their own, they must be prepared to put their hands in their pockets and pay for him.[2] Sometimes, however, a vicar was more complaisant (or more easily bullied), for in 1482 the rector of Burford agreed to allow the inhabitants of Boraston an annual sum with glebe towards the support of a priest for the chapel, to be paid "without demur and with all arrears."[3] Chaplains were supposed to assist at the parish church when their duties at the chapel were finished, but they often proved very refractory, making frivolous excuses not to serve, preferring to take their ease in taverns and towns.[4] Bishops were constantly being appealed to to bring these chaplains to order, and *make* them obey their vicars; with the result that severe monitions were frequently issued against them, and idle chaplains were threatened with suspension.[5]

Another class of clergy existed, more objectionable still to

[1] *Reg. Mayew*, p. 130. [2] *Reg. Mylling*, p. 18.

[3] *Reg. Mylling*, p. 82, cf. *Reg. Spofford*, p. 23.

[4] *Concilia*, III, 335, for the complaint of Convocation in 1411 about chaplains.

[5] *Reg. Lacy*, pp. 422, 452–3, 456, 713, 806. In 1392 a chaplain, having a grievance against his vicar, went so far as to carry off the latter's goods to the value of £10 by the aid of "swords, bows and arrows," *Reg. Fordham*, f. 117.

the parish priest—the private chaplain. People were expected to attend their own parish church and not go gadding about to other churches, but very often rich people had their own private chapel and chaplain. In the episcopal registers there are numerous cases of licences given to private individuals to have their own private chapel or oratory, though the proviso is usually added that there should be no prejudice thereby to the parish church.[1] In 1415 Bishop Bubwith granted a licence to Elizabeth, relict of Edward Stadelyng, to have masses and other divine offices celebrated in a low voice in her chapel in her house of Halsway, in the presence of herself and her household. In the year 1400 a licence was granted to Richard Wallop and Alice his wife in Hampshire to hear divine service in their private chapel during the Bishop's pleasure.[2] Can we not see in this custom traces of the discontented parishioner? Probably Richard Wallop (or *more* probably Alice his wife) had quarrelled with his parson, and revenged himself by hearing divine service in a private chapel. They *had* to go somewhere, or the Bishop would have been down on them. Nowadays the discontented parishioner leaves the Church, withdraws his subscriptions, and is "done" with religion, without fear of ecclesiastical censure or admonition or excommunication.

The private chaplain.

As time went on, these private chaplains multiplied, and it became the regular fashion to have one's private chaplain. Some of these were mere loafers, with nothing to do but wait upon the ladies of the household, toady to their patron, make themselves ridiculous, and bring the priesthood into contempt. Others, however, occupied an important and useful position in the household. They were chosen not so much on religious grounds as for their business capacity, and they became the secretaries, agents, bailiffs, stewards,

[1] *Reg. Lacy*, pp. 420, 21. This injunction, however, was not always observed, and many who had their own private chapels refused to support their parish church or contribute their share to the upkeep of the fabric and the services. Bishops had often to come to the aid of the parson and act sternly. The Archbishop of York, in 1466, issued an injunction that unless such people supported their parish churches their chapels would be prohibited altogether, *Concilia*, III, 599, Constit. of Neville.

[2] *Reg. Bubwith*, p. 223; *Reg. Wykeham*, II, 520.

and general advisers of their patrons. Sir Thomas Gloys and Sir Thomas Howes were private chaplains to the Pastons and exercised great influence over the affairs and fortunes of the family. The fifth Earl of Northumberland had eleven chaplains, who "seem to have been almost the only persons capable of exercising any office of skill or science; so that the Surveyor of my lord's lands, his Secretary, and the Clarke of his foreign expences were all Priests; notwithstanding which, the last Officer was weekly to make up his accounts on Sunday."[1]

Chantries and prayers for the dead.

Another class of clergy who brought little honour to the clerical Order was the mass priests. The medieval doctrine was that the soul which was not eternally lost passed into a place called Purgatory, where it was punished for those sins committed while on earth which had not been entirely or sufficiently expiated by penance. It was also cleansed by purifying fires and so rendered fit for heaven. The time spent in Purgatory depended upon the state of the individual soul; and it was held that this period of purgation could be lessened and its pains alleviated by prayers of the living offered on behalf of the dead. To pray for the dead had been the custom of the Church from the earliest days of Christianity, and the great Fathers undoubtedly lent the weight of their authority to the belief that the prayers and intercessions of the living had great efficacy in bringing repose to the soul of the departed, and possibly also relief from actual suffering. In the 14th century this doctrine was universally held in the Western Church, and a regular system grew up of providing intercessory prayers for the dead. People left money for the erection of chantries, and for the endowment of chantry priests to say masses for the repose and relief of their departed souls.[2] These chantries were built everywhere, usually in parish churches or in cathedrals or in abbeys, but sometimes also as separate buildings. When they were attached to a church they were generally built in the nave, and formed a kind of chapel containing the tomb of the departed. Very graceful and beautiful in their delicate and

[1] *The Earl of Northumberland's Household Book*, p. vii.

[2] For instances of foundations of chantries see *Reg. Stanbury*, pp. 100–4; *Reg. Spofford*, pp. 281–8; and two very good instances in the *Liber Albus*, Nos. 704, 1193.

elaborate tracery some of these chantries are, though comparatively few remain.[1]

The custom of praying for the souls of the departed is beautiful and ancient, but unfortunately the chantries which were erected for the purpose gave rise to one of the worst abuses of the later Medieval Church. The mass priests who served them did not always bear a high character. Sometimes they acted as curates to the parish church; sometimes they were schoolmasters; more often they spent their time in idle loafing. After mass was sung they had nothing to do, and to while away the time they often resorted to taverns and even to less respectable places.[2] Many of them were very negligent of their duties, and the bishops had to call them to order. In 1416 Bishop Bubwith deprived Edmund Stopp, a chantry priest at Limington, because he had wilfully absented himself for six years and refused to reside. The Bishop of Hereford in 1483 sequestered the revenues of Pyrton chantry on account of the chaplain's neglect and absence. The Archbishop of York in 1466 issued regulations for the mass priests, ordering them to be subservient to the parish priest, not to take the part of the parishioners against them, and not to extort excessive fees.[3] But the evil continued to flourish. The saying of mass became a trade, like shoemaking or bricklaying, and mass priests swarmed everywhere. They caused so great trouble to Colet when he was Dean of St. Paul's that he declared that they were a disgrace to the Church and brought grave discredit upon the priestly Order. Erasmus, too, is very severe upon them. Writing in 1530 to the Bishop of Hildesheim, he angrily complains of the lives and conversation of the mass priests. "Nowadays when the Celebration is over the man who has offered the Sacrifice adjourns to drinking parties and loose talk, or to cards and dice, or goes hunting and lounging in idleness. While he is at the altar angels wait upon him; when he leaves it he seeks the refuse of mankind. It is not decent."[4]

Mass priests.

[1] There are some beautiful chantries in the Cathedral Church of Winchester. See Vaughan, *Winchester Cathedral*, cc. 4 and 5.

[2] *Concilia*, III, p. 605.

[3] *Reg. Bubwith*, p. 246; *Reg. Mylling*, p. 143; *Concilia*, III, p. 604.

[4] Froude, *Lectures on Erasmus*, p. 386.

bad roads and difficulties of communication, the dull monotony of a country parson's life was too much for many of these medieval clerics, who jumped at any excuse to get away. It was by no means always idleness or love of pleasure that led men to absent themselves from their cures. The financial responsibilities of the parson, especially the duty of almsgiving, sometimes proved too great for the slender resources of the benefice; and no doubt many were only too glad to escape for a while from the clamour of disagreeable, quarrelsome and fault-finding parishioners. Of course, a man was not supposed to leave his parish without a licence from the Bishop; but if the latter refused, one could easily be bought from the Pope, who was only too willing to earn an honest penny by such means. In 1402 Bishop William of Wykeham granted the rector of Bletchingley leave of absence for three years, and when the licence was about to expire he refused to renew it. This did not at all suit the rector, who obviously shrank from parochial work; but the matter was easily remedied, for he just brought the matter before Pope Boniface IX, who readily sold him a leave of absence for another seven years.[1] Bishops were not unnaturally very suspicious of these papal licences. In 1523 George Sidnan, rector of Shorewell, Isle of Wight, was cited to show cause why his rectory should not be sequestrated because of his dilapidations and non-residence. The rector tried to foist off upon the Bishop a papal dispensation; but on inspection it was found to have run out, for it was only for the year 1521.[2] But if a man could not get a licence from his Bishop and was too poor to buy a papal dispensation and too honest to forge one, he simply played the truant and went off on his own. When the Bishop heard that one of his clergy had left his parish without permission he promptly ordered him back; but this was more easily said than done, for sometimes the absentee rector was able to escape detection. In the year 1400 a commission was issued by the

The medieval clergy very restless and anxious to leave their cures.

Episcopal and Papal licences.

Playing the truant.

[1] *Reg. Wykeham*, II, 482, 498.

[2] *Reg. Fox* (Winton), V, f. 52. In 1526 a rector flourished before the Bp. of Hereford a papal dispensation, allowing him to hold two incompatible benefices, *Reg. Bothe*, I, 176. There are several instances in this register of sequestration for non-residence.

Bishop of Winchester to the Rural Dean of Sombourne and the vicar of Romsey to cite the rector of Michelmersh to return into residence within fifteen days. The missing rector, however, could not be found, though it was reported that he was wandering about somewhere in the diocese of Bath and Wells. The only thing to do, therefore, was to sequestrate his living.[1] Certainly for criminals or debtors or negligent clergy the Middle Ages were a very convenient time in which to live; for in days when there were no railways, motors, or telegraphs it was the easiest thing in the world to hide, if only in the next county.

Episcopal attempts to enforce the residence of the parochial clergy.

Many attempts were made to stop the evil of non-residence. In 1401 Archbishop Arundell ordered all vicars and rectors to reside, as their absence meant the neglect of souls, decline of Church life, and the scandalisation of the laity; but the injunction had little effect and complaints are of frequent occurrence.[2] In 1438 the parishioners of Childon, in Devonshire, complained that their vicar neglected his duty and continually absented himself without licence. To their delight the living was sequestrated.[3] Archbishop Morton in 1487 tried hard to make the clergy reside. After enumerating the evils of non-residence, he insisted that clergy *must* reside and set a good example to their parishioners. If they had a licence to hold more than one living they were to reside in each in turn; papal dispensations for non-residence were to be carefully scrutinised (for certain of the clergy were not above forging them), and if they were found to be genuine the Archbishop insisted that suitable vicars should be left in charge.[4]

Bishop Fox.

Bishop Fox who, until the end of his life, never attempted to reside for more than a few weeks at a time (if at all) in any of his many dioceses, was very perturbed at the practice of the lower clergy not residing in their cures and failing to give personal attention to their pastoral duties. It was (he said) a thoroughly bad practice and ought to be stopped. Accordingly, when he was Bishop of Durham (1494–1501), he sent monitions to non-resident clergy, ordering them to return at once and

[1] *Reg. Wykeham*, II, 501.
[2] *Concilia*, III, 267, 275.
[3] *Reg. Lacy*, p. 714, cf. p. 650 and *Reg. Mylling*, pp. 70, 80; *Reg. Spofford*, pp. 38, 41, 49, 103, 138, 159, 195, 221; *Reg. Stanbury*, pp. 116, 125.
[4] *Concilia*, III, 619.

reside in their benefices. So keenly indeed did he feel (in the case of the lower clergy) the evils of non-residence that he determined to *make* his nominees reside. Before he would institute a man to a benefice, in order to insure his continual residence, he made him sign a bond for a large sum of money which he was to forfeit if he left his parish without leave.[1] When a few years later he became Bishop of Winchester he employed the same drastic methods. In 1508 he issued (so easy is precept) a monition to the Archdeacon of Winchester to order certain rectors, who were absent without leave, to return to residence at once under pain of deprivation.[2] The evil, though checked, still flourished; for it was one of the complaints of the Commons against the Spirituality in 1529.[3]

The medieval clergy were constantly on the move.

A very striking characteristic of the medieval parson was his dislike to remain for long in the same place. He is always moving about, and livings are continually changing hands. For example, between 1430–52 the rectory of Goodleigh, near Barnstaple, changed five times; and in the space of twenty years (1432–52) the rectory of West Worlington in Devonshire changed no less than seven times, four rectors having resigned and three having died. Later in the century the same frequent changes are found. In the diocese of Hereford between 1477–92 there were as many as five rectors of the parish of Stockton (one of them being deprived for his immoral life); while in seventeen years the rectory of Whitbourne in the same diocese changed hands no less than six times. During the wars of the Roses the parish of Elstree in Herts had nine rectors in sixteen years; while Shephall in the same county had five in six years.[4] A great many clerical moves were due to exchanges.

Exchanges.

[1] e.g. the rector of Ryton gave him a bond of £100 (=£1200) to secure his continued and personal residence, *Reg. Fox* (B. and W.), p. 56.

[2] *Reg. Fox* (Winton), II, f. 98; cf. *Reg. Mayew*, p. 190, for a similar monition in 1513. Wykeham frequently ordered the non-residents to return, *Reg. Wykeham*, II, 22, 51, 144, 308, 349–51. In 1383 forty-four parishes are mentioned where the rectors were absent without leave. For absenteeism in Herts in 1426–7 see Rushbrook Williams, *History of Abbey of St. Albans*, p. 199.

[3] *L. and P.*, IV, 6043.

[4] *Reg. Lacy; Reg. Mylling*, pp. 185–202; Rushbrook Williams, p. 218.

Both bishops and lay patrons encouraged such exchanges and did all they could to expedite them. In this respect the Medieval Church was wise, for the frequent moves of the clergy made for vitality, and undoubtedly did much to prevent that stagnation and loss of efficiency which are the inevitable result of men staying too long in one parish. During the 14th and first half of the 15th centuries exchanges were very frequent, but for some reason or another grew rarer towards the close of the Middle Ages.[1] During the episcopate of Wykeham (1367–1402) exchanges were very usual, two moves out of every five being due to this cause. In the diocese of Ely during the ten years' episcopate of Arundell (1378–88) there were eighty exchanges; under Bishop Fordham, between 1388–1408, there were 186. In the diocese of Hereford at the beginning of the 15th century there were ninety-nine exchanges in twelve years, several of the livings being exchanged three or four times. In 1410 in the diocese of Bath and Wells out of fifty-eight moves twenty-seven were due to exchanges. This is perhaps above the average; yet we find that in 1423 out of thirty-six moves thirteen were due to exchanges. The medieval parson seems (to judge from the record of registers) to have been in a continual fret to move on and get out of one benefice into another. But he did not always like it when he had got there. He sometimes found that he had made a mistake, and, finding his new sphere less ideal than he had anticipated, hastened to exchange again. Sometimes men changed their diocese only to discover that they wished they had not. On May 30th, 1410, Walter Olney, vicar of Horton in the diocese of Rochester, exchanged with John Grenelane, rector of Writelyngton in Somersetshire; but apparently he did not care for his new diocese or diocesan; for in August he changed back again into the diocese of Rochester.[2] The

A typical medieval parson.

Rev. Thomas Pounde was a typical 15th-century parson. On June 29th, 1430, he was instituted to the rectory of Combe Pyne in Devonshire on the presentation of the lord of the manor, to whom he had probably acted as a private chaplain; but he very soon got

[1] Thus during the eighteen years' episcopate of Bishop Bothe of Hereford (1517–35) there were only four exchanges, *Reg. Bothe*, pp. 331–49. There were few exchanges during the long episcopate of Fox at Winchester.

[2] *Reg. Bubwith*, pp. 9, 11.

tired of his cure, and a year later exchanged livings with the vicar of Toller-Fratrum in Dorsetshire. Here he remained for nearly seven years, when he again became restless and, feeling he would like a move on, effected another exchange, this time with the vicar of Salcombe Regis in his old diocese of Exeter; but eight years of Salcombe Regis were quite long enough for any man and he once more felt it was high time he should be moving on again. Accordingly he arranged an exchange of benefices with the vicar of Dunsford in Devonshire, where he remained until his death a few years later.[1] This constant movement among the parochial clergy was hailed with delight by their parishioners, who, after some years of one man, felt that it was perhaps possible to have at times too much of a good thing, and who were as eager for fresh faces as the clergy were for fresh places. Who will blame them? It is putting too great a strain upon human nature to expect any congregation to stand more than ten years of the same parson. More than half the ills from which the Church of England is suffering to-day are due simply to the clergy staying too long in one parish. Hence stagnation.

Choppe-churches.

But exchanges were not always of this innocent type. In the latter half of the 14th century a class of men made themselves notorious by erecting traffic in livings into a regular trade. These clerics were known as *choppechurches*, and derived a good income by defrauding others by crafty and grossly unjust exchanges, or by robbing them of their benefices altogether. In 1392 Archbishop Courtenay issued a mandate against these choppechurches, denouncing their idleness, extravagance, and simony. Stringent measures were to be taken to put down the abuse, and stern punishment was denounced against "all fraudulent holders of churches and dignities, all sons of iniquity commonly called choppechurches, whose iniquities the clergy condemn, the people abominate and the generality of both sexes detest." After the close of the 14th century less is heard of this abuse.[2]

A number of vacancies were caused by resignation. Very frequently when a man resigned he was given a pension to be paid out of the income of the living, and most of the

[1] *Reg. Lacy*, pp. 126, 132, 235, 311. There are several similar instances in the registers.

[2] *Reg. Fordham*, f. 115.

clergy who resigned did so (*sub spe pensionis*). Some bishops insisted that retiring clergy should always have a pension, perhaps not so much out of pity for the man as for the good name of the Church. Bishop Lacy in 1425 assigns a pension of six marks out of the living to the retiring vicar of St. Mervyn in Cornwall, "lest," he adds, "being destitute he be compelled miserably to beg his bread to the scandal of the priestly Order." The pensions were as a rule small, but then the livings were small, too, and it is a wonder that they could stand the charge, but vicars *had* to pay under a threat of excommunication and sequestration. This is one of the (many) Church abuses which has survived to the present time. The whole thing was (and is) a scandal, for the payment of a pension out of the scanty resources of the benefice is a grave handicap to Church work.[1]

Resignation and pensions.

Occasionally the Bishop, instead of assigning a fixed sum as pension, gave permission to the retiring incumbent to bargain with his successor about the matter, not (one would imagine) a very satisfactory arrangement for either party. In 1514 the vicar of Lugwundine felt compelled to resign through age and infirmities. He resigns solely "*sub spe pensionis*"; but in spite of his age, infirmities, and merits the Bishop of Hereford only gives him permission to bargain with his successor and do the best he can for himself in his old age. One can imagine the unseemly haggling which must have taken place, the sense of grievance on both sides, the uncharitable feelings engendered, the fervid language used, and the edification of all concerned. One wonders what the wretched man got in the end, and how long he lived, a burden to himself and a vexation to his successor.[2] A curious case occurred in 1420. The vicar of Chilton in Somersetshire resigned, and the Bishop of Bath and Wells assigned him the not unsatis-

Some curious examples of pensions.

[1] *Reg. Lacy*, p. 526. The highest pension I have come across is one of 20 marks assigned in 1494 by Bishop Fox to the retiring vicar of Chard, *Reg. Fox*, p. 104; cf. p. 55, where the vicar of Knestoke receives only 4 marks. In 1424 the retiring Archdeacon of Hereford got a pension of £20; in 1432 the rector of Hopesay got 10 marks out of a living worth 30 marks, *Reg. Spofford*, pp. 52, 148.

[2] *Reg. Mayew*, p. 192; cf. pp. 200, 201, 206, 207; *Reg. Fox* (B. and W.), p. 114, for other instances. There are several instances of bargaining for a pension in *Reg. Bothe*.

factory pension of twelve marks a year, that he should not "to the scandal of the priestly Order" have to beg his bread in public; but this is not all, for (doubtless to raise the spirits of his successor) he also "assigned him a chamber on the north side of the rectory with the common use of the hall, kitchen and garden." To which arrangement (so we are told) the new vicar "freely consented." It was thought wise, however, to fortify his free assent with a solemn oath to pay.[1] Poor man! It would be bad enough to have his pensioner residing in the same parish, a daily reminder of an intolerable grievance; but in the same house, using the same rooms, meeting daily, perhaps hourly! The experiment was not repeated, for this is the only instance recorded of such an arrangement.

Patronage.

It may not be uninteresting to note how patronage was held, and how it was exercised in the Middle Ages. Take an example. Bishop Lacy was Bishop of Exeter for thirty-five years (1420–55), and during that period there were 1276 vacancies of livings. Of these vacancies the Bishop appointed to 156, the Dean and Chapter to 106, the Crown to 69, monasteries and collegiate bodies to 334, and private patrons to nearly all these put together, 611. There were 120 exchanges.[2] There were often cases of disputed patronage, and commissions were appointed which rendered elaborate and very verbose reports to the Bishop. In 1481 there was a dispute with reference to the patronage of the chantry of the Blessed Virgin Mary at Dilwyn. An inquiry was held, but Sir Richard de la Bere, one of the claimants, so intimidated and bullied the jury that it refused to return a verdict.[3] Some of the bishops were careful not to appoint the nominees of private patrons without careful inquiry about their fitness. But there was great laxity at times. Sometimes private patrons appointed men to livings in their gift, not for their spiritual qualifications or fitness for the parish, but simply because they felt they would be useful to them personally as stewards, or book-keepers, or surveyors, "such as can surelie and wiselie be your receivours of your rents

Abuse of patronage.

[1] *Reg. Bubwith*, p. 389.

[2] *Reg. Lacy*, II, *passim*. See also *Reg. Fox* (B. and W.), p. 28. During his episcopate of 2½ years there were 104 vacancies: bishops, 18; monasteries, 48; lay, 38.

[3] *Reg. Mylling*, p. 68.

and revenues and, rather than fail, will boldie distraine a poore man's cattle and drive them to pounde till they starve for hunger."[1] Benefices were often given to young boys. In 1508 Thomas Slade, a lad of eighteen, obtained a dispensation from the Pope, permitting him to hold a benefice. No doubt he had to pay, for we are told of another boy who was charged £3 (=£36) for a licence to hold a benefice at the age of sixteen.[2] In the Petition of the Commons in 1532 great complaint was made of the bad practice of bishops giving benefices to young boys. "And also whereas the said spiritual ordinaries do daily confer and give sundry benefices unto certain young folks, calling them their nephews or kinsfolk, not apt or able to serve the cure of any such benefice; whereby the said ordinaries do keep and detain the fruits and profits of the same benefices in their own hands, and thereby accumulate to themselves right great and large sums of money . . . and so the cures and other promotions given unto such infants be only employed to the enriching of the said ordinaries and the poor silly souls of your people and subjects which should be taught, for lack of good curates do perish without doctrine or any good teaching."[3]

Dilapidations in the Middle Ages.

The question of dilapidations vexed the soul (and pocket) of the medieval parson as it vexes his successor to-day. He was supposed to keep his house and buildings in good repair, and, if he were a rector, to maintain the chancel as well; but in many cases the livings were so small that the parson found the greatest difficulties in finding the money. Still, they were legally responsible, and if they failed to carry out their obligations the ecclesiastical authorities came down upon them pretty sharply. The frequent appointment of commissions to deal with the question of dilapidations shows the unpopularity and difficulty of the whole system among the parochial clergy. In 1441 a new rector was appointed to the living of St. Martins-by-Loo in Cornwall; but on arrival he found everything in ruins—chancel, rectory, outbuildings. He at

[1] In the *Paston Letters* the vicars of the parishes in the gift of the Pastons often acted as agents to these patrons and made themselves generally useful. This sometimes brought them into conflict with their other parishioners. See the vicar of Paston's letter, *P.L.*, 438.

[2] *Reg. Mayew*, p. 88; *L. and P.*, IV, 2360.

[3] Gee and Hardy, p. 150.

once brought the case before the Bishop, who appointed a commission with the Archdeacon of Cornwall at its head to hold an inquiry. An elaborate survey was made and estimates obtained. The total cost of the repairs, caused by previous neglect, would, it was found, amount to £40 (=£600).[1] Monitions were frequently issued by the ecclesiastical authorities, warning the clergy to maintain their buildings in good repair, and not to allow them through carelessness or neglect to fall into decay. In 1403 Archbishop Arundell ordered the clergy to repair their houses and especially the churches, many of which were in such a state of ruin and decay that divine service could not be held in them.[2] If an incumbent refused or was unable to do his dilapidations, little mercy was shown to him. In 1421 John Waryn, rector of Parkham, had allowed the church and rectory to decay. The Bishop of Exeter orders his living to be sequestrated. In 1428 he did the same in the case of the benefice of Rattery, because the appropriators, an abbey in Wales, and the vicar had between them allowed the church to fall into such disrepair that divine service could not be properly performed. In 1423 Bishop Bubwith sequestrated all fruits, rents, profits, and other emoluments whatsoever of the parish church of Woky and of Master Nicholas Mockyng, rector of the same, whether in barns or fields, for the proper repair of palpable defects in the chancel of the church and in the manse and buildings pertaining to the same.[3]

[1] *Reg. Lacy*, p. 783, cf. *Reg. Mayew*, p. 72; *Reg. Bubwith*, p. 18; *Reg. Bothe*, I, 171.

[2] *Concilia*, III, 276.

[3] *Reg. Lacy*, pp. 480, 548; cf. 679, 708, 715; *Reg. Bubwith*, p. 436; *Reg. Fox* (Winton), f. 52, for the case of the rector of Shorewell. In 1424 the buildings at Bayton, "in ruinositatem, deformitatem, collapsum, et irreparabilem dilapidacionem notorie collapsa sunt," *Reg. Spofford*, p. 175. Deans and Chapters were often very careless about dilapidations, *ibid.* pp. 112, 221, 259. Sometimes men took the money for dilapidations from their predecessors and spent it upon themselves, *Concilia*, III, 721. In 1368 the Archdeacon of Surrey (who was also rector of Farnham), appropriated for his own use stone left by his predecessor for repairs, *Reg. Wykeham*, II, 67. The Visitations of Archbp. Kempe reveal many complaints of absenteeism and dilapidations of parish churches, *Surtees Soc.*, cxxvii, p. 212, 13; but in a great number of cases the parishioners in reply to inquiries answer "*Omnia bene.*"

What was the general relation between the parson and his parishioners ? In very many cases, undoubtedly, it was excellent ; but there were exceptions. Then, as now, there was sometimes friction and unpleasantness, and the fault was not always on one side. Quarrels (generally about trifles) were not uncommon. A few instances will suffice. Thus in 1413 an ash tree was blown down during a gale in the churchyard of Westbury in the diocese of Bath and Wells. The vicar at once claimed it as his own, and lost no time in getting it removed into his own garden. This indecent haste caused great annoyance to the parishioners, who declared that the tree belonged to *them* and that the vicar had no business to remove it. The dispute ran so high that an appeal had to be made to the Bishop. The vicar, it appears, though hasty and tactless, had the law on his side, for the Bishop pronounced in his favour.[1] The same year the vicar of Wedmore, Robert Tanner, had defiled his churchyard by the shedding of blood. This had caused a great scandal in the parish. The vicar had to be excommunicated, and was only released after he had given complete satisfaction to the parishioners, whose feelings he had so violently outraged.[2] Churchyards and the trees in them seem to have been a constant source of friction, for in 1423 John Dyer, rector of Clapton, charged two of his parishioners with wilfully and illegally cutting down trees in the churchyard, and asked the Bishop to excommunicate them. The Bishop did so ; and they are only absolved on their undertaking to hand over the trees to the rector, give four pence to the poor, plant fresh trees, lie prostrate in the churchyard during Mass, and promising never to repeat the offence.[3]

Relation between clergy and people.

Causes of friction.

There were many other causes of friction between parson and people, and sometimes the latter in their anger took the law into their own hands and inflicted summary punish-

[1] *Reg. Bubwith*, p. 134. Tithes were a frequent cause of friction ; see *Reg. Spofford*, p. 212, where the Bp. had to interfere. Excommunication was pronounced against those who withheld their tithe, *Reg. Arundell*, ff. 37, 57 b. ; *Reg. Wykeham*, II, 144. John Myrc, in *Instructions for Parish Priests* (E.E.T.S., p. 11), writes :—

Teche hem also well and grethe
How they schule paye here teythe.

[2] *Reg. Bubwith*, p. 141.

[3] *Ibid.*, p. 432.

ment upon the obnoxious cleric.[1] Thus, for example, in the year 1486 the parishioners of Bosbury in the diocese of Hereford were so exasperated for some reason against the rector of Munsley that they made a violent personal assault upon him. In this they were, of course, in the wrong. The rector knew it; and he took good care that they should be paid out. Much might be forgiven; but an assault upon a member of the clerical caste partook of the nature of an unforgivable sin; and the delinquents only obtained absolution on promising to go on a pilgrimage to the shrine of St. Thomas. Our sympathies are at first with the rector until we read a little further on that, on his death four years later, all his ecclesiastical property had to be sequestrated because of his neglect, a fact which leads us to suspect that the parishioners may have had more to say for themselves than is at first sight apparent.[2]

Violence on the part of parishioners.

It is more pleasant to turn from sordid details like these, which after all are the rare exception, to the parochial life and work of the Church. A parish priest was (after the lord of the manor) the chief person, the *parson*, of the parish, and as such he occupied a prominent and important position among his people. In remote villages he was probably the only educated man in the place, and people would come to him for advice in worldly as well as in spiritual matters. He might act as lawyer, as doctor and as the general friend and adviser of his parishioners. It was his duty to look after the poor, and to provide for them out of tithes and offerings. He was required to show hospitality, exhortations to which are very frequent, and which in a poor benefice made so great a demand upon the slender resources of the clergy. In all these and many other secular duties he was expected to take the lead, and to exercise his influence for the good of the people and in the interests of the Church.

Important position of the parson in his parish.

[1] For very violent assaults upon unpopular parochial clergy see *Reg. Spofford*, pp. 9, 16, 36. For cases of violence and rowdyism in Church porches and during divine service see *Yorks Visit.* (Sur. Soc., cxxvii, 220, 1); *Paston Letters*, 179, and 434 where in 1460 the vicar of Paston writes: "And the great fray that they mad in the tyme of masse it ravyched my witts and mad me ful hevyly dysposyd."

[2] *Reg. Mylling*, pp. 107, 128. Clerical neighbours sometimes quarrelled. Thus in 1533 the rector of Ribbesford is warned not to interfere with the rights of Cleobury Mortimer, *Reg. Bothe*, p. 278.

But the chief work of the parish priest was, then as now, care for the spiritual welfare of its children. The duty of worship was diligently preached and (for the most part) regularly practised. On Sundays and Feast Days the parishioners came to church to hear Mass. There was, besides, daily Mass, for it was the rule for the priest to say Mass daily as well as the seven canonical hours and the lesser offices of B.V.M. The Italian traveller who visited England in 1500 tells us that daily Mass was regularly attended.[1] Particular stress was laid upon the teaching office of the Church. In the 13th century three or four sermons a year were all that were required or expected, but in the latter part of the 14th century many of the more energetic of the clergy, fired by the example of the Friars and Wycliffites, devoted themselves to preaching and became expert at the art. Many of these sermons, full of homely anecdotes, consisted of fervent appeals to the emotions, dwelt with dramatic power upon the Passion of our Lord, and were evangelical in the best sense of the word.[2] Every priest, whether he was a preacher or not, was required to teach his parishioners the Creed of the Church and the way of good living. In the Constitutions of George Neville, Archbishop of York, it was ordered that, in view of the spread of heretical opinions, due largely to ignorance of the true Faith, every priest shall four times a year (*per se vel per alium*) preach upon the Lord's Prayer, the Ten Commandments, the two precepts of the Gospel, the Seven Works of Mercy, the Seven Deadly Sins, the Seven Principal Virtues, and the Seven Sacraments. They must thoroughly learn all these and teach them to their flock.[3] The clergy were also required to teach children the Lord's Prayer, the Salutation of the B.V.M., the Apostles' Creed, the Psalm *De Profundis*, the usual Prayers for the Dead, the Ten Commandments, the Seven Deadly Sins, the Seven Sacraments, the Seven Gifts of the Holy Ghost, the Seven Works of Mercy, and the manner of confession. For those who could read (and could afford them) there were primers and books of devotion written in English and fairly accessible. These contained

Spiritual duties of the parish clergy.

[1] *Italian Relation*, p. 23.

[2] For examples of such preaching see Mirk's *Festial*, Ed. Erbe (E.E.T.S.), a collection of homilies for Festivals.

[3] *Concilia*, III, 599.

chapters from the Bible,[1] the canonical hours, the commandments, the Lord's Prayer, the penitential Psalms and a litany together with certain private devotions and instructions. By the aid of these primers worshippers could follow the services in church, even though they could not understand Latin.[2] Finally, it was the duty of the priest to urge his flock to confess their sins at least three times a year; to visit the sick; and to carry the last Sacraments to the dying, reminding them to make their will and not omitting to hint at a legacy both to the Church and to the parish.[3]

Such, at any rate, was the *theory* of the work of the Church. How far the theory was put into practice in the later Middle Age is another matter. The theory of the Church is always excellent, even if its practice is at times somewhat lax; for it often happens that men's ideals are higher than their mode of carrying them out. It seems somewhat doubtful, with the large number of non-resident rectors and ill-paid vicars and chaplains, whether theory and practice were able at all times to coincide. Dr. Edward Lee, who succeeded Wolsey as Archbishop of York, is reported to have said that in the

Divorce between precept and practice.

[1] For the vexed question of Bible reading in English in the later Middle Ages see Deanesley, *The Lollard Bible*, esp. pp. 319–60. The subject matter of the Bible was well known in the Middle Ages, for literature is full of references to it.

[2] The earliest mention of the Primer is 1294. A 15th-cent. Primer is published by E.E.T.S., *The Prymer or Lay Folks' Prayer Book*. This gives the hours B.V.M., certain Psalms and Offices, the Ave Maria and a Litany. Primers were quite common and are frequently mentioned in wills. See also Maskell, *Monumenta Ritualia Eccles. Angl.*, II, 1–242 and Introd. For the Mass, *The Lay Folks' Mass Book*, ed. Simmons (E.E.T.S.) in rhyming verses, early 14th century. For medieval services generally see C. Wordsworth, *Notes on Med. Services in Eng.*, 1898; Wordsworth and Littlehales, *The Old Service Books of the English Church*; Maskell, *The Ancient Liturgy of the Church of Eng.*, with various uses in parallel columns. Archbp. Thoresby (1352–74) wrote *The Lay Folks' Catechism* (ed. Simmons and Nolloth, E.E.T.S.), a simple, devout and very practical instruction for the laity.

[3] See *Instructions for Parish Priests*, by John Myrc (ed. Peacock, E.E.T.S.). This book, in the form of a poem, gives sound practical advice upon the duties of a parish priest, inculcates a high standard of religion and morality, and is a good exposition of the medieval *ideal* of pastoral work. See also Gasquet, *Parish Life in Medieval England*; Manning, *The People's Faith in the time of Wyclif*, cc. 1–4; Bennett, *The Pastons and their England*, c. xiv.

whole of Yorkshire he only knew of twelve parochial clergy who were able and willing to preach and to teach their people. But perhaps the Archbishop, like many other prelates of the period, had but a limited knowledge of the capacities and labours of his clergy.

Illiterate Clergy.

It is certain, however, that some of the medieval clergy were imperfectly educated. Grosseteste, Bishop of Lincoln (1235–54), laid down as the minimum knowledge requisite for a priest ability to teach the Lord's Prayer, the Hail Mary, the Three Creeds, the Ten Commandments, the Seven Deadly Sins and the Seven Sacraments. He was also expected to have sufficient knowledge of grammar and song to enable him to sing and understand the Mass. There were some, however, who failed to reach even this standard. Peckham in 1281 dwelt upon the harm done by the ignorance of so many of the clergy; while the episcopal registers of the 14th and 15th centuries afford proof that some of the clergy were very ignorant. In 1381 William Wichot, rector of St. Peter's, Winchester, was appointed to the benefice of Newnham, and before institution he took his oath in the presence of the Bishop that he would regularly attend a Grammar School, and would there diligently learn grammar and song. Four years later another Winchester cleric, the rector of St. Michael's, was sworn to get by heart the Creed, the Ten Commandments, the Sacraments, the Works of Mercy and the Deadly Sins. One hundred and forty-one years later, in 1526, the Prior of St. John of Jerusalem presented William Marshall to the living of Sawston. The Bishop of Ely was of opinion that, being very ignorant, he should diligently study for two years and should then appear again. His institution was to depend upon his attainments.[1] Archbishop Bourchier in 1455 says of the clergy in Kent that some are "ignorant and unlearned, unskilled or almost destitute of letters, not without grave peril and great danger to souls";[2] and Bishop Pecocke thought that the growth of heresy was due to a dearth of clergy able to expound the Scriptures. At the beginning of the 15th century Bishop

[1] *Reg. Wykeham*, II, pp. 116, 371; *Reg. Alcock*, f. 34. For earlier cases see *Educ. Charters*, pp. 147, 155. In 1225 the new vicar of Hanworth was ordered by the Bp. of Lincoln to attend a Grammar School because of his ignorance.

[2] *Concilia*, III, 573.

Bubwith instituted Robert Russe, priest, to the vicarage of Henstrygge; but the poor man was hopelessly ignorant, even of the rudiments of the Faith, and could only just manage to read. The Bishop did not see his way to refuse institution, but he made him give a sworn undertaking to procure at the earliest opportunity a book containing the elements of the Christian Faith, and learn and understand the contents of the same.[1]

As the century advanced the standard of learning among the clergy certainly became higher, and the very fact that indignant attention was drawn to the illiteracy of certain priests points to the better education of the rest, and to the feeling that intellectual attainments were essential for the work and influence of the priesthood. Still, matters were far from satisfactory on the very eve of the Reformation, for the Chancellor of York complained of the great harm done to the Church by the ignorance of the clergy, and one of the grievances of the Commons against the clergy in 1529 was against "unlearned ministers."[2]

The clergy were diligent in extracting money from the laity.

But whether the clergy neglected the duties of preaching and teaching or not, there was, at any rate, one duty which they certainly did *not* neglect, the duty of extracting money from the pockets of their parishioners. The laity were exhorted and warned; and, when warning and exhortation failed, were *forced* to give. It was the custom for all parishioners to give regularly and systematically to the Church; and this they did, for the most part willingly and gladly, from love to their Church and from belief in their religion. At the same time it is only fair to add that episcopal registers reveal another side of the question. These offerings were by no means *always* voluntary. People in the Middle Ages *had* to give, whether they liked it or not. If they did not fall into line, means were soon taken to *make* them do so. By a Bull of Pope Nicholas V in 1453 every householder who was

[1] *Reg. Bubwith*, p. 139.

[2] *L. and P.*, IV, 6043. See also Deanesley, pp. 157, 193, 195, 196. In the synods called by Bishop Bothe at Wolsey's orders the articles and constitutions for reform were read to the clergy "in vulgari, pro faciliori et uberiori eorundem intellectu"—a sign that the Latinity of the clergy of the diocese of Hereford was somewhat weak, *Reg. Bothe*, pp. iii, 67.

rented at ten shillings per annum had to pay one farthing to the Church every offering day; those whose rent was twenty shillings paid a halfpenny; and so on in proportion to their means. In 1388 the parish of Farnham was raising money for the purchase of church bells; the parishioners were duly and properly assessed; but some, it appears, objected (on "principle," of course) to pay. The Bishop soon hears of it, and issues a mandate to the vicar to admonish certain parishioners under pain of ecclesiastical censure to pay to the collector their quota.[1] A few years earlier, in 1375, the Bishop had sent a mandate enabling the rector of Lambeth to *enforce* payment for a rate for the repairs of the parish church. "Rector of Lambeth enjoined to admonish certain children of iniquity, whose names are on a scroll attached to the mandate, to pay their contributions henceforth, under pain of excommunication."[2] "Pay, or be excommunicated," was the medieval method of raising money. People, too, were often frightened or bribed into leaving money or gifts to the Church in their wills. They certainly believed that the right disposal of their goods had much to do with their eternal happiness, for they were promised relief in Purgatory if they would make a will favourable to the Church. In the will of Sir John Fastolf in 1459 we find that he leaves money to the Church and to the poor, and beseeches his executors to pay it as he willed: "I exhorte, beseeche and preye all mine executors, in the virtue of our Lord Jesu Cryst, and in virtue of the aspercion of His holy Blood, shed out graciously for the salvation of all mankinde, that for the more hasty delyveraunce of my soule from the peynefull flammes of the fyre of Purgatory" . . . they will do as he wishes.[3] Posthumous charity is, so far as the giver is concerned, a complete fraud. It is not any very real generosity to give away one's money when one has no further worldly use for it; and such charity is often only a means of obtaining notoriety at the expense of the rightful heirs. Still, whatever the motive, the gift proves very acceptable.

Pressure often resorted to in extracting money.

[1] *Reg. Wykeham*, II, 419.

[2] *Reg. Wykeham*, II, 217; cf. *Reg. Fordham*, f. 201, where parishioners who refused in 1405 to contribute to a new missal for the Church of Downham were threatened with citation before the Bishop.

[3] *Paston Letters*, I, p. 459.

These were more or less legitimate methods of raising funds; but there was another method more open to objection. One of the most serious charges brought with such frequency and insistence against the clergy of the period was their practice of demanding fees for the performance of spiritual duties. Fees were charged for almost everything they did. There was a fee for baptism, a fee for churching, a fee for extreme unction, a fee for absolution, a fee for consecrations, a fee for burials, a fee for everything. Money was the golden key which alone (it seemed) could unlock the spiritual treasures of the Church. These fees were at first purely voluntary offerings; then they became customary; at last they were obligatory, for the clergy refused to perform their spiritual duties without them. Some fees were paid without much complaint; but others were the cause of very bad feeling. The fees which provoked the greatest dissatisfaction, which were the cause of endless friction and dispute, which led to the interference of the Bishops, of Convocation and, lastly, of Parliament, were the fees connected with burials. These fees were known as *mortuaries*. The parson had the right of taking the best beast, or the best jewel, garment, cloth or piece of furniture belonging to the dead man as his fee for performing the rite of burial. Some of the clergy were in the habit, as soon as they heard of the death of a parishioner, of invading the house of mourning, not so much to utter words of comfort as to secure the mortuary; and many of them positively refused to bury the body until the fee had been handed over. Thus a corpse was often left unburied for days while the parson and the relatives were engaged in an unseemly bickering about the mortuary. The evil had for long engaged the attention of the authorities of the Church. Archbishop Langham in the 14th century had made an attempt to regulate the abuse of mortuaries; Church Councils had condemned the system again and again; while individual bishops were often called upon to settle disputes. Thus in 1425 a violent wrangling took place between the rector of Kingsbridge and his parishioners with respect to the burial fees which were being charged; and the matter caused such trouble that the Bishop of Exeter had to interfere and pour oil on troubled waters. There was some

Clerical fees.

Mortuary fees.

Dispute about burial fees at Kingsbridge.

very plain speaking, and the rector was told a few home truths. The Bishop spoke indignantly about the scandal of corpses remaining unburied, and of the unpopularity which the Church incurred by the exactions and the cupidity of many of the clergy.[1] The famous case of Richard Hunne in 1514 arose out of a mortuary dispute, Hunne refusing to give the priest the bearing sheet which the latter demanded for the burial of an infant. The dispute raged with such violence and led to such complications that it aroused everywhere very deep feeling. It was in connection with this case that the inhabitants of London made a formal complaint about the exactions of their clergy. They complained of the exorbitant fees demanded for tapers at mass; for marriages, burials and churchings; for friends prayed for in the Bede roll; for howsell at Easter and for devotions on divers days. The House of Commons took the matter up and made a strong protest against the extortions of curates and parish priests, more particularly with reference to the burial of the dead.[2] In the following year the cupidity of the clergy was brought to the notice of the King, who sympathised with the laity in the matter, and Parliament, with a view to remedying the grievance and removing danger of infection from unburied corpses, asserted "That no parish priest was to refuse to bury; that every curate was to administer the sacraments of Holy Church when required to every sick person in his parish, and shall receive into his church or churchyard the corpse of every person dying in his parish under a penalty of £40; and that no curate shall demand mortuary fees or gifts from those lacking goods."[3] The evil was certainly checked, but it still continued to exist; cupidity was the vice of the age; and the clergy clung with much eagerness to their fees.

Case of Hunne.

The bishops in 1529 urged the advisability of limiting exactions[4]; but apparently they were unsuccessful; for one of the complaints of the Commons in 1532 was the excessive fees demanded by the clergy. "And where also the said prelates and ordinaries daily do permit and suffer the parsons, vicars, curates, parish

Complaints in 1532.

[1] *Reg. Lacy*, p. 524; cf. p. 693; also *Reg. Fox* (B. and W.), p. 99; *Reg. Mayew*, p. 222. There are several instances.
[2] *L. and P.*, I, 5725. [3] *Ibid.*, II, 1315. [4] *Concilia*, III, 717.

priests and other spiritual persons having cure of souls, within this your realm ministering, to exact and take of your humble and obedient subjects divers sums of money for the sacraments and sacramentals of Holy Church, sometimes denying the same without they be first paid the said sums of money, which sacraments and sacramentals your said most humble and obedient subjects under the protection of your highness do suppose and think ought to be in most reverend, charitable and godly-wise freely administered unto them at all times requisite, without denial or exaction of any manner sums of money to be demanded or asked for the same."[1]

Evil effects of clerical fees.

A moderate system of fees would not have raised such an outcry, for without fees (so great was the poverty of some of the livings) the clergy could not have lived at all. But the fees had become extortionate. Spiritual gifts were prostituted to money making, and became an affair of barter like produce in the mart. Nothing did the Church so much harm, nothing made the clergy so unpopular, and nothing so paved the way for the Reformation as the fees demanded by the Medieval Church. Well might Archbishop Morton declare in his speech to Convocation in 1487 that the laity were always hostile to the clergy.[2] Well might the Bishop of London tell Wolsey in 1515 that the Londoners were so hostile to the clergy that no London jury would acquit a clerk charged with murder, were he as "innocent as Abel."[3]

Another side to the question.

But to this question there is another side which has often been overlooked. If the clergy were oppressors, they were in turn no less oppressed; and, indeed, it is not altogether unreasonable to conclude that the exactions imposed upon them were not seldom the cause of their own rigorous insistence upon fees. "The

[1] Gee and Hardy, pp. 145–53. The Petition originated with the Court and not with the Commons; but there is no reason to think that it did not represent popular opinion. For two cases of objectors to clerical fees violently interrupting High Mass in 1461 see Thornley, *England under the Yorkists*, pp. 191–2.

[2] *Concilia*, III, 618.

[3] *L. and P.*, II, 2. See Smith, *Church and State in the Middle Ages*, pp. 22, 23. Simon Fish in 1528 wrote the *Supplication of Beggars*, which contained a violent diatribe against the clergy for extortion and greed.

clergy of England are rich," wrote Gregory XI in 1375 to the Bishop of Winchester.[1] This was certainly true of the higher clergy and of those who were fortunate enough to hold valuable rectories, though the number of the latter cannot have been large, since the more valuable rectories were appropriated. In the Register of Wykeham we have a list of the approximate value of the livings in the diocese of Winchester. Assuming that a mark in that age had the purchasing value of £10 in the year 1913, and a pound the value of £15, we find that few rectories were then worth less than £150 a year, while the average was between £300 and £400. There were some very valuable benefices. Several were worth £1000 a year. Kingsclere was worth £1500 ; the rectory of Farnham (attached to the Archdeaconry of Surrey) brought the Archdeacon some £1850 a year ; while the rectory of Downton was valued at £2000. In the case of appropriated rectories the difference between the incomes of the absentee rectors and the resident vicars who were responsible for the work of the parish was very marked. Thus the appropriators of Andover received £1100, their vicar £100 ; the Abbey of Tarrant pocketed £800 a year from Hurstbourne Tarrant, while their wretched vicar was passing rich on £65. Similar cases might be quoted indefinitely.[2]

But so far as the parochial clergy were concerned the income was by no means all clear gain. There was much to come out of it—first-fruits, procurations, tenths, subsidies, papal dues, besides a number of occasional exactions for royal or papal purposes. A large part of Wykeham's Register is taken up with elaborate directions for getting money from the clergy ; and we can see the extreme difficulty which the clergy often had in finding the cash. They were continually and severely harassed by these exactions, and many of them could not pay. No wonder if, in return, they were rigorous in their insistence upon their own fees. They often *had* to be so in self-defence. A great part of episcopal duty seems to have consisted in raising money, and severe penalties were threatened against defaulters. Churches were put under an interdict ; livings were sequestrated ; and defaulting clergy were suspended and excommunicated.[3] In 1371 the Bishop

Charges upon clerical incomes.

[1] *Reg. Wykeham*, II, 245. [2] *Ibid.*, I, Appendix I.
[3] *Reg. Arundell*, f. 103 b. ; *Reg. Wykeham*, II, 136, 139.

of Winchester ordered the rector of Puttenham and the vicar of Farnham to sequestrate the goods of the Archdeacon of Surrey for non-payment of £8, his assessment as rector of Farnham. In 1390 the Archdeacon of Ely was threatened with sequestration because he was a defaulter in the matter of tenths for the years 1388–90; while on March 12th, 1375, Bishop Arundell of Ely writes to the King informing him that nine abbots, two abbesses, twenty-one priors, three prioresses, four rectors and three vicars refuse to pay the tenth lately granted by the clergy to the King. They have all been under excommunication for sixty days, and still have the hardihood to refuse. Will the King kindly intervene and supplement spiritual threats with material force.[1] Is it matter for surprise that the clergy were oppressive when they themselves were so oppressed? Accusations of greed must be qualified by these considerations.

Character of the parochial clergy in the later medieval church.

What was the general character of the parochial clergy in the 15th and early part of the 16th century? Contemporary writers do not always paint them in a very favourable light, and it is quite certain that (like the laity) they had their failings. One of the charges brought against them was that they *would* dress and live as laymen. Whether this is a failing or not depends, perhaps, upon the point of view. At any rate, it caused the bishops great distress; Archbishop Bourchier in a Council in London held in 1463 denounced the extravagant dress of the clergy,[2] and so completely, indeed, do some of the clergy seem to have disguised themselves that Archbishop Morton complained that it was actually impossible to distinguish them from the laity either in appearance or in manners. They dress (like the laity) in a "foppish" manner, wearing their hair long and their coats short, and they usually carry swords.[3] Some were regular sporting

They imitate the laity.

[1] *Reg. Wykeham*, II, 138; *Reg. Fordham*, f. 111; *Reg. Arundell*, f. 6.

[2] *Concilia*, III, 585. He wisely says: "Veremur ne populus nobis subjectus vitam et mores nostros sermonibus et prædicationibus nostris discrepantes animadvertant, ac inde occasione capta verbis nostris minus confidentes ecclesiam Christi, quod ipse avertat, ejusque ministros ac eorum sacram doctrinam et auctoritatem contemnere excitentur."

[3] Neque utatur ense, vel sica, nec zona aut marcipio deaurato vel auri ornatum habente, *Concilia*, III, p. 620; see also *Reg. Mayew*,

parsons, went hunting and hawking with their lay friends, and were devoted to games and even dice. Still more serious charges were sometimes made. Some used to spend much time in feasting and drinking in taverns when they ought to have been visiting their parishioners. A few (of the baser sort) did not always observe the proprieties, and occasionally seem to have indulged in that extra glass which separates complete respectability from irretrievable loss of character. An occasional lapse from the strict path of temperance might, perhaps, have been overlooked by their parishioners, to whom the same frailty is attributed; but the line had to be drawn somewhere, and too frequent lapses offended the morals, roused the ire and at length provoked the interference of the parishioners. Thus, for example, the vicar of Bridport, in Dorsetshire, was reported to be "drunk every day," and the Bishop had to issue a commission of inquiry. It was held in the presence of a "copious multitude" of the parishioners; and twelve townsmen (obviously parson-baiters of a well-known type) acted as "witnesses." It is satisfactory, however, to know that the vicar was a foreigner.[1]

Are fond of sport.

But more serious charges than these are brought against a few of the medieval clergy. Isolated cases of wrongdoing prove nothing beyond the fact that human nature is liable to err and that, in taking Holy Orders, a man does not put off his humanity. To frame an indictment against the clergy generally upon the evidence of occasional entries in episcopal registers is to be guilty both of drawing conclusions by the use of an imperfect induction and of displaying partiality and bias. Thus when we read of two cases of theft in the Register of Bishop Arundell in 1376,[2] we are not to conclude that the clergy of the diocese of Ely were thieves. Or when we read the well-known letter that Margaret Paston wrote to John

Character of some of the medieval clergy.

p. 108, where is given Archbishop Warham's decree (1509), empowering the Bishops to punish and reform the clergy's inordinate display in the way of dress; see also Regulations of Synod of Ely, 1528, *Concilia*, III, 712.

[1] Mrs. Green, *Town Life in 15th Cent.*, I, 157. The income of the wretched man was only £x, xii, ii a year (*Valo Eccles.*, I, p. 231). Perhaps he took to drink in desperation.

[2] *Reg. Arundell*, f. 19 b, 26 b.

Paston in 1461, urging him to send down a commission "to sit upon the parson of Snoryng and on such as was cause of Thomas Denysys' death, and for many and gret horebyl robberries";[1] or when we read that in 1465 John Mallery, vicar of Lewesham, "violently in the pulpit incited his parishioners to attack and murder the sheriff or any other royal officer who attempted to execute any royal writ or mandate, and led his parishioners with swords, clubs, bows and arrows,"[2] are we to jump to the conclusion that the average parson of that date was a disorderly ruffian. No historian would draw general conclusions from such isolated instances; but unfortunately there is available evidence founded on a wider basis; and there can be little doubt that at *certain epochs* and in *certain localities* the general standard was not satisfactory. In the Register of John Whethamstede, Abbot of St. Albans in the 15th century, there occur "grave charges of murder, treason and apostacy both against the regular and the secular clergy."[3] Canon Bannister, who has so admirably edited the Hereford Registers, writes in his introduction to the Register of Mylling (1474–92): "The clergy are equally immoral with their parishioners and the cases of clerical crime in this register are more in number and worse in character than those in previous records. On January 5th, 1475, in the city court of Hereford five clerics are presented for night-walking with swords. In 1478, at the same court, two chaplains are presented for a similar offence, and three other clergy (including the vicar of All Saints, Hereford) for common bawdry. After these and the like instances of wrong-doing it is something of a surprise to read of the vicar of Goodrich being deprived for hunting on Good Friday. There are in this Register convictions of clergy before secular courts of rape, robbery, burglary, murder, theft, wounding and embezzlement. In each case the convicts are duly claimed by the Bishop, and after purgation released. This clerical immunity (for the formalities of purgation with the recurring names of those who may almost be called professional compurgators were now little more than the assurance of immunity) was doubtless responsible for countless cases of crime. Some

[1] *Paston Letters*, II, No. 406.
[2] Thornley, *England under the Yorkists*, p. 183.
[3] Rushbrook Williams, *Hist. of Abbey of St. Albans*, p. 218.

clerical offenders when reclaimed from the secular authorities were apparently allowed to escape from the Bishop's prison; for on November 13th, 1481, the Bishop is pardoned 'for all escapes of persons convicted of felony from his custody'; and at the next appointment of the keeper of the prison the new official pledges himself by four sureties in £100 to strictly guard the prisoners in iron ankle bands, arm-bolts and neck-chains and other kinds of chains."[1] Fortunately there was a very great improvement in the diocese as the Reformation drew near, for in the Register of Bishop Bothe (1516–35) there is little mention of crime or immorality.

Felonies and crimes were, among the parochial clergy at any rate, certainly local, occasional and exceptional. This unfortunately can scarcely be said to be the case with respect to clerical immorality. The standard of morality was not always a high one. As Bishop Stubbs says: "The records of the spiritual courts of the Middle Ages remain in such abundance and in such concord of testimony as to leave no doubt of the facts." The attempt to enforce celibacy was never wholly successful, and the practical results were often disastrous. "Instead of personal purity there is a long story of licensed and unlicensed concubinage, and, appendant to it, much miscellaneous profligacy and a general low tone of morality in the very point which is supposed to be secured."[2] The higher clergy were as a rule free from such scandals, though there were a few conspicuous exceptions; but among a certain number of the clergy there was considerable laxity, and the registers and records of the period contain instances of unworthy clergy. Things were at their very worst in the middle of the 15th century. In the year 1455 Archbishop Bourchier issued a commission for reforming the clergy in his diocese of Canterbury, and the document is most damaging to the character of the clergy of that diocese. "There are," he writes, "some vicars and rectors who neglect and scorn the cure of souls; and like vagabonds and profligates run about through the kingdom and apply themselves to worldly gain, to revellings

Clerical morality.

Archbishop Bourchier on the clergy, 1455.

[1] *Reg. Mylling*, pp. iv, v.
[2] *Constit. Hist.*, III, 384, 385. See also the *Lollard Conclusion* of 1394, printed by Gee and Hardy, p. 126.

moreover, to drinking bouts, and to wicked adulteries and fornications; and besides spend their time in all manner of vice, to the neglect of their parish, the ruin of their churches, and the scandal of the parishioners." The evils of all this neglect and immorality are obvious. "Whence it follows that very many crimes are daily committed by our people to the contempt of God and holy religion; the dignity of the clergy is disgraced; the health of souls is dangerously neglected; the hope of the poor fails; decay and all manner of ruin attack church buildings; church goods are vainly and uselessly spoiled and wasted; priests unlearned, untaught, unknown and unrecognised, and often times without Orders, or suspended from fulfilling their Orders, do by presumptuously administering sacraments and sacramentals bring the souls of our subjects to ruin and captivity; many illicit and criminal concubinages, fornications, and adulteries are encouraged among our people; and the last wills of testators are very often wickedly set aside and made void."[1]

This was the nadir. As the country recovered from the anarchy of the 15th century matters steadily improved, and measures were taken to raise the standard of clerical life and work.[2]

In discussing the character of the clergy of this period two considerations must be kept in mind. There was, to begin with, the low moral tone of the age, due rather to the civil strife and general lawlessness of the time than to neglect on the part of the Church. Those who condemn the failings of the later Medieval Church sometimes speak as though it were an immoral Church in a virtuous age; as

[1] *Concilia*, III, 573, translated in Gee and Hardy, p. 141. See also *Kempe's Visitation* (1428), Sur. Soc., cxxvii, 217, 18. Also *L. and P.*, III, 1122 for Bishop Fox on the clergy of the diocese of Winchester. Colet's fierce denunciation of the clergy is well known, Lupton, p. 71. See also *Reg. Bubwith*, p. 131; *Reg. Wykeham*, II, 222–3; *Concilia*, 360.

[2] Synods passed excellent rules, and bishops exhorted, rebuked and punished. An Act was passed in the first year of Henry VII (1 Henry VII. c. 4) which gave bishops power to punish by imprisonment for moral offences; and in the Provincial Council of Prelates held in 1529 severe penalties were enjoined for breaches of the moral law. See *Concilia* III, p. 721, also pp. 360–5, 370, 528–9, 618; and the Commissions of Bishops to their Archdeacons and Vicars-General, e.g. *Reg. Mylling*, p. 27. Medieval ideas of marriage may perhaps have led to some distortion of the moral perspective.

though the Church tried to corrupt an age which rose up like a Hebrew prophet to rebuke its vices. This was not the case. The 15th century was a period of moral corruption, and there was a conspicuous want of refinement in both sexes and in all classes. Both Gower and Gascoigne clearly tell us that weakness in the Church was due to the corruption of the age. Bishop Pecocke says that, bad as the age was, it would have been much worse if it had not been for the influence of the Church. The truth is that the tone of the age had invaded the Church, which had not offered sufficient resistance.

In the second place, it must not be forgotten that, though the available evidence relating to the later Medieval Church does undoubtedly point to decline, yet that evidence is in no sense exhaustive. There is a large amount of material, mostly in the shape of episcopal registers, which is hidden away in diocesan archives, and is practically accessible only to local experts. The published registers of the 15th century relate chiefly to remote dioceses, such as Exeter, Bath and Wells, and a border county like Hereford. Before we can obtain a complete picture we require to know more about the life and work of the parochial clergy in the chief centres of population in, for example, the dioceses of London and Norwich. In Norfolk, after the Black Death, there was a great outburst of church building, and magnificent parish churches in the Perpendicular style were built all over the county. This certainly does not indicate failure on the part of the Church or of the parochial clergy. Our knowledge is thus incomplete, and it must not be forgotten that the clergy treated of in this chapter are necessarily drawn from a comparatively small area. It is, therefore, of great importance that care should be taken, in reading the contemporary documents relating to the history of the Church in the period succeeding the Black Death, not to mistake the exception for the type; not to place too much reliance upon the picturesque and pungent criticisms of prejudiced satirists and opponents; above all, not to draw general conclusions from insufficient data, or pass sweeping moral judgments upon a whole community on the strength of admitted and well proved instances of frailty in a percentage of its members. Exactly what proportion of evildoers in any society or community would justify us in branding that society or community with an epithet expressive of its general characteristics is a nice point to decide. It is certain that quite a small number of evil-doers is often sufficient to bring disgrace upon the whole community. This is certainly true in the case of the Christian Church, where a high standard is always expected.

It is necessary to bear in mind these considerations, if we are to keep a right perspective, more particularly in an age of decline when obvious faults distract attention from unobtrusive virtues. Sweeping moral judgments generally err on the side of exaggeration ; the sins of other people must not be allowed to monopolise our whole stock of righteous indignation ; and (besides) Christian charity cannot be outraged, whether in history or in life, with permanent impunity. The Christian standard of morality remains, of course, the same for all ages, but the degree of guilt attached to lapses from that standard can only be adequately estimated by reference to the difficulties, temptations and general conditions of the age. The 15th century cannot be judged by the standards of the 20th. To expect the same high standard of morals and duty in a distant, ignorant and brutal age, with an unenlightened public opinion, with little healthy publicity, with many temptations and few restraints, is to expect what is obviously (human nature being what it is) more or less impossible.

The faithful parish priest.

There remains, in conclusion, one type of the later medieval parish priest of whom we hear too little, both then and at the present time. The evidence of frailty must not blind us to the existence of a large body of clergy who not only led blameless lives, but protested vigorously against the moral evils of their day. Of these men we hear nothing in the episcopal registers, which from the nature of their contents indicate faults rather than virtues ; and, while noting defects, pass over in silence all evidence of faithful parish work. We shall look in vain in those dry records for notices of unobtrusive Christian service. And it is for this reason that caution is required in drawing, from episcopal registers and conciliar injunctions, general conclusions upon the life, work and character of the parochial clergy. This must be gathered from other sources as well. Unlike the 18th century, which was, at any rate during certain decades, likewise a period of spiritual inertia and ecclesiastical abuses, the 15th century is somewhat weak in evidence for the brighter side of Church life. Satirists and moralists in all ages have a tendency to exaggerate defects and to emphasise the darker side of the social and religious life of their times; and, unfortunately, we do not possess sufficient contemporary literature to give us more intimate knowledge and to balance the picture drawn by unfavourable hands. Yet, in spite of all that can be urged against the clergy of the later Medieval Church, in spite of the evidence of dark spots and grave defects, in spite of failures and failings which can admit of no dispute, we cannot doubt that, even in the darkest times and in the worst places, there were parish clergy who were faithful to the ideal of Christian life, who kept the torch of faith and religion burning, who were as lights shining in a dark place, as a city set on a hill, as rivers of water in a thirsty land. While failures and abuses at once attract the eye, arouse attention and fire indignation, such men often escape notice, though their influence remains as a power for righteousness. If there had been no faithful parochial clergy, Church life could scarcely have continued as it did; and we should be blind to the teaching of all experience, as well as to the dictates of common sense, if we ignored the brighter and higher aspects of clerical life after the Black Death. It is a pleasing task to be able to turn aside from the dry and lifeless entries in episcopal registers; from injunctions, regulations, rebukes and threats; from the denunciations of satirists and enemies; even from the moral indignation of good men like Colet, to the living picture of a great master. Chaucer satirised many of the ecclesiastical types of his day, but he had a tender place in his heart for the humble parish priest. In his "Poor Parson of a Town" we have portrayed for us one of the most attractive characters of the Middle Ages, a character which is, we would fain hope, a type rather than an exception :—

> "A good man was there of religion
> And was a poor parson of a town;
> But rich he was of holy thought and work,
> He was also a learned man, a clerk,
> That Christe's gospel truly would preach
> His parishioners devoutly would he teach.

Wide was his parish and houses far asunder,
But he ne lafte nat,[1] for rain nor thunder,
In sickness nor in meschief[2] to visit
The farrest in his parish much and little,
Upon his feet and in his hand a staff.
This noble ensample to his sheep he gave
That first he wrought and afterward he taught.
A better priest I trow that nowhere none is.
He waited after no pomp and reverence,
Nor maked him a spyced conscience,
But Christe's lore, and His apostles twelve,
He taught, and first he followed it himself."[3]

[1] Never omitted.
[2] Trouble.
[3] *Prologue*, ll. 479 f.

CHAPTER IV

GROWING TENSION WITH ROME

IT is impossible to understand the position of the Medieval English Church without reference to the ideas which dominated the political and religious thought of the medieval world.[1] According to these dominant ideas there was to be one great Christian society composed of a world-wide Empire and a world-wide Church, which were to embrace all mankind in their sway; which were to deal, the one with man's secular, the other with his religious life; and which, as they were but different aspects of one and the same idea, were to act together in perfect harmony. The idea of separate and independent nations or churches was foreign to medieval thought. Society was a unity looked at from two points of view, the temporal and the spiritual, and governed respectively by Emperor and Pope, who were thus the complements of each other. Each was the agent of God; for to each was entrusted the oversight of the world in one of its twofold aspects. Each had his own jurisdiction, his own laws, his own sphere of action; but these two spheres were so mutually interdependent and so closely connected that it was difficult to define the duties and powers which belonged respectively to Emperor and to Pope, and to assign to each his proper function in such a way that there should be no overlapping, no jealousy and no interference. It was the failure to carry out this theory in practice which led to that bitter feud between Pope and Emperor which distracted medieval Europe, weakened the Empire and dissipated the spiritual energies of the Church.

Medieval conception of Church and Empire.

[1] See Gierke, *Political Theories of the Middle Age* (trans. Maitland), pp. 9–21, 36. R. W. and A. J. Carlyle, *A Hist. of Med. Political Theory in the West*, 4 vols., esp. Vol. IV; Taylor, *Medieval Mind*, II, 275–80, and c. 43, The Med. Synthesis; Lane Poole, *Illustrations of the Hist. of Med. Thought*, c. ix; Dunning, *A Hist. of Political Theories, Anc. and Med.*, cc. vi, vii.

When in the later Middle Ages the Papacy fell into disrepute these ideas gradually underwent a transformation; and there arose a general questioning of the foundations upon which the whole conception of the Medieval Church had been based. The teaching and influence of Wycliffe, the papal residence at Avignon in French territory, the Conciliar movement of the 15th century, the voting by nations at the Council of Constance, the increasing power and conception of the State, the growing revolt against the trammels of scholasticism and medieval ideas generally, together with the growth of national literatures and the rise of national states, led to the idea of the formation of national churches more or less independent of the Papacy. The movement was assisted by the great unpopularity which in the 14th and 15th centuries the Papacy incurred. Dependence upon Rome, which in earlier days had been a blessing, had now become a yoke; its advantages were doubtful, its inconveniences certain. The revolt from Rome was no bolt from the blue suddenly descending upon an unsuspecting Church at Luther's instigation in 1517. It had been growing steadily during the 15th century, having its origin quite as much in political ideas as in theological abuses, being, in fact, the inevitable result of the break-up of the great conception of Empire and Papacy, upon which medieval society had been based, and to which the Papacy owed so much of its authority and power.

Growing revolt against Rome during the 15th century.

To understand how the breach with Rome in the reign of Henry VIII was rendered possible it will be necessary to trace briefly the relations between England and the Papacy, and to show in what ways the latter interfered with the liberties, incurred the resentment, and at last forfeited the respect of English Churchmen.

One of the links that bound the English Church to Rome and made it an integral part of the Catholic Church of the West was the use of Roman canon law in the English Church courts. This law, which deals not with questions of faith and doctrine but with morals and discipline, had been gradually built up from various collections of ecclesiastical rules, customs and traditions, from portions of the civil law of Rome, from the canons and decrees of synods and councils, from forgeries

Growth of the Roman Canon Law.

and false decretals, and from rulings and decretals issued from time to time by the Popes in their capacity as heads and lawgivers of the Church.[1] Thus from the earliest days there had grown up a vast mass of rules and regulations, intended for the guidance and moral government of the Church. In the 6th century the monk Dionysius made a collection of canons, which became the basis of later Roman canon law; but it was not until the 12th century that any real attempt was made to reconcile or explain the immense number of papal rulings and synodal canons. This was done by Gratian, a Benedictine monk at Bologna, who published in Rome (*c.* 1142) a treatise, *Concordia discordantium canonum,* generally known as the *Decretum Gratiani,* in which he attempted to codify, explain and reconcile the many conflicting, doubtful and difficult canons which had been current in the Western Church under the general name of canon law. This treatise at once superseded all other collections, and took its place as the standard textbook in the Universities and law schools of the West.

The Corpus Juris Canonici.

But this collection made no pretence to finality; and, in view of the increasing number of canons and decretals which were being constantly issued, the *Decretum* of Gratian was during the next three hundred years enlarged and supplemented by Gregory IX, Boniface VIII, Clement V, John XXIII, and finally by Sixtus IV in 1483. The whole of this collection of ancient and medieval canons is generally known as the *Corpus Juris Canonici.* This canon law was Roman in two senses of the word. It was issued with all the authority of the Papacy; and it was based largely upon the principles and the methods of the Roman civil law. It was thus a very high branch of law, one instance among many of the debt which Europe owes to the ancient empire of Rome, and its intrinsic value gave it an authority quite independent of the Papacy and the Church.

[1] "*Canon law*" is variously regarded. Thus it is spoken of as:—

(*a*) The system of papal jurisprudence and legislation from the 12th cent. to the Reformation.

(*b*) So much of the above as was retained by Henry VIII and still remains part of the Ecclesiastical law of England.

(*c*) The *Codex Juris Canonici,* the canon law for the Roman Church at the present time.

This Roman canon law was the common law, the *jus commune*, for the whole of the Western Church. Its authority was recognised everywhere; and each new Roman canon or papal decretal became, as soon as it was promulgated, the law of the Catholic Church, as a matter of course, without questioning and without any formal acceptance on the part of any branch of the Church, however remote from the centre, or however ambitious of independence. The English Church, as an integral part of the Catholic Church, came within the jurisdiction of this universal canon law, which had supreme authority and binding force in the English ecclesiastical courts. The late Professor Maitland[1] went so far as to state that "in all probability large portions (to say the least) of the canon law of Rome were regarded by the courts Christian in this country as absolutely binding statute law." The latter phrase is misleading. The Roman canon law never formed part of the statute or common law of England, but, like the Catholic faith, which likewise was never embodied in statute law, was regarded as equally binding upon the English Church. It had behind it the authority not of King or of Parliament or of any temporal power, but the unquestioned authority of the Papacy, the general consent of Western Christianity and the whole moral and spiritual force of the Catholic Church.

The authority of Roman Canon Law in the English Church.

But the operation of this canon law of the Universal Church, for all its prestige and authority, was in England partially limited both by statute law and by local ecclesiastical custom. Contrary to Roman canon law, the common law of England laid down that children born out of wedlock were not legitimised by the subsequent marriage of their parents; that benefit of clergy was to be confined to felony; and that questions of patronage, probates and wills should be dealt with in temporal and not in spiritual courts; while the great statutes of *Provisors* and *Præmunire* limited, not always successfully, the scope of the Roman canon law and placed some restraint upon the power and authority of the Papacy in England. These points were not always gained without considerable opposition on the part of the Spirituality, the anti-papal legislation of the 14th century,

Roman Canon Law limited: (a) By the common law of England.

1 *Canon Law in the Church of England*, p. 2.

more particularly, not being allowed to pass without protest (renewed from time to time) from prelates and clergy, as derogatory to the dignity of the Pope, and as infringing upon the liberties of the Church; but when national law came into collision with the general law of Christendom it was the latter which had to give way; for without the consent of the temporal power papal decrees could not be enforced in the country. Compared, however, with the great body of canon law these limitations by the national legislature were by no means numerous, the temporal power being as a general rule chary of interference with spiritual jurisdiction; and thus the universal law of the Church was, with a few exceptions, allowed free play in England.

(b) By local customs of the English Church.

The canon law of Rome was also to some small extent modified or expanded by certain local customs of the English Church. Roman law, valuable as it was, did not always meet the requirements of distant parts of the Church, where, as in England and Germany, certain native usages and rules, embodied in the canons of local synods, had grown up supplementing and at times even superseding the universal law in cases where local circumstances indicated the need of special legislation. This native canon law was called *Consuetudo;* and it was clearly admitted by the Roman canon law that, where a collision occurred between the *jus commune* and native custom, the latter should, if it had the force of time and national support behind it, prevail; so that local custom, being thus allowed and provided for by Roman canon law, might be said itself to be part of Roman canon law. English native canon law consisted of certain canons promulgated in the 13th century by the papal legates, Otho and Othobon, but fully accepted by English synods; of papal rulings specially given to meet the needs of the English Church; and of constitutions issued during the 13th and 14th centuries in synods held by the Archbishops of Canterbury; all of which native English canon law was collected and published in 1433 by William Lyndwood, Bishop of St. David's and Dean of the Arches, in a famous treatise known as the *Provinciale.*[1] Thus there was in England, as in Germany

[1] *Provinciale, seu Constitutiones Angliæ.* This, a large and closely printed volume, not easy to read, contains the provincial constitutions

and in France, a certain amount of authoritative native canon law; but this was based upon the methods and principles of the Roman canon law; it was comparatively small in extent; it was merely supplementary, was permitted by the Papacy, and by itself forms a very insignificant and inadequate body of laws.[1]

Appeals to Rome and attempts to check them.

The universal use of canon law in the ecclesiastical courts naturally involved an acknowledgment on the part of the English Church of the appellate jurisdiction of the Apostolic See. Ever since the Norman Conquest there had grown up a regular system of carrying appeals to Rome. Italian lawyers were more learned in the canon law than English, and were often better qualified from their learning and experience to settle legal points of great intricacy; and so long as the papal court was able to deliver more weighty judgments, and

of 14 Archbishops of Canterbury from Langton to Chichele, together with the Legatine Constitutions of Otho and Othobon, with a commentary and notes by William Lyndwood. The best-known edition is that of 1679, printed at Oxford.

[1] English usage differed from Roman in several minor particulars, especially in the matter of fees, ritual, repairs of churches and legacies of clergy. Much has been made of Archbishop Peckham's so-called refusal to enforce Gregory X's decretals against pluralism. It was not opposition on the part of the Archbishop, but simply his inability to carry out the decretal as it stood. With statesmanlike wisdom he modified its application to render it practical; but he was careful to apologise humbly to the Pope for even seeming to go against his decretals. Canon law is a subject of extreme difficulty and acute controversy, canonists, lawyers and historians differing considerably in their conception of the scope, meaning and validity of canon law. There is a large literature dealing with the subject. See Pollock and Maitland, *Hist. Eng. Law*, I, 88–114, c. iv, Roman and Canon Law; Phillimore, *Eccles. Law*, I, 18, 19, for relation of medieval canon law to the present law of the C. of Eng. Crosse, *Authority in C. of Eng.; Report of Royal Commiss. on Eccles. Courts*, 1883. Stubbs, *Seventeen Lectures*, 13 and 14; Carlyle, *Hist. Med. Political Theory in West*, II, esp. c. ix.

Maitland, in *Canon Law in the Church of England*, controverts the position taken up (under the influence of Stubbs) in the *Report on Eccles. Courts*, and denies the alleged independence both of the Med. Eng. Church and of native English canon law. In 1912 Mr. Ogle published *The Canon Law in Medieval England*, in which he criticises Maitland's views, and sets out to prove that the English Church possessed a native canon law "of substantive authority, and valid on occasion even against the decretals." Reichel has just published (1922, S.P.C.K.) the first vol. of *The Canon Law of Church Institutions*, a work of great learning and value.

to deal with matters for which the English courts provided no satisfactory remedy, little objection could be made against the system of carrying appeals to Rome. But as the study of canon law became more advanced in England, and as the court of Rome became more venal and grasping, the need for appeals became less apparent and the practice came to be regarded with deep resentment. In the Constitutions of Clarendon, Henry II endeavoured to make appeals to Rome subject to the consent of the Crown, but he was compelled to drop the proposal. In 1353 and again in 1393 the great statutes of *Præmunire* were passed, and decreed forfeiture and banishment against all who carried an appeal to Rome. The statutes had considerable effect in checking the system, while the scandal of the great Schism considerably diminished the number of appeals taken to the papal court, with the result that they grew fewer as the 15th century advanced, and in course of time became restricted simply to questions relating to wills and marriages. Dispensations for marriages formed a constant source of appeals to Rome. In 1473 Sir John Paston was very anxious to obtain a dispensation of marriage with Mistress Anne Hault, who was his kinswoman. He appealed to Rome, and received an answer that there was certainly there "the well of grace and salve sufficient for such a sore," and that he could receive a dispensation; *but* (the real crux being a matter of money and not of morals) his proctor in Rome demands 1000 ducats for the favour. At the same time Sir John is given a hint that the proctor is open to a deal, and he therefore hopes to get off with 100 or 200 ducats at the most.[1] It is interesting to remember that it was in connection with a marriage appeal to Rome that England broke with the Papacy. Henry VIII's appeal for a divorce did not succeed. He revenged himself on the Pope by renouncing his allegiance to the Papacy.

Instances of appeals to Rome.

The interference of the Pope in the matter of the appointments to bishoprics and other preferments was another link that bound England to Rome, and which was deeply resented. An Archbishop received from the Pope the gift of the pall, and until this arrived he was not regarded as fully qualified to

Interference of the Papacy with appointments in the English Church.

[1] Sir John is also told that "Papa hoc facit hodiernis diebus multociens," *Paston Letters*, Nov. 22, 1473.

exercise his authority. The Pope, therefore, had it in his power practically to veto the appointment of an Archbishop by refusing to send the pall. Disputed elections to bishoprics were referred to the Pope, who in such cases claimed the right of appointing whom he liked. The case of Stephen Langton will readily recur to the memory, though in this case Innocent III's appointment proved a blessing to the nation. The Pope claimed the sole right of translating bishops from one See to another and of filling up the vacancies thus created, as well as the right of appointment when a bishop died in Rome. But this was not all. In the 13th century a system of provisions and reservations had grown up; and under this system the Pope claimed the right of *providing* for his friends by putting them into English benefices, dignities and bishoprics which he caused to be "reserved" for his own use, thus contemptuously trampling upon the rights of patrons, both clerical and lay, whom he frightened into acquiescence by a threat of excommunication, or by withholding licences, dispensations and indulgences.[1] A whole host of unwanted foreigners was thus thrust into valuable and important positions in the English Church. The proportion of aliens among abbots and priors and papally appointed cathedral clergy was at times very considerable, and the presence of a number of foreign abbots in Parliament was detrimental to the interests of the nation. Fortunately, however, owing to the practice of non-residence their benefices and their dioceses did not see much of these undesirable aliens.[2]

Provisions and Reservations.

This system of provisions and reservations was very unpopular, and became still more so in the 14th century, when the Pope took up his residence at Avignon. So intolerable became the abuse of a Pope, who resided in the territory and under the influence of England's enemy, "providing" to English benefices, sees and abbeys that Parliament determined to check the practice. In 1351 it passed the famous *Statute of Provisors*,

[1] For a good instance of a papal provision see *Liber Albus*, 240, p. 45; and for a provision for a boy of thirteen given by Clement V in 1309, *ibid.*, 446, p. 92.

[2] Thus we are informed that the rector of Godalming, Cardinal James de Ursinis, whose procurations were becoming due, had gone away and forgotten to leave his address, *Reg. Wykeham*, II, pp. 243–4.

which laid down that all persons receiving papal Provisions were liable to imprisonment, and that all the preferments to which the Pope nominated were to be forfeited for that turn to the King. The Act was renewed forty years later, but it proved quite powerless to stop the evil.[1] The lords spiritual refused to give their assent to the Act; the two Archbishops made a formal protest against its enactment; and in his oath of allegiance to the Papacy the Archbishop of Canterbury retained his promise to respect papal reservations and provisions.[2] The Popes were very angry about these statutes and complained bitterly about them. Boniface IX threatened the Archbishop with excommunication unless he procured their repeal.[3] In 1426 Martin V sent an insolent letter to Archbishop Chichele demanding the repeal of the statutes; so fierce and threatening was he that the Archbishop urged Parliament to repeal them; but the Commons refused to give way, and the Pope in his anger actually deprived the Archbishop of his legatine authority and threatened England with an interdict. In the end, however, he was compelled to yield.[4]

The Act of Provisors a dead letter.

But in spite of Parliament the Act remained, at any rate so far as the appointment of bishops was concerned, a dead letter. During the 183 years from the passing of the first Statute of Provisors in 1351 to the assumption of royal supremacy by Henry VIII in 1534, 321 appointments were made to the 21 Sees of England and Wales; and out of these 321 episcopal appointments only 23 (and of these 23 nine occurred in the Welsh dioceses) were made by that system of free election without interference from Rome, which had twice been solemnly ordered by the national Parliament.[5] The fact was that the

[1] The second *Statute of Provisors*, 1390, is printed in Gee and Hardy, p. 112. The Acts were due to the Temporal Power, not to the Spirituality asserting its independence of the Pope. In *Reg. Arundell*, ff. 10, 14, 17 b., there are cases of the sequestration of benefices on discovery that they were obtained by papal provisions.

[2] *Concilia*, III, 647. [3] *Reg. Wykeham*, II, 484.

[4] *Concilia*, III, 471–86, for the correspondence. Also *Gascoigne*, LXIII.

[5] *Dict. of Eng. Church Hist.* The figures may be verified by referring to each diocese. The lists do not always agree with Stubbs, e.g. Exeter, 1395. Stubbs says it was made without papal interference, *Constit. Hist.*, III, 326. Ollard and Crosse say it was a case of papal provision, *Dict.*, p. 218.

Acts of Provisors were only enforced when it suited the King, who found it convenient to keep on good terms with the Papacy. In return for a free hand in dealing with the Church, he agreed to share with the Pope the appointment to English Sees; and when King and Pope thus worked in collusion, they were able to override the rights of patrons and snap their fingers at the liberties of the Church and the statutes of Parliament. Both Henry VII and his son (in his early days) took great pains to keep on good terms with the Pope, and had their regular agents and proctors at Rome to prosecute all promotions and to see that the recommendations of the Crown met with success.[1] The result was that all episcopal appointments were made by papal provision at the request of the King, who thus succeeded in increasing the hold of the Crown over the Church, and who, by placing his own favourites and nominees in the most important ecclesiastical dignities as a reward for secular work, was responsible for many of the worst abuses of the day. Such collusion was, of course, absolutely fatal to the rights, liberties and well-being of the Church.[2]

Papal authority over English prelates.

In addition to his power over the appointments to English Sees the Pope took good care to exercise severe authority over the bishops and make them duly subservient to the Holy See. All bishops on their appointment took a very stringent oath of obedience and submission. When Mayew was appointed to Hereford in 1504 he commenced his episcopate with a solemn oath to the Pope: "I Richard, Bishop of Hereford, will be faithful and obedient to blessed Peter and to the holy Apostolic Roman Church and to my master the lord Pope Julius II and his successors. I will take no part by word or deed in any plot whereby they may come to loss. I will reveal to no one their plans. I will defend the rights of the Roman See against all men."[3] The Archbishop of Canterbury took the same oath in an even stronger form. He promised that he would defend and advance the rights,

[1] Campbell, *Materials for the reign of Henry VII*, I, 176.
[2] For examples of such appointments see *L. and P.*, I, 4722, 5411, 5412, which mention Papal Bulls nominating Wolsey to Lincoln and translating him to York. See also III, 1759, where Henry promises he will write to the Pope to get the Abbey of St. Albans for Wolsey.
[3] *Reg. Mayew*, p. 4.

honours, privileges and authority of the Roman Church and of the Pope; that he would hinder, as far as lay in him, anything which might prove to their detriment and hurt; and that he would uphold with all his strength, and see that others upheld, the rules of the holy Fathers, the decrees, rules, sentences, dispositions, reservations, provisions and mandates of the Popes.[1]

There was another hold, too, which the Pope had over the Archbishop of Canterbury. From the year 1221 the Archbishops had always been ex-officio *legati nati*, that is, they possessed in the legatine authority the visitatorial jurisdiction of the Pope; and this power, placed in the hands of the Primate, forced the Crown to recognise the supreme jurisdiction of the Holy See. It had another effect, too. The Archbishop did not stand upon his own authority as Head of the English Church. What authority he had over the Church, apart from his own diocese, was delegated, or at any rate had the appearance of being delegated, from Rome; and this, together with the right of appeal from the Archbishop to the Pope, made very apparent the dependence of the English Church upon the Church of Rome.

The Pope and the Archbishop of Canterbury.

But there was another tie between England and Rome which became the cause of still more serious complaint. The Papacy was always in need of money and was always trying to squeeze it out of Europe. Indeed, the greed and venality of the papal court were notorious, and contemporary literature is full of complaints of the avarice and extortions of the Papacy, which came to be regarded more as a money-making than a spiritual agency. In England (as elsewhere) papal exactions pressed heavily upon clergy and laity alike, and led to serious discontent.[2] There were three ways in which the Pope raised money. (1) There were *the regular contributions*. From the clergy he demanded the whole of the first year's income from any preferment (annates), and afterwards a yearly payment (tenths). The tax was severely felt by the poorer clergy. In the Act

Financial exactions of the Papacy.

Annates and Tenths.

[1] *Concilia*, III, p. 647.

[2] For an instance of papal extortion see the way in which Innocent VIII treated a new Bishop of Lichfield. Brown, *Venetian Calendar*, I, 614, p. 209.

for the conditional restraint of annates (1532) it was stated that "great and inestimable sums of money have been daily conveyed out of this realm for annates, which have been taken for archbishoprics and bishoprics, and for confirmations, elections, admissions, postulations, provisions, collations, dispositions, institutions, installations, investitures, orders, holy benedictions, palls or other things requisite and necessary to the attaining of these promotions"—with the result that the nation had been impoverished and the friends of those promoted often ruined. During the fifty years preceding the Reformation as much as £160,000 (=£2,000,000), besides "other great and intolerable sums," have been conveyed to the court of Rome.[1] This was (obviously) more than any self-respecting monarch could stand, so first-fruits and tenths were taken from the Pope by Henry VIII, who, instead of giving them to the Church, coolly appropriated them for the Crown.[2]

(2) From the whole nation, lay and clerical alike, the Pope demanded *Peter's Pence*. This had become fixed at a sum which would be now worth about £4000 a year. The Pope had a duly authorised collector in England, but, in spite of this, Peter's Pence seems to have been very irregularly paid, and its collection to have caused considerable friction. We hear many complaints about arrears of payment. The lower clergy were, as might be expected, often behind hand, but the dignitaries of the Church were frequent offenders as well. In 1399 the Papal Nuncio complained that the Archdeacon of Winchester had not paid his Peter's Pence for the last eleven years. The Archdeacon of Surrey was, apparently, more honest than his brother, for he paid "when he could," or perhaps when he felt inclined; but even *he* has not paid for 1395, 1397, 1398 and 1399. The Bishop of Winchester felt he must make inquiries and answer the complaint. He tells the Nuncio that the Archdeacon of Winchester has been "monished." The Archdeacon of Surrey is dead, and his executors have not been cited because they could not be found. Several priors and abbots have paid up; others, who have not, have been excommunicated and their goods sequestrated. Nor

Peter's Pence.

[1] Gee and Hardy, p. 178.

[2] They were afterwards restored by Queen Anne, and called Queen Anne's Bounty.

was the payment made any more willingly as time went on, for we find Polydore Vergil, writing from London on March 3rd, 1514, to Rome, "Very few will pay Peter's Pence."[1]

Irregular Papal exactions.

These, however, were regular enactions, and if the Papacy had been content with these there would have been fewer complaints; but unfortunately the Pope was always wanting money for special objects of his own, and was continually sending demands to the English prelates to make collections either to provide him with money for some of his numerous worldly schemes, or to pay the expenses of some nuncio who was to visit England. In 1517 Leo X wrote to Cardinal Wolsey and to the Bishops of Winchester, Exeter and Lichfield, enjoining them to collect money from all persons in their dioceses to assist his Holiness. What for? For some crusade, or religious purpose, or good work? By no means, but simply for his own private, selfish, ambitious and unscrupulous war against the Duke of Urbino and his friends, "the sons of iniquity and children of perdition."[2] These demands were very unpopular, and great difficulty was often experienced in getting in the money. In 1519 Silvester told Wolsey that the Pope was very angry because he had not received the money which he had demanded, and adds, "The clergy are powerful in England, and it is not possible to extract money from them as in other countries."[3] The great Bishop of Winchester, William of Wykeham, was on one occasion severely rebuked for his half-heartedness in meeting a papal demand, and was actually threatened with excommunication unless he sent off the money within thirty days.[4]

The Pope had other means as well of raising funds. He derived a large income from licences to break ecclesiastical rules; from dispensations, pardons, indulgences and fees; above all, from the sale of offices, livings, prebends, abbeys

[1] *Reg. Wykeham*, II, pp. 484–5; *L. and P.*, II, 215; cf. *Reg. Bubwith*, pp. 321, 402, where the Dean and Chapter of Wells and several priors are cited to pay procurations (some of several years standing) on pain of excommunication; also *Reg. Arundell*, f. 113. The Bp. of Hereford's Peter's Pence for 1517 amounted to £6, *Reg. Bothe*, p. 33.

[2] *L. and P.*, II, 3617–20. Leo gives Wolsey full power to punish defaulters.

[3] *Ibid.*, III, 149.

[4] *Reg. Wykeham*, II, 224–5. See also the account of Papal taxation for a crusade with the assessments of each diocese, *Concilia*, III, 646.

and bishoprics. Anything that was saleable was sold. The sacred office of the cardinalate was sold by Julius II, Leo X. and, of course, by Alexander VI, who is said to have raised in the year 1500 the sum of 120,000 ducats by the appointment of twelve new cardinals. In 1523 a correspondent from Rome wrote to Wolsey: "The Cardinals are poor, and no wonder! for they gave all their money, some forty or fifty thousand ducats, to be made Cardinals."[1] Even the Papacy itself, the very highest office in the Church, could be purchased for money; for it is well known that Alexander VI and Julius II obtained it by heavy bribery; and Wolsey, as we have already seen, when a candidate, urged his friends to spare no expense to get it for him, and not to let it go for want of 100,000 ducats. Nothing, in fact, could be obtained without money at the papal court, which was, on the eve of the Reformation, little better than a gang of greedy and unscrupulous officials, who framed a number of regulations not to protect morals, but to make money. In 1515 the Bishop of Worcester wrote that he had bribed Cardinal St. Quattuor to expedite certain bulls, but "these great men expect great reward for their labours"; two years later he told Wolsey that nothing could be effected in the court of Rome without gifts; and another correspondent clinched the matter when he said, "He that hath no money in Rome is but a beast."[2] If the money so raised had been well spent less objection would have been made. But it was not. Large sums were collected for crusades, which were never started, or even intended to be started. The extravagance and luxury of the Renaissance Popes and Cardinals were notorious. The money squeezed out of poor parsons and wealthy laity went, not to fight the infidel or to promote religion, but to meet the Pope's extravagance, or to wage ambitious and selfish wars, or to swell the pockets of extortionate officials. Nothing made the Papacy so unpopular as this system of extortion, especially in England, where these constant demands for money were bitterly resented. People grumbled but *had* to pay, for the Pope could make it exceedingly unpleasant for those who crossed his path. Was it any

Greed and corruption of the Papal Court.

[1] *L. and P.*, III, 2891.

[2] *Ibid.*, II, 1105, 3781; III, 2772; cf. I, 4936, where Silvester tells Wolsey it would cost £1000 to obtain a certain faculty.

wonder, then, that the Papacy was unpopular, or that it had forfeited respect, or that the Pope came to be regarded as an extortioner rather than the Holy Father of Christian people? Was it any wonder that, when the nation got the chance, it determined to put an end to the whole system of papal exactions? In 1534 an Act was passed forbidding papal dispensations and the payment of Peter's Pence. It mentioned "the intolerable exactions of the Bishop of Rome, called the Pope, as well in pensions, censes, Peter-pence, procurations, fruits, suits for provisions, and expedition of bulls for archbishoprics and bishoprics, and for delegacies and rescripts in causes of contentions and appeals, jurisdictions legatine, and also for dispensations, licences, faculties, grants, relaxations, writs, rehabilitations, abolitions and other infinite sort of bulls, briefs and instruments of sundry natures, names and kinds."[1]

The financial exactions of the Papacy rendered it extremely unpopular.

And yet we must make allowance for the Pope. He inherited the system, and was not by any means his own master. Wolsey and other prelates had their friends and agents at the papal court, who could only promote their interests by heavy bribes to the cardinals and papal officials, who ran the Curia for their own profit. The Renaissance Popes readily acquiesced in the abuse; even had they desired reform they were nearly helpless; and the system, in spite of its flagrant evils, was too profitable to be abolished. Only one Pope of this period, Hadrian VI (1522–3), raised his voice and attempted reforms. He did not live long. In a year he died—of poison. A high-minded autocrat is often the most impotent of mortals.

We have, fortunately, a contemporary document which throws considerable light upon the aims and methods of the Curia. It was drawn up in the secret consistory of cardinals, which met after the death of Alexander VI (1502) to elect his successor. The document consists of a number of articles which were to be observed by the new Pope in his dealings with the College of Cardinals. They were not to be "taxed or prosecuted or interfered with" without the express consent of two-thirds of their number; they were to remain in the undisturbed possession both of their benefices and their property, "how-

Aims and methods of the Curia.

[1] Gee and Hardy, p. 209.

ever ill-gotten it may be"; and (if needy) they were to receive from the Pope two hundred gold florins a month. All irregularities were to be overlooked. The Pope was to absolve them from all crimes and offences hitherto committed, "however exorbitant, enormous and great they may be," that thus they might become as innocent "as when the whole curia came from the baptismal font." All present in the Conclave solemnly swore that whoever of them should be elected Pope should immediately after his election bind himself by a solemn oath faithfully to observe the agreement. He will incur *ipso facto* eternal damnation, if he break any of these clauses. The document was signed by thirty-four cardinals and ratified by the new Pope, Pius III (1503).[1] Such were the aims of the papal court. Their idea of ecclesiastical reform consisted solely in the substitution of a selfish oligarchy for the autocracy of the Pope. There was no talk of raising the standard of religious life, improving morals or correcting ecclesiastical abuses. What good would such a reform have been to the Church? Its rulers were blind, and nothing but a revolution could have opened their eyes. Without the Reformation there would have been no Catholic reaction and no Council of Trent.

Power of the great medieval Popes.

But besides these special causes of discontent there was another, more general and more serious. On the eve of the Reformation the Papacy had lost the respect of Europe. Gregory VII (1073–85) and his successors had raised the Papacy to a position of great eminence, laying claim to supremacy alike in temporal as in spiritual things. They deposed kings, gave the law to Europe, carried on a long and successful contest with the Empire, organised the spiritual forces of the Church against the anarchy and brutality of the age, and, in spite of pride and ambition, directed their influence to the support of civilisation, religion and learning. By the middle of the 13th century the Pope had become supreme; but while the Papacy conquered the Empire, the world conquered the Papacy. The victory of the Popes proved to be their ruin. Zeal for the welfare of the Church became a mere pretext for increasing the wealth, the personal power and the temporal possessions of the Holy See. The arrogance of the Papacy

[1] A summary of this document may be found in Bergenroth, *Spanish Calendar*, I, 371, p. 311.

culminated in Boniface VIII (1294–1303), who at the jubilee of 1300 is said to have placed himself upon the papal throne and, arrayed in the imperial trappings, to have cried out, "I am Emperor, I am Cæsar." Three years later a very different scene took place; and at Anagni the pretensions of the Papacy were humbled to the dust by Philip the Fair. The Pope never recovered the shock, and died shortly afterwards in Rome "in a frenzy of rage and revenge."[1]

The long residence at Avignon, the Great Schism and the Conciliar movement weaken the Papacy.

The Popes of the later Middle Ages were very inferior to their predecessors both in character and ability. The 14th and 15th centuries produced no Hildebrand, or Innocent III, or Alexander III, or Gregory IX, but in their stead mere ecclesiastical officials and self-seekers. Papal rule was so bad that Rome became an unsafe place even for the Popes themselves. In 1309 Clement V left the city, and for nearly seventy years the Popes resided at Avignon; and as this was in French territory the Papacy ceased to be European and became French. The English lost respect for Popes who lived under the influence of their hereditary foes, and a series of anti-papal laws in the second half of the 14th century marked the hostility of King and Parliament. The attacks of Wycliffe both voiced and inflamed the dislike, and inflicted a blow upon papal authority from which it never recovered. The return of the Papacy to Rome was immediately followed by the Great Schism, and Europe was scandalised by two, and at one time three, rival Popes, each claiming to be the Vicar of Christ, each appealing for the allegiance of Europe, and each attacking his rivals with a vigour worthy of a better cause. The Great Schism gave rise

[1] For the career of Boniface VIII see Milman, *Latin Christianity*, Book XI, cc. 7, 8, 9. Gibbon says of him: "His memory is stained with the glaring vices of avarice and pride. He entered like a fox, reigned as a lion and died as a dog," *Decline and Fall*, VII, 243 (ed. Bury). Dante beheld his great vision in 1300, three years before the death of Boniface, but his arrival in hell was confidently expected. See *Inferno, Canto XIX*, 52 *seq.*; *Canto XXVII*. Even Simon Magus had a better place in Hell than Boniface.

> But from his holy office soon shall God
> Expel, and drive him down to that foul place
> Where Simon Magus hath his curst abode—
> To depth profounder thrusting Boniface.
>
> (*Paradiso, Canto XXX*, 145, trans. Wright.)

to the Conciliar movement of the 15th century, a movement which questioned the whole basis of the Pope's position. General Councils were summoned at Constance and Basle to prepare a scheme of reform for the Church, but the only reform which they could suggest was the transference of the autocracy of the Pope to a close oligarchy of bishops and cardinals. The scheme came to nothing, and the Conciliar movement, though it did away with the scandal of the Schism, ended, so far as reform was concerned, in a dismal failure. The Pope (Martin V, 1417–31) outwitted the Council, and became more autocratic than ever; but his position, though apparently secure, was in reality highly precarious. Belief in papal claims had been rudely shattered by the scandal of the Schism, and by the revolutionary opinions which had been so freely expressed by Wycliffe, by Huss, and even in the Councils themselves.

The Renaissance Popes.

But respect for the Papacy was destined to receive a yet ruder shock. In the latter half of the 15th century there arose that series of Pontiffs who are generally known as the Renaissance Popes, men who so lowered the tone of the Papacy that it became a byword and a scandal.[1] The Pope ceased to be the Father of Christendom and joined the ranks of the Italian despots. He entangled himself in the unscrupulous politics of Italy and, moved by greed of territory, engaged, like the secular princes of the day in bloodshed and war. The scandal reached its climax in Alexander VI. It is always dangerous to deal in superlatives in describing either virtue or vice; but by the testimony of all who knew him Alexander VI was, in spite of his fine presence, his great ability and his charm of manner, a notorious evil liver, a worse man even than John XXIII.[2] Alexander VI scandalised even his own age, which was not exactly sensitive on the subject of morals. At his death in 1503 there was a general desire for the appointment of a better man, and Ferdinand, writing to the Duke of Estrada, speaks of the "injuries inflicted of late upon the Church and upon Christendom on account of there not being a good Pope."[3]

Alexander VI, 1492–1503.

[1] Pius II (1458–64) was an exception. See Creighton, *Papacy*, Bk. IV, and Ady, *Life and Times of Pius II*.

[2] See *Decline and Fall* (ed. Bury), c. 70, p. 289.

[3] Bergenroth, *Spanish Calendar*, I, 372, p. 314.

The Italian Renaissance culminated in that cultured unbeliever Leo X, the son of Lorenzo the Magnificent, a man characterised by the artistic feeling, the passion for beauty, the intellectual refinement and the utter worldliness and religious scepticism which were the prominent traits of the leaders of Italian humanism. Leo X stands for the very embodiment of the Revival of Letters. At thirteen he was Cardinal; at thirty-seven Pope. Florence seemed to have removed to Rome, and his court became the most brilliant in Europe. Greek and Latin letters, sculpture, painting and architecture found in Leo their most munificent patron. Literary and artistic gifts were the surest means of obtaining ecclesiastical preferment, and both bishops and cardinals were chosen from the ranks of the humanists. To the court of Leo, as to that of his father before him, there flocked the learning of Europe. Rarely has the world seen any society so cultured, so brilliant in the highest artistic achievement and so indifferent to religion, piety and morals as the society which surrounded Leo X during the second decade of the 16th century. All that was most beautiful in art and most grand in architecture, all that was most pleasing to the senses and most attractive to the cultured, seemed to centre round the papal court. It was the brightest hour before the shadows began to lengthen. The Italian Renaissance went out in a blaze of glory. Little indeed could any of that brilliant and cultured society have foreseen the terrible doom which was soon to descend like a thunderbolt upon the city. But it was near at hand. In 1527 came the hordes of Charles V and the sack of Rome. The godless days of the Renaissance Popes had passed away.

Leo X, 1513-21.

How could Europe seek guidance in religion and morals from Pontiffs who were openly immoral like Alexander VI, or rude warriors like Julius II, or cultured unbelievers like Leo X? Is it surprising that there was corruption in the Church, seeing its rulers set so bad an example, or that many good men were led to the conclusion that, as it would not reform itself from within, the only remedy was a violent revolution from without? The Papacy lost its hold upon Europe when it forfeited its respect. Nothing can make up for the loss of character, not great place nor brilliant gifts nor charm of

Evil influence of the Renaissance Popes.

manner. When character is lost all is lost, for it is only by moral qualities that the Church can influence the world. When it relies upon moral and spiritual weapons it is a great religious power, however much men may dispute its doctrines or resent its interference. When it descends to the weapons and methods of the world it is sure to fail. All ecclesiastical history teaches this lesson which, though a truism, needs to be learnt by each generation. The decline of the later Medieval Church was due not so much to corruption in doctrine or to superstition in ceremony as to the loss of those high ideals which its Founder taught; and nowhere was this loss more conspicuous or more fatally exhibited than in the Papacy itself.

CHAPTER V

THE POWERS AND PRIVILEGES OF THE LATER MEDIEVAL CHURCH

THE Medieval Church wielded a power which is not easy to understand in a day when the State is all-powerful. It stood in a unique position of privilege ; and with its temporal advantages, its spiritual weapons and its great authority it constituted a veritable *imperium in imperio.* To begin with, the Church had its own special Courts of law. Before the Norman Conquest the same courts served for clergy and laity alike. The Bishop sat side by side with Ealdormen in the Shire Courts, declaring the law and pronouncing the sentence in all cases in which ecclesiastics were concerned ; the Archdeacon in like manner assisted in the jurisdiction of the Court of the Hundred ; and Church and State were so far one that the same law, the same courts, the same rewards and the same punishments served for all classes of the community.[1]

Church Courts.

This state of things was altered at the Conquest. William I wished to bring the Church in England more into line with the Church on the Continent, and among other reforms which he made he effected a complete separation between Church and State in all questions affecting the administration of justice. He laid down the rule that, henceforth, all ecclesiastical causes and persons were to be tried only by ecclesiastical judges, and that bishops and archdeacons, being no longer permitted to use the local courts, should be given special courts of their own, the decrees of which were to be enforced by the strong arm of the Crown, and were to be as

William I established separate Ecclesiastical Courts.

[1] The bishops had their own private courts for clerical discipline and purely spiritual matters.

binding and as authoritative as the decrees of secular judges.[1]

There now arose an elaborate and ascending group of Church Courts. These were the Court of the Rural Dean, to try petty cases; the Court of the Archdeacon, concerned chiefly with moral lapses on the part of the laity; the Diocesan or Consistory Court of the Bishop, which constituted both a court of first instance and a court of appeal from that of the Archdeacon, and was presided over by the Bishop's official, the Chancellor. Lastly, there were the Provincial Courts of the two Archbishops, the Archbishop of York having two courts; the Archbishop of Canterbury having four, the Court of Arches, so called because it was held in the church of St. Mary-le-Bow (de Arcubus), a very important court both of appeal and, in certain cases, of first instance; the Court of Audience, which was held at St. Paul's; the Court of Prerogative, which dealt with probates[2]; and the Court of Peculiars, which was concerned with parishes outside ordinary episcopal jurisdiction.

Their growth.

These spiritual courts dealt with all purely spiritual and ecclesiastical questions, heresy, clerical discipline and morality; but they had a much wider jurisdiction than this; for a great part of what now comes before secular courts, breach of contract, marriage, probate and the morals of the laity, then lay within the province of these ecclesiastical courts, which had "over the clergy an exclusive, and over the laity an extensive jurisdiction." Their power was great, for the law of the Church was just as powerful and even more far reaching than the law of the land. To-day religion is optional. People are free to accept it or to reject it as they like. The Church cannot enforce its discipline upon unwilling members. It can only exhort and persuade. In the Middle Ages things were very different. The law of the Church applied to all alike. If men refused to obey the rules of the Church or to accept its correction, the Church had the power to *make* them; and it could do this by means of

The jurisdiction of the Ecclestical Courts.

[1] For William's ordinance see Stubbs, *Select Charters*, p. 85.

[2] This court was peculiar to England. Elsewhere in the Church the question of wills was a matter for the secular courts. As a fair exchange the latter took over in England questions of advowsons and certain other temporalities.

the ecclesiastical courts. Was a man leading an immoral life? The Church could hale him before its courts and impose upon him a severe penance. Did a layman refuse to pay the fees demanded of him? The parson could bring him before the courts and *make* him pay. Had a man broken his bond? The Church would soon take him in hand. Did the relatives wish to prove a will? It could be done only by the authority of the Church.

Rivalry between secular and ecclesiastical courts.

But it was not the jurisdiction of the ecclesiastical courts that made them so unpopular. At first their establishment had been a distinct gain, for they administered a better law, and awarded more humane penalties than the secular courts. But it soon became apparent that this dual system of jurisdiction was open to grave objection and led to great abuses. Henry II tried to remedy the evil by the Constitutions of Clarendon, but failed dismally. An angry rivalry soon sprang up between the courts of the Church and the courts of the King. Each side complained of encroachments upon their respective jurisdictions, and disputes were incessant. There arose a conflict between canon law and common law which, as the latter grew in extent and improved in method, caused great friction between Church and State. The clergy complained again and again of the infringement of their privileges. People bought "prohibitions" in the temporal courts, and by their means stopped processes in the spiritual courts. Lawyers made subtle attacks upon the liberties of the Church, and by strange interpretations turned the Statutes of Præmunire and Provisors to "the intolerable hurt and prejudice of prelates and spiritual judges."[1] Occasionally violence was resorted to and justice was rendered impossible. In 1481 Sir Richard de la Bere came into court with armed followers and intimidated the jury.[2] In 1512 the Mayor of Hereford and his officials openly molested persons having business in the court of the Bishop, and the Crown had to send a mandate directing him to permit free access to the ecclesiastical courts.[3]

Such incidents afford evidence of the great dislike in which the spiritual courts had come to be held. They were

[1] *Concilia*, III, 555. See also Stubbs, *Seventeen Lectures*, p. 366.
[2] *Reg. Mylling*, p. 68; cf. *Reg. Lacy*, pp. 628–9.
[3] *Reg. Mayew*, p. 135.

in truth unpopular everywhere, and bitter complaints were made about them. They were slow, expensive and uncertain; their fees were exorbitant and their exactions shameful. Sir Henry Guilford complained in 1529 that he had to pay one thousand marks to prove the will of Sir W. Compton, for whom he was acting as executor.[1] The courts swarmed with petty lawyers, who made a living out of the misfortunes of their victims. The Archdeacon's court was particularly unpopular. It dealt with the morals of the laity, and in order to obtain business the officials sanctioned an odious system of spies and informers, who crept into houses, wormed out secrets and reported breaches of morality or of canon law. No one felt safe, for the easiest way of paying out a rival was to lay an information against him in the Church Courts. The Summoner was constantly at the doors of the laity with his summons to attend some ecclesiastical court, often at a great distance, and generally for trivial and vexatious causes[2]; the Summoner, pictured for us by Chaucer with his red face, his love of strong wine red as blood, his accessibility to a bribe, his *significat* and *questio quid juris*. And if all other charges failed, there still remained the fatal charge of heresy which (as in the famous case of Hunne) it was always possible to trump up, and which at once rendered the man an object of suspicion for the rest of his life.

Unpopularity and abuses of the Church Courts.

Towards the end of the Middle Ages the condition of Church courts was a veritable scandal. Colet speaks of the "scandals and vices of the courts." "What loss of religion, what diminution of authority, what neglect of Christ, what blaspheming of God ensues from these disputes and litigations. Nay! they might see how the very thing they call the Church's goods, which they imagine themselves to be keeping or else recovering by their lawsuits, are slipping away little by little every day and can with difficulty be retained. For they are trying

Colet on Church Courts.

[1] *L. and P.*, IV, 6043. This was perhaps an exceptionally high charge, as he had to pay both in the Archbishop's Court and in the Legatine Court of Wolsey. But the usual fees were excessive, especially in the Courts of Arches and Audience. See "*The Petition of the Commons*," 1532, Gee and Hardy, p. 145, where a list of fees is given.

[2] "The Clerks for their own proper lucres doth upon every light surmise make out processes," Pollard, *Henry VII*, III, 200. See also Gee and Hardy, p. 147.

to retain them by force rather than by men's liberality and good will; and nothing can be more unworthy of the Church than this."[1] Archbishop Warham was fully alive to the evils of the Church Courts. In 1507 he issued nine injunctions for the reform of the Court of Audience, protecting poor suitors, ordering despatch of business and limiting the number of proctors.[2] Some years later Wolsey tried his hand at reform. He wished his Legatine Court to supersede the Provincial Courts of the Archbishop, but his imperiousness and want of tact only led to friction with the Archbishop, who felt himself aggrieved and his privileges attacked.[3] The result was utter confusion and all the evils of a dual control. All efforts at reform were a failure; and so oppressive, so tyrannical, so unscrupulous had the administration of the ecclesiastical courts become in the 15th and 16th centuries that men readily paid hush money and gave enormous bribes to the officials to keep them out of the courts. The gulf between clergy and laity steadily widened; the ecclesiastical system became daily more unpopular, until at last Henry VIII opened the flood-gates, and the long pent-up discontent of the laity burst forth in an irresistible torrent, which threatened to engulf the whole medieval ecclesiastical system.[4]

Warham and Wolsey.

Growing abuses of the Courts.

Another special privilege of the Medieval Church was that known as *Benefit of Clergy*, a privilege which belonged to that "bird of ill omen" (as Maitland calls him) the criminous clerk. The clerical Order was, as we have seen, a very large one, and comprised men of all classes and of all characters. Even those in the lowest Orders, who were practically laymen, were ranked as clergy, and crimes committed by them were regarded as a stain upon the good name of the clerical Order. So in a sense they were; but when historians speak about criminous clerks we must bear in mind that these were for the most part men in the lowest Orders, and that among the clergy proper (in our sense of the word), and especially among the parochial clergy, the proportion of criminals was by no means

Benefit of Clergy.

[1] Lupton, p. 73.
[2] *Concilia*, III, 650.
[3] See *Concilia*, III, 660, 661, 681; *L. and P.*, III, 77, 98, 127; Hook, *Lives of the Archbishops*, New Series, I, 234–43.
[4] For Eccles. Courts see Mackower, *Constit. Hist. C. of Eng.*, pp. 384–464; Reichel, *Manual of Canon Law*, II, 174–230.

large. Not, indeed, that the parochial clergy were blameless. Far from it. The episcopal registers contain many entries relating to criminous priests, though such men were probably to be found rather in the remoter parts of England, on the rough borderland between England and Wales, in the wilds of Yorkshire, away from civilisation and public opinion rather than in the more populated and more civilised parts of the country. In some districts, certainly, especially during the anarchy of the 15th century, things were very bad; and there are several instances of the conviction of parish clergy for the crimes of perjury, theft, violence, rape and even murder. The Bull of Clement VII in 1528 giving Wolsey authority to deal with criminous clerks states that "some priests both among the secular and regular clergy do not hesitate at times to commit frightful crimes."[1]

The chief reason for the extent of clerical crime in the Middle Ages was, undoubtedly, the absurd system which prevailed of dealing with the criminous clerk. After the Conquest the clergy were tried in their own courts for all offences, both civil and ecclesiastical; but as these courts could not inflict any punishment which involved loss of life or limb, it is clear that clergy convicted of serious offences got off lightly.

After the Conquest the clergy were tried in their own courts.

Owing to the lightness of the penalty imposed and to the confusion which prevailed during the greater part of the reign of Stephen, the number of serious crimes committed by members of the clerical Order increased to such an extent as to become a menace to society, since the clergy might commit murder and other grave crimes almost with impunity. The scandal had become so great that Henry II, soon after his accession, determined to deal with the evil. By the Constitutions of Clarendon he proposed that clerks (or those that passed themselves off as clerks) should, when accused of a crime, be brought straightway into the King's Court. Two questions had to be decided by the court—Was the man a clerk? Was the charge one of felony? If, after due examination, the court was satisfied on these two points, it was to proceed no further with the trial, but was to hand over the accused to the Ecclesiastical Court, to the jurisdiction of which the case now belonged; and, in order to prevent the man

The Constitutions of Clarendon.

[1] *Concilia*, III, 713.

escaping, the trial was to be conducted under the eyes of a royal official. If found guilty, the Church was to offer the criminous clerk no further protection. He was to be degraded from his Holy Orders and reduced to the status of a layman; he was then to be brought back as a layman into the King's Court; and as he had already been found guilty, he was to be condemned to the layman's barbarous punishment of mutilation and death.[1] As Roman canon law ordered the separate treatment of clerks and laymen, Becket, after some hesitation, refused to accept the proposed reforms. A violent quarrel ensued. The result was disastrous both to Church and State. The Archbishop was murdered and became a martyr. Henry had to drop the obnoxious clauses, and the scandal of clerical crime went on practically unchecked.

Procedure in dealing with criminous clerks after the death of Becket.

From the time of Becket up to the Reformation the practice of dealing with a criminous clerk seems to have been as follows: He was brought before the secular courts, tried and, if found guilty, condemned. He was then taken in charge by the Bishop's officials appointed for the purpose, and placed in the Bishop's prison. Thereupon he immediately appealed to the Bishop, pleaded not guilty and claimed the right of proving his innocence by means of purgation, which meant asking his friends to appear as witnesses and bear testimony to his innocence. If these appeared (as they generally did), the criminal clerk was released without further fuss. If, however, his guilt was too apparent even for his own cronies to swear to his innocence, he was kept for a short time in the episcopal dungeon, from which he was soon allowed quietly to escape. There are several instances in the 15th century registers of this mode of procedure. Thus, for example. In 1475 a purgation was held by the Vicar-General of the diocese of Hereford of one Gitto Glane, a clerk, who had been convicted by a secular court of rape and robbery.

[1] Constitutions of Clarendon, c. iii, *Select Charters*, p. 138. The clause is so concise and so obscure that no two writers agree as to its exact interpretation. Stubbs admits that "the matter is far from clear, and was not clear at the time." See *Constit. Hist.*, I, p. 501; Taswell-Langmead, *Eng. Constit. Hist.*, p. 73; Medley, *English Constit. Hist.*, p. 168; and, above all, Maitland, *Canon Law in the Church of England*, where a whole chapter (iv) is devoted to the subject.

As no witnesses appeared against him, though due notice of the proceedings had been published by the Rural Dean of Ludlow, he was acquitted and released.[1] Four years later the chaplain of Diddlebury, a priest, had been convicted by the King's justices of a very shocking case of rape. He was taken by the Bishop's official, declared his innocence, demanded and obtained purgation and release.[2]

Friction between ecclesiastical and secular courts,

Officials were regularly appointed by the bishops to watch the trial of clerks in the King's Courts and protect them "according to the sacred canons, rights and laudable customs of the realm of England"[3] from the danger of falling into the clutches of the secular authority. The presence of these episcopal officials was very necessary, for secular courts were only too delighted whenever a chance came their way of getting their own back and inflicting summary vengeance upon a peccant clerk. In 1402 the Convocation of Canterbury asserted that clergy convicted of felonies had been tried and executed by the secular courts. The same complaint was made by the clergy in 1475, 1478 and 1483, and appeals were made to the Crown to stop the abuse. In 1485 Innocent VIII complained to Henry VII that clergy have been tried before the secular courts, and have (against all canon law) been subjected to torture and mutilation. The royal authority was called in to uphold an ecclesiastical abuse, and give royal protection to the undeserving.[4]

Benefit of clergy, a danger and a farce.

In its fight for privilege the Church brought upon itself a fitting nemesis. The custom of allowing the criminous clerk to be tried by the milder law of the Church, which in rougher days had been a protection against the barbarity of secular tribunals, became in time an abuse, and was responsible for much of the clerical crime and disorder which were so prevalent in the later Middle Ages. At length the practice was reduced

[1] *Reg. Mylling*, p. 14.

[2] *Ibid.*, p. 52, cf. pp. 42–3. Bishops could withhold purgation if they thought fit. By the constitution of Archbishop Boniface every bishop must have one or two prisons for criminous clerks. For good example of the purgation of a criminous clerk see *Liber Albus*, p. 31.

[3] *Reg. Meyew*, p. 143; cf. *Reg. Bubwith*, p. 59.

[4] *Concilia*, III, 270, 608, 612, 614, 617. Cf. the complaints of Sixtus IV, p. 609. See *Reg. Bothe*, I, 119–23, for charter of liberty and privileges granted to the clergy by Edward IV in 1461.

to an absurdity. When a man was brought before the secular court, accused of a felony, he at once pleaded his "clergy"; and as it was not easy to discover (so wide was the clerical Order) whether he was in Holy Orders or not, a simple test was applied. The judge asked him to read a verse from the Bible. This was supposed to be a sure test, as at one time only the clergy could read. Hence it came about that anyone who could read, or even (so absurd was the whole procedure) repeat from memory a Biblical text, was at once allowed Benefit of Clergy without further investigation.[1] The custom became at last so great a scandal that Parliament took the matter up. In 1489 an Act was passed to "take awaye the benefytt of clergye from certayne persones." It stated that "whereas many have been the more bold to commit murder, rape, robbery, theft and all other mischievous deeds because they have been continually admitted to the Benefit of Clergy, it is enacted that every person not being in Holy Orders who has once claimed Benefit of Clergy may not do so a second time; that every murderer and felon be branded on the thumb in open court by the gaoler before being sent to the Church Court; and that any clerk on a second charge must produce his Letters of Orders before the Court, and if he cannot do so, he is to lose the Benefit of Clergy."[2] Eight years later (in 1497) Parliament passed another law dealing with the same subject, and enacted that any lay person who murdered his master should not be permitted (even if he could read) to claim the Benefit of Clergy, but that he should at once be executed as a layman.

Attempts to remedy the abuse.

During the early days of Henry VIII the question caused a violent collision between Church and State. In 1513 an Act was passed enacting that all murderers and robbers should be refused the Benefit of Clergy unless they were actually priests,

Collision between Church and State on the question in 1513.

[1] Cf. *Italian Relation*, p. 35. "In another way also the priests are the occasion of crimes; in that they have usurped a privilege that no thief or murderer who can read, should perish by the hands of justice . . . if he can read he is liberated from the power of the law, and given as a clerk into the hands of the Bishop." The fact that so many criminals succeeded in passing themselves off as clergy has led to an exaggerated idea of the extent of crime among the medieval clergy.

[2] 4 Henry VII, c. 13; 12 Henry VII, c. 7, given by Pollard, *Henry VII*, III, 193.

deacons or sub-deacons. The Act was temporary and was to expire in 1514; but even so it stirred the Church to fury at the bare idea of this unscrupulous encroachment upon its privileges by the State in its desire to limit disorder and crime. Better, thought the baser sort, anything than restriction of Church privilege. The Abbot of Winchcombe was put forward as champion of Church abuses. He preached a sermon at St. Paul's, in which he denounced the action of Parliament as outraging both the Word of God and the rights of the Church, and threatened vengeance against all who had passed it. Standish, Warden of the Greyfriars, was put up to champion the rights of Parliament. He denied the moral right of the clergy to plead exemption from royal jurisdiction in criminal cases, and rounded on the bishops for neglecting their spiritual duties. Convocation at once replied by citing him for heresy, the invariable charge against those who attempted Church reform. But the King interfered; Standish was snatched from the fury of his enemies; and, though the Act was not renewed, Henry asserted the authority of the Crown: "By the permission and ordinance of God we are King of England; and the Kings of England in times past never had any superior but God only. Therefore know you well, that we will maintain the right of our crown, and of our temporal jurisdiction, as well in this as in all other points, in as ample a manner as any of our predecessors have done before our time."

The privilege abolished.

But the evil had become so notorious that something had to be done. Even the Papacy attempted reform. In 1516 Leo X issued a Bull inhibiting anyone for the next five years from being admitted to Minor Orders unless he be promoted simultaneously to the office of sub-deacon, "as many persons enter Minor Orders simply to enjoy Benefit of Clergy."[1] In 1532, when Crown and Parliament were united in an attack upon the Church, the Act of 1513 was renewed; while in 1536 the privilege was withdrawn from those in Major Orders who were charged with certain grave offences. By this time the power of the Church had been broken, and though the privilege nominally lingered on until comparatively recent times, after the Reformation it ceased to be an abuse.

[1] *L. and P.*, II, 1532.

Another of the privileges of the Medieval Church which led to much abuse was that of *Sanctuary*. Certain places, generally churches, were looked upon as sanctuaries—that is, as places where a criminal who was fleeing from justice might find refuge and protection. When he had reached the sanctuary, and as long as he remained there, he was safe. No one dared to touch him. The Church offered him its full protection, and visited with severe penalties those who refused to respect the privilege. This lasted forty days, and if during that period the criminal wished to leave the country, he was allowed to do so. He was stripped to the shirt by the chief magistrate of the place, a crucifix was placed in his hand, and he was conducted to the sea, where he was allowed to take ship and depart. The Italian writer, to whom we are indebted for these details, tells us how people bewailed his unhappy lot at having to leave England, "as though England were the whole world," and out of England life was not worth living.[1]

The Right of Sanctuary.

Durham Cathedral was a very famous sanctuary. Men escaping from justice or from the vengeance of their pursuers fled to the North Door of the Cathedral, famous for its knocker, and knocked loudly for protection. Certain men were always on duty in the chamber over the door, stationed there to open the door for refugees at any time of the day or night. When the refugees had been admitted the Galilee bell was rung that all might know that someone had claimed the right of sanctuary. The Prior then ordered them to be kept in the church and to be clad in a black gown made with a cross of yellow cloth called St. Cuthbert's cross, set on the left shoulder. A special room was provided for them and they were fed and cared for at the expense of the Abbey.[2]

In its origin the custom was good, being designed to prevent injustice. In days of anarchy and violence, when the administration of justice was barbarous and uncertain, and when the wronged often took the law into their own hands, the right of sanctuary was a very real protection for the innocent, or for those who

Its liability to abuse.

[1] *Italian Relation*, pp. 34, 35, and Note 54.

[2] *Rites of Durham*, pp. 41–2. The circuits of sanctuaries were usually marked with crosses. See also *Reg. Sanct. Dunelm.* (Sur. Soc. V.)

were fleeing from their enemies. But at the same time the privilege was liable to grave abuse. Debtors took advantage of it, and from the safety of their sanctuary defied their creditors. The worst criminals often escaped their due punishment. A privilege, which was established to check lawlessness and injustice, soon became itself a means of spreading the very evils which it was designed to remedy, and the Church was accused (not without truth) of obstructing justice and of harbouring criminals. Sanctuaries became the resort of thieves, murderers, "malicious heinous traitors." In 1459 a man sought sanctuary in Ely Cathedral, and openly confessed that he had lately killed his servant by beating him with an iron instrument, that he had feloniously stolen a bay horse and that he was an abettor and harbourer of thieves and robbers.[1] Westminster Abbey acquired an evil notoriety for harbouring dangerous criminals, who used to steal out at night, brawl in the streets, devise new robberies, kill, destroy, and then come in again as though the Church gave them not merely protection from the crime which they had already committed, but licence to commit still worse. The abuse became so great that Henry VII was compelled to deal with it. In 1487 Parliament put a stop to the practice of debtors defrauding their creditors by abusing the privilege of sanctuary; while in the same year the King obtained a Bull from Innocent VIII which limited the privilege to first offenders. In 1504 Julius II took it away from persons suspected of high treason; and it was finally abolished for criminals in the reign of James I, though certain places, such as White Friars, were regarded as sanctuaries, so far as civil processes were concerned, for some years later.[2]

Measures to regulate it.

But perhaps the power of the Medieval Church was displayed with the greatest effect and on the largest scale in the use of those spiritual weapons of reward and punishment which made the Spirituality so formidable a foe to provoke, and enabled it not merely to hold its own with the Temporal Power, but at times (by the mere force of spiritual weapons) to terrorise it into complete

Penance.

[1] *Reg. Gray*, f. 117.

[2] Scott in the *Fortunes of Nigel* has described Alsatia a kind of London Sanctuary for criminals. For Innocent's Bull see *Concilia*, III, 621.

submission. The first way in which the Church could make its power felt was by the infliction of penance. Perhaps some of the practices which were most severely condemned at the Reformation were those connected with the doctrine of sin, its nature, its punishment and its pardon. The Church had a very clear notion of sin. It was a definite act; a definite breach of the laws of God and the Church; and as such it must be atoned for by contrition, by confession and by punishment. These three acts were called penance; and submission to penance was held to atone for the sin, to pardon the guilt and to remove, or at least to mitigate, the punishment which the sinner will receive from God in the next world. In early days penance usually took the form of corporal punishment, though it took other and milder forms as well, such as going upon a pilgrimage, or engaging in some pious and charitable work. The penance was on a sliding scale in accordance with the nature of the sin, and was usually performed in public. Even the very highest had to submit to public penance. In the days of the Early Church, St. Ambrose, Bishop of Milan, imposed a severe penance upon the Emperor Theodosius for having permitted the massacre of the rebellious Thessalonians[1]; the Emperor Henry IV in 1077 was kept waiting barefooted in the snow outside the Pope's palace at Canossa, because he had dared to cross the path of Hildebrand; and our own King Henry II submitted to a humiliating penance at Canterbury, where he was publicly scourged by the monks as an atonement for the murder of Becket.

Instances of Penance.

In the year 1394 we have two characteristic instances of medieval penance. John Brabourne of Streatham had taken sanctuary in the porch of the parish church. Richard Wylkyn and John Brokere arrested him there and carried him off to Guildford goal. It was a very serious matter to interfere with the right of sanctuary; and the Bishop issues a mandate that a very severe penance should be inflicted upon the offenders. On three consecutive Sundays they are to walk in procession, stripped to their shirts and carrying lighted tapers, Wylkyn, the principal, a taper of a pound weight; Brokere one of smaller size. One of the parties charged with carrying out the penance, clad in a surplice, is to flagellate the offenders

[1] See *Decline and Fall* (ed. Bury), III, 175.

with a rod, at the same time declaring to the people the reason for the penance. After which the penitents are to kneel in the middle of the church at High Mass, repeat the *Magnificat* in audible voice, and pray for forgiveness. This penance is to be performed at Streatham, at St. George's, Mitcham, and at Mitcham parish church on successive Sundays.[1] In 1419 Philip Peynton, of Hulle Episcopi, near Taunton, was haled before a secular tribunal for an offence within the cognisance of the Church Courts. This was a grave offence, and the Bishop of Bath and Wells came down very heavily upon the offender for daring to infringe the liberties of the Church. He orders him to pay all expenses, to give twelve shillings to Philip Peynton and to submit to three "fustigations through the church of Hulle and three in the market place of Taunton."[2]

Penance takes the form of a money payment.

But as this sort of penance was found by the laity, and especially by the well-to-do laity, to be somewhat oppressive and humiliating, a custom grew up in the 14th century of substituting for corporal punishment some other expiation for sin, less humiliating to the individual and at the same time more profitable to the Church. This generally took the form of a money payment. Instead of submitting to corporal punishment, the sinner might atone for his sin by a fine, somewhat after the custom of the Anglo-Saxon wergeld.[3] Sins were graduated, and each had its price. The worst immorality could be condoned for money. It became simply a calculation of ways and means, how many sins, or what kind of sins, could a man *afford* to commit. The rich were obviously at a great advantage in this respect, since their licence to sin was only limited by the size of their purses. The Church found the system profitable, and made a large income out of it. It was generally willing to smile upon the sinner and welcome him back to the fold, if he produced the ready cash. The bait proved irresistible, and money was rarely refused. The Later Medieval Church desired not the death of a sinner, but rather that he should

Evil results of of this custom.

[1] *Reg. Wykeham*, II, 454.

[2] *Reg. Bubwith*, p. 353. The episcopal registers contain many interesting cases of penance.

[3] For a good instance of this see *L.V.*, II, p. lx, where the punishment of whipping was easily commuted for a cash payment of 20s.

pay and live. The result was fatal to its spiritual and moral force. Who could look up to a Church for guidance in ethics and religion which in practice (though perhaps not in theory) asserted that sin could be easily atoned for by a money payment, and which regarded breaches of the moral law not so much as an offence in the sight of God, but rather as the easiest means of raising funds ?[1]

From this custom of commuting penance for ready money arose one of the greatest abuses of the Medieval Church, the system of Indulgences. The Church had two weapons for enforcing its will, persuasion and force. It tried persuasion first, and if this failed it resorted to force. Its method of persuasion took the form of Indulgences ; its method of force that of Excommunication. Excommunication and the Interdict were, indeed, powerful weapons in the days when men believed that the Church possessed the key to Heaven, and could, if necessary, condemn a man eternally. We must not blame the Church for employing these methods, for they were the only weapons either for aggression or for defence which it possessed. In days of brute force and unchecked licence, the Church had only spiritual weapons with which to meet the cruelty and violence of the age. In the interests of civilisation, morality and religion it *had* to make its voice heard and respected, and how could it do this except by the assertion of its spiritual powers to bless and to condemn ? It could certainly have been wished, however, that it had exercised these powers more often on behalf of righteousness than in defence of its own immunities and privileges. The Church was not always over scrupulous in the use of its spiritual powers. The system certainly had its legitimate uses ; but it kept the laity in bondage, led to bitter complaints and contributed greatly to the overthrow of the ecclesiastical system in the 16th century.

Two powerful weapons of the Church—Excommunication and Indulgences.

Both Excommunication and the Interdict were frequently resorted to by the Papacy. When a country was laid under an Interdict the sacraments could not be administered, public worship could not be celebrated, and the burial service could not be used ; and these

Excommunication and the Interdict.

[1] The better churchmen disliked the system. Archbishop Thoresby (1352–74) in his *Lay Folks Catechism*, p. 49 (E.E.T.S.), strongly condemns the condoning of sin for a money payment.

were in the Middle Ages very real punishments. It will be remembered that Innocent III laid England under an Interdict for five years because King John refused to receive Langton as Archbishop of Canterbury. In the long contest between the Empire and the Papacy the Pope relied largely upon the power of excommunication, which, as Henry IV of Germany found to his cost, was a very serious thing in those days. In 1488 the Pope sent to Henry VII a Bull which contained a solemn excommunication of the rebels who were threatening his throne, and which proved very useful. That interdicts and excommunications were very dangerous things to quarrel with we have the testimony of Henry VII himself. In 1487 a soldier, John Swift by name, began robbing and plundering after the battle of Stoke. " On being remonstrated with he said, 'What signify censures of Church or Pontiff? Do you not see that interdicts of that sort are of no weight whatever, since you see with your own eyes that those very men who obtained such in their favour are routed, and that the whole anathema has recoiled upon their own heads?' On pronouncing these words he instantly fell dead upon the ground, and his face and his body immediately became blacker than soot itself, and shortly afterwards the corpse emitted such a stench that no one soever could approach it. Verily we give thanks to Almighty God, who of His ineffable mercy has exhibited in our Kingdom so great a miracle concerning the Christian faith."[1]

Instances of Excommunication in the episcopal registers.

In the episcopal registers we hear much of excommunication. People were excommunicated for all sorts of reasons. Food had been refused to certain who had taken refuge in sanctuary, and excommunication was the penalty. A layman had so far forgotten himself that he had actually dared to lay violent hands upon the sacred person of a clergyman, and the Bishop immediately excommunicated him. Some miscreants have gone poaching, and that too in the Bishop's park. Let them be excommunicated. People were even excommunicated for refusing subscriptions to Church objects; clergy who refused to pay the papal enactions were excommunicated; even the great Bishop of Winchester himself, William of Wykeham, the Chancellor of England, was

[1] Henry VII to Innocent VIII, *Letters and Papers of Henry VII*, I, 94–6.

threatened with excommunication, unless he sent off within thirty days the sums demanded from the papal Nuncios. That this is not a mere threat is shown by the fact that the Bishop sends off an urgent mandate to his Archdeacon to get the money in as quickly as possible.[1]

The other weapon of the Church was persuasion. This generally took the form of an Indulgence. The subject is a difficult one, and it is important to distinguish carefully between the *theory* of Indulgences and the way in which they worked out in actual practice. The theory was this. The Church had a large spiritual treasure, acquired partly as the Bride of Christ, and partly from the good deeds, the works of supererogation, of saints and martyrs. These good deeds could be set over against the evil deeds of sinners to make the balance even, and thus to preserve that happy mean of virtue, so dear to Aristotle and to the Medieval Church. The Church could make use of this treasure to lighten the load of punishment incurred by sinners ; but of course it was not prepared to do this without some substantial *quid pro quo* (money preferred) from the sinner. In *theory*, at any rate, whatever may have been the popular idea, the Church did not by its system of Indulgences grant either forgiveness of sin or permission to sin. It simply, for a monetary consideration, remitted some or all of the sinner's punishment in this world ; and, when the doctrine of Purgatory became established, it shortened the time, or lessened the intensity, of punishment for those who, not being eternally lost, must go through the purifying fires of an intermediate state before they can be fit for the Kingdom of Heaven. Indulgences could in *theory* only be given to the truly penitent. When the sin had been atoned for by genuine repentance, the Indulgence remitted part or all (plenary or partial indulgence) of the temporal punishment due for the sin. The difficulty, however, lay in the

Indulgences.

[1] See *Reg. Wykeham*, II, 217, 225, 228, 289. *Reg. Lacy*, p. 751 ; *Reg. Mylling*, p. 140. There are many instances. An excommunicated person was expected to submit to the Church within forty days. If he did not, the secular arm was called in. For an instance see *Reg. Bubwith*, p. 420. If a man died excommunicate he was refused Christian burial. If by chance he were buried the churchyard was regarded as defiled and had to be reconciled, *Reg. Mylling*, p. 37. In Wykeham's Register there is an instance of the absolution of the corpse of an excommunicate to allow Christian burial, *Reg. Wykeham*, II, 69.

fact that there was no test for gauging the reality of the sinner's inward feelings. Such was the theory, but in practice (so nice was the theological definition) people regarded Indulgences as forgiveness of sin in return for a money payment, and (so easy were Pardons and Indulgences to buy) as a virtual permission to sin again on the same easy terms of expiation.[1]

Indulgences, generally of forty days, were offered for all kinds of purposes. People were encouraged and bribed to give by the offer of Indulgences. Exeter Cathedral is badly in need of repair and funds are required. If people will only subscribe, they may have an Indulgence of forty days. Everyone who has read Kingsley's *Westward Ho* knows the famous bridge of Bideford. In 1425 the citizens of Bideford were collecting money to build it, but funds were not very plentiful and a little encouragement was needed. The Bishop of Exeter comes to the rescue and offers an Indulgence to stimulate generosity. Henry VIII is preparing for an expedition against France; the reigning Pontiff is the warlike Julius II, who thinks wars are things to be encouraged; all, therefore, who take part in the expedition or in any way help it shall have a plenary Indulgence. And so on. There were Indulgences for those who contributed to the upkeep of abbeys, cathedrals, churches, chapels, shrines, roads and bridges; for those who will help the poor, the sick, the suffering, the unfortunate, and even contribute to relief of criminous clerks. There is an Indulgence for those who will redeem a Portuguese from the hands of the Saracens, or go on a Crusade, or repeat the Lord's Prayer and the Hail Mary at break of day, or (descending to mundane matters) help to build a vicarage. Indulgences are even offered for those who will attend the sermons of a preacher! Perhaps if the custom were revived we should not hear so much about dull sermons. One wonders if the wretched man obtained an

Instances of Indulgences.

[1] The subject of Indulgences is an extremely difficult one. See Lea, *History of Auricular Confession and Indulgences,* III; Creighton, *Hist. Papacy,* Bk. VI, c. 3; *Camb. Mod. Hist.*, II, 121–9; Coulton, *Social Life,* pp. 203–7. There is a very interesting article upon Pardons and Indulgences by the late Canon Wordsworth in the *Yorks. Arch. Journal,* XVI, 369–423, where the theory of Indulgences is discussed, the literature of the subject given, and examples of Yorkshire Pardons and Indulgences recorded.

audience even with this incentive. Medieval churchmen were taught the duty of giving, and, that virtue might not go unrewarded and to make the donor realise that generosity was a pleasure as well as a duty, an Indulgence was generally thrown in. The plan certainly had its advantages. A medieval bishop did not head the subscription list; he knew better; he offered Indulgences to induce others to give.[1]

But the system of Indulgences was chiefly used by the Papacy as a means of raising money. In 1300 Boniface VIII decreed a Plenary Indulgence for those who, in that year and every hundredth year following, visited Rome. This was found so useful a method of filling the papal coffers that Clement VI reduced the Jubilee period from 100 to 50 years; Urban VI reduced it to 33; and Paul II to 25 years.

The Papacy and Indulgences.

Indulgences and Pardons were freely sold in England. In 1440 Peter de Monte came to England and sold Indulgences, causing much scandal and indignation. He made a great deal of money, which he refused to hand over to the Pope until he had been made Archbishop of Milan. In 1501 Alexander VI sent to England to be distributed unto the King's subjects by the hands of his "dear and well-beloved William Battes, student in the University of Cambridge," a Papal Bull which granted "indulgence, pardon and grace with remission of all their sins" to those who would contribute money to the crusade which the Pope was at that time meditating against the Turk. Every facility and encouragement were to be given for paying. The Commissioners were empowered to change all manner of vows "into alms." Those who were ill and unable to visit the churches, where the money was to be paid and the Indulgence granted, could have the "said indulgence, remission and grace" provided that they first "compounded effectually" with the Commissary or his deputy. Each was to pay according to his means; and in order that there should be no mistake in the matter, the Pope sent a detailed list of incomes and appropriate charges. Any sin (apparently) could be atoned for; but a speciality was made of usury, theft, simony and irregularity in singing

Sale of Indulgences in England.

[1] *Reg. Wykeham*, II, 476, 495, 496, 523, 545; *Reg. Lacy*, pp. 471, 484, 506, 512, 668, 742; *Reg. Mayew*, pp. 285–7; *Reg. Boulers*, p. 15; *Reg. Stanbury*, p. 91; *Reg. Bothe*, pp. 76, 175, 207; *L. and P.*, I, 3602.

Mass, or in ministering the other holy Sacraments. To make it still more encouraging, it was added that thieves might, if they preferred, keep their ill-gotten goods instead of returning them to their owners. But in all cases this very important proviso was added—" always provided that the said persons make a composition unto the said commissary."[1] The scandal reached its height when Tetzel came into Saxony in 1517, armed with a papal Bull to grant Indulgences in return for contributions towards the expense of rebuilding St. Peter's at Rome. It was this which led to Luther's protest, and was the spark which fired the Reformation.

The selling of Indulgences was a regular profession. Pardoners, as these sellers were termed, went all over the country hawking their wares. Chaucer has given us an immortal picture of a typical pardoner:—

Pardoners.

" A gentil Pardoner,
That straight was come from the court of Rome,
His walet lay biforn him in his lappe
Bret ful of pardoun come from Rome al hot.
He had a croys of latoun full of stones,
And in a glass he hadde pigge's bones.
But with these relikes, when that he fond
A poor person dwelling upon lond,
Upon a day he gat him more money
Than that person gat in monthes tweye.
And thus with feigned flattery and japes
He made the parson and the people his apes."[2]

On the occasion of some great papal Indulgence these pardoners went about in companies. On arriving at a town they were met by the town officials, and with music and song marched through the streets in solemn procession, holding aloft the papal Bull. The system led to the greatest abuses. Gascoigne[3] has some very strong remarks to make upon the subject. People, he tells us, did not hesitate to commit the grossest sins, because they knew that, with the greatest ease and swiftness, they

Evil effects of the sale of Indulgences.

[1] *Letters and Papers Henry VII*, II, 93–100. For Indulgences for contributions to the building of St. Peter's, Rome, see *Reg. Fox*, II, f. 140 ; *L. and P.*, II, 3767.

[2] *Prologue*, ll., 670 *seq.*

[3] Gascoigne, p. 123.

could for a few pence buy a pardon from the Pope. "The sellers of these pardons rush all over the country, selling pardons for a few coppers, or even for a good draught of wine; some even for carnal love." "Rome came to people's very doors." Alfonso, King of Arragon, said to Pope Eugenius IV (1431–47), "The Church of Rome is like a harlot, which sells herself to anyone who gives her money." In 1517 a writer stated that pardoners in France preached that whoever put into their money-box ten sous would go straight to Paradise; and added his opinion that such Indulgences are ruinous to the King and the poor. Erasmus, writing to Warham the next year, said: "The court of Rome is shameless. What can be more gross than these continued Indulgences? A war against the Turk is made the pretext when the real purpose is to drive the Spaniards from Naples."[1] There were a great many false pardoners who made money by forging Indulgences and selling them *avaritiæ veneno inebriati.*[2] Life must certainly have been easy in those days for well-to-do sinners. All they had to do was to buy a pardon, and then they might go on sinning as much as they liked, or rather as long as their money lasted. This may not have been the theological doctrine of Indulgences, but this was pretty much how the system worked out in practice.

[1] *L. and P.*, II, 3818, 3991.

[2] *Concilia*, III, 599. In 1414 the University of Oxford protested against the growing scandal of Indulgences, *ibid.*, 360. For medieval views of Indulgences see Coulton, *Social Life*, pp. 203–7.

CHAPTER VI

COLET AND THE NEW MOVEMENT FOR EDUCATIONAL REFORM

PART I

MEDIEVAL ENGLISH SCHOOLS

UP to the end of the 19th century a very hazy and mistaken idea was held with respect to education in medieval England. The general notion was that the only education available, until the foundation of Winchester, Eton and St. Paul's, was due to the zeal of the monks. Medieval England was, according to tradition, plunged in darkness and ignorance except where glimmerings from the monasteries enlightened the land. To each abbey there was attached (so we were led to believe) a thoroughly efficient and flourishing school, maintained by the monastery, taught by the monks and available for the general public. We pictured to ourselves the good monk, pious, ascetic, zealous and learned, diligently instructing the youth of England in the faith of the Church, in the morals of religion and in the humaner letters. At the Dissolution all this, of course, came to an end, and an irreparable blow was in danger of being struck at the sacred cause of education, when Henry VIII and Edward VI, children of the Renaissance, patrons of learning and self-denying philanthropists, came to the rescue, and out of their privy purse founded in all parts of England grammar schools bearing their name, and giving a far more enlightened instruction both in the Faith and the Humanities. It was an attractive and delightful picture; and the fact that it leaned to the side of fiction did not make it any the less delightful or attractive. It was left to a modern iconoclast to explode these ideas, draw aside the veil which

Mistaken ideas about education in medieval England.

had for so long concealed the truth, and rewrite the history of medieval education. Mr. Leach in numerous books (aided by later writers in the same field) has shed the light of truth upon the subject, and with great zeal, research and learning has destroyed many a reputation, thrown over many an obscure country grammar school the glamour of remote antiquity, and shown that medieval England, so far from being a land of ignorance, or dependent upon the monk for instruction, possessed in practically every centre of population flourishing schools, which catered for the needs of the majority of the people and gave an education, narrow and imperfect indeed, but, when judged by the limitations of the age, often surprisingly good.[1]

Antiquity of schools.

The truth is that schools, so far from beginning with William of Wykeham, are among the most ancient of all our institutions, and begin in England with the coming of St. Augustine at the close of the 6th century. From the very first the teaching office of the Church was recognised by its leaders. A liberal education was regarded by the more enlightened of them as essential for the study and comprehension of Christian theology; and to secure this, the Church (though not without serious misgivings) allowed its children to attend the very efficient schools, themselves modelled on those of Athens and Alexandria, which abounded throughout the Roman Empire. When Rome fell before the barbarians its schools perished; but the Church, when opportunity offered, established Christian schools on the model of the imperial schools. Indeed, wherever Christianity spread, a school was invariably founded as an integral part of the work of the Church.[2] It is not therefore surprising to find that Augustine

[1] See also Rashdall II, 600 f. In Andover, however, a very ancient town, careful research by local antiquarians has failed to find any record or trace of a medieval school. See Adamson, *Short Hist. Educ.*, p. 76, where he says that the number of children in medieval schools was much smaller than the entire child-population. For the antiquity of obscure country grammar schools, Leach, *Early Yorks. Sch.*, and his list of schools with dates at the end of *English Schools at the Reformation.*

[2] The relation between the pagan and Christian schools is a matter of controversy. The Church was not consistent in its attitude to pagan literature, but it became more hostile as time went on. See Adamson, *Short Hist. Educ.*, c. 1; and pp. 190 f. in *Med. Contributions to Modern Civilisation;* Cubberley, *Hist. Educ.*, pp. 82–104; Parry, *Educ. in*

regarded as one of the first duties of his missionary enterprise the establishment of a school, which became the model of other English schools and which, under the name of the King's School, Canterbury, is flourishing at the present day.[1]

As Christianity spread in England education spread too. Archbishop Theodore, a Greek (668–93), did much to encourage secular learning, and especially the study of classical authors. Indeed, there was a high standard of education in England at this time. Aldhelm, who was probably educated at a grammar school in Winchester, writing *c.* 680 mentions his elaborate scheme of studies. York possessed a very flourishing and efficient school in the 8th century. Alcuin, a native of the city, was both a pupil and a master here before he went to the court of Charlemagne. He tells us that the curriculum at York was grammar, rhetoric, law, music, astronomy, geometry, theology, architecture; and for literature Virgil, Lucan, Statius, Cicero, Pliny, Aristotle and the Christian poets, Sedulius and Juvencus. The Danish invasions were a check both to Christianity and to education, but Alfred tried to revive an interest in learning, which had sunk incredibly low. He made many translations and established palace schools. Dunstan was also an educationalist, and was himself for a time a teacher at Glastonbury.

Schools in Saxon times.

The Norman Conquest gave a great impetus to Church life and to church building. A large number of Collegiate Churches were founded, which included among their other duties that of providing free grammar schools, while the Cathedral grammar schools (likewise free) were strengthened and improved. A school became an integral part of a Cathedral establishment, and a special officer, the Chancellor, was appointed to supervise its educational activities.

Schools after the Conquest.

Middle Ages, p. 2. The duty of bishops and clergy to keep schools was laid down in many Councils. That of Eugenius II in 826 ordered bishops to establish Grammar Schools for teaching the liberal arts "because in these chiefly the commandments of God are manifested and declared." The Lateran Council in 1179 and Innocent III in 1215 ordered every cathedral to provide free schools for poor scholars. The Council of Westminster in 1200 decreed "ut presbyteri per villas scholas habeant et gratis doceant." *Educ. Charters*, pp. 20, 122, 138, 142.

[1] See Woodruff and Cape, *Hist. King's School*, c. i.

Among the most numerous, though not the most efficient, medieval schools were those which were known as *Chantry Schools*. It is not always easy to determine whether chantries were founded for the primary purpose of education, or whether schools became attached to chantries already founded. The former is certainly true of many schools. Thus Chelmsford Grammar School was founded as a chantry school in 1375 by Sir John Mountney, who left money for a chantry priest to serve the chantry and act as schoolmaster. It is probable that parish church schools were little more than classes held in the church for the purpose of instruction in elementary knowledge, and that to make this education more systematic and more efficient chantries were founded in connection with the parish church, the primary duty of the chantry priest being to act as a schoolmaster. The Chantries' Acts of 1548 dissolved colleges, chantries, gilds and brotherhoods. Hence the schools (over 300) maintained by these were abolished or crippled. Those schools which were retained (under pressure) lost their lands and received instead a monetary income ; and as the value of money went down and that of land increased the disendowment of the schools became very apparent. Had they retained their original endowments, many a struggling grammar school would have been to-day a wealthy and flourishing institution.

Chantry Schools.

There is an interesting document in the register of Spofford of Hereford describing the foundation of a chantry school at Newland by Johanna Greyndoore in the year 1446. The chaplain is to be skilled in the "art or science of grammar," and his assistant sufficiently well skilled in the same. The school is to be open to all who live in the place, or care to come there for the purpose of education. The fees for elementary education ("their alphabet, matins and psalter") were to be fourpence a year; for instruction in grammar the fees were double. There were to be four holidays a year : a fortnight at Easter, a week at Whitsuntide, six weeks in the summer and a fortnight at Christmas. It is somewhat strange to learn that the age of entrance is to be eighteen, so that it is not a school at all in our sense of the word, a fact which makes us wonder how many so-called schools of medieval England resembled this one. The scholars were to be of

Instance of a Chantry School.

honest conversation, intent upon their studies and obedient to the master, who was to see that their whole time was devoted to education.[1] If they were disobedient and refused to submit to discipline, they were to be expelled. Their religious duties were severe. Twice every day they were to recite the Psalms, *Deus misereatur* and the *De Profundis* (the latter kneeling), the Lord's Prayer, the *Ave Maria;* and were to pray for the foundress and her husband.[2]

Other classes of schools.

There were other classes of schools as well. *Gild Schools* made their appearance in the 13th and 14th centuries. To each gild there was generally attached a priest whose duty it was to hold the gild services and pray for the souls of departed members; but in addition to these duties he was often required to keep a school, the primary object of which was the education of the sons of the gild members, who needed instruction in the vernacular, but which was generally thrown open to the general public. There were, in addition, a few schools maintained in connection with hospitals, such as that of Banbury, which at the beginning of the 16th century was famous for its very efficient method of teaching. There were also schools at the Universities in connection with some of the colleges, intended to serve as a training ground for the Universities. Of these College schools that of Merton College, Oxford, is a good example.[3]

Decay of the older schools in the 15th century.

These schools, however, were not independent institutions, for they were part of a larger body and generally owed their foundation to more or less accidental circumstances. But towards the close of the 14th century a new class of school arose, which owed its existence to the generosity of private founders, and which was established for the sole purpose of the education of youth. Schools were founded by kings, nobles, ecclesiastics and city merchants. The 15th century was a

[1] 'Quod per capellanum ad aliqua ministeria exercenda non ponantur, sed erudicione et studio continue vacare compellantur.'

[2] *Reg. Spofford*, pp. 281–8. See also *Reg. Stanbury*, pp. 21–33 for a similar instance.

[3] For some interesting and enlightening extracts from the accounts of Merton College schoolboys, 1277–1310; 1347–95, see *Educ. Charters*, pp. 211–23, 299–305. "Extras" were not (it appears) a hateful device only of modern school authorities for bleeding parents, for we find "extras" even in the fourteenth century.

great age for school foundations. There is good reason to believe that in the first half of the century the general standard of education among the older foundations had, with some notable exceptions, greatly deteriorated. It was a time of demoralisation and unrest, and all institutions seem to have been suffering from a wasting disease—the Church, the Universities, the Religious Houses, the Mendicants, the constitutional government of the country. In this general collapse the schools did not escape. Many of the older grammar schools fell into decay; Cathedral Chapters were often in such a disgraceful state that the efficiency of their schools suffered; the supply of good teachers rapidly fell off. In 1439 William Byngham reported how in a journey from London to Coventry and Ripon he had found, owing to a scarcity of competent masters, at least seventy grammar schools in decay which fifty years previously had been flourishing institutions. To remedy this scarcity he petitioned the King that he might found *God's House* (afterwards Christ's College) in Cambridge for the training of grammar school masters. In 1447 the rectors of four important London churches petitioned Parliament to allow them to establish grammar schools in their parishes on the ground that schools were decaying. Previously, they declare, there had been both in London and in all parts of the realm a great number of grammar schools, "and how few there be in these days, and the great hurt that is caused by this." After the close of the civil wars matters improved. The Renaissance crossed the Alps; a new spirit was abroad; and it only remained for enlightened and munificent founders, of whom fortunately there was no lack, to seize the opportunity for a new era in education.

Private founders.

Even before this there had been a few founders. In 1432 William Sevenoaks founded Sevenoaks Grammar School, placing it under the trust of the rector and churchwardens, who were to secure as headmaster at ten marks per annum "an honest man sufficiently advanced and expert in the science of grammar, B.A., by no means in holy orders."[1] In 1443 John Abbot, a mercer of London, founded a school at Farthinghoe, and, nearly eighty years before Colet, entrusted it to the care of

[1] Infra sacros ordines minime constitutum. *Educ. Charters*, p. 4. To have a layman as headmaster was a very revolutionary proposal.

the Mercers. In 1487 Sir John Sha founded a school and placed it under the Goldsmiths; and to the same Company was entrusted his school at Cromer which Sir Bartholomew Read founded in 1505. In 1502 Sir John Percyvale founded a Free Grammar School at Macclesfield for "gentil manne's sonnes and other good men's children," and entrusted it to seventeen lay trustees.[1]

But the majority of private foundations were due to the generosity of ecclesiastics. Archbishop Chichele founded a college at Higham Ferrars in 1425 and incorporated into it the local grammar school. Archbishop Kempe of York founded a school at Wye in Kent ten years later; Waynflete of Winchester founded in 1459 a grammar school at Wainfleet, his native place, and another in connection with his College of Magdalen at Oxford (1480). Rotheram founded the College of Jesus for six boys to be educated in song, grammar and writing until their eighteenth year. Of Colet's contemporaries, Fox founded schools at Taunton and Grantham; Oldham of Exeter refounded the Collegiate Grammar School of Manchester; while Wolsey planned a magnificent school at Ipswich which, if its endowments had not been confiscated, would have been one of the most efficient and enlightened schools in Europe.

But of these private foundations the most famous and the most magnificent are the Colleges of Winchester and Eton.

Winchester.

In 1382 William of Wykeham, Bishop of Winchester, founded "Seinte Marie College of Wynchestre," to consist of "70 poor and needy scholars, clerks, living college-wise therein, and studying and becoming proficient in grammaticals, grammar being the foundation, gate and source of all the other liberal arts." To these seventy scholars ten commoners were added, and the whole establishment amounted to about one hundred persons. The aim of Wykeham was to ensure a supply of learned clergy, as the number had lamentably fallen off, to the great hurt of the Church, by reason of "plague, wars and other miseries." Winchester College was at one time referred to as our oldest educational establishment; but, of course,

[1] There are several other instances. For London schools and their founders see Stow, *Survey* (Everyman ed.), pp. 66–70, 96–107. For other cases of schools placed under City Companies see Watson, *Gr. Sch.*, pp. 22–3.

compared with Canterbury or York or many an obscure country grammar school, it may be regarded as modern. Nor was the idea original, for Wykeham had both foreign and English models. But it was, nevertheless, a landmark in the history of English education. Its size, its dedication to a single purpose, the grandeur of the scheme, the magnificence of the buildings, its rich endowments, the beauty of the site in the ancient capital of England, its many famous sons, its long and continuous history in the same school buildings from the 14th century to the present day have given it a pre-eminent position among the schools of England.[1]

Eton.

Fired by the example of Wykeham and Chichele, Henry VI in 1440 founded in the parish church of Eton "the King's College of oure Ladye of Eton besyde Wyndesore," to consist of a Provost, 10 Fellows, 6 choristers, 25 poor and needy scholars to learn grammar, and 25 poor and disabled men. The 25 scholars were soon increased to 70, and 20 oppidans allowed. It was to be a free grammar school open to the whole nation.[2] These two great colleges of Winchester and Eton have had the good fortune to survive and become famous. They might easily, like many other scholastic institutions, have been despoiled in the days of Henry VIII and Edward VI, their buildings destroyed and their names obliterated. Institutions (like individuals) owe more than it is always agreeable to recognise to accident and good luck.[3]

The monk and education.

In this scheme of medieval education where does the monk come in, for at one time it was held that *he* was the only educator of the period? When in early days monks engaged, like St. Augustine, in missionary

[1] Foundation deed in *Ed. Charters*, pp. 320–8. See also Leach, *Hist Winchester College*; Kirby, *Annals*, cc. 1 and 2; Mackenzie-Walcott *William of Wykeham and his Colleges*; Cook, *About Winchester College* Adams, *Wykehamica*; Moberly, *Life of Wykeham*, c. ix; and fo school teaching and life in the early part of 16th century, *V.C.H. Hants*, II, 296 *seq.*

[2] *Educ. Charters*, pp. 404–14. See also Maxwell Lyte, *Hist. Eton College.*

[3] Both Eton and Winchester were founded for the less wealth classes, since the sons of the nobility were in the Middle Ages not sen to school but to the households of nobles and ecclesiastics for thei education and training. John Paston was educated in the househol of the Duke of Norfolk. His cousin William was sent to Eton.

enterprise, they no doubt took part in the secular education of their converts; and in the 7th and 8th centuries, under the influence of Irish monasticism and, later, under that of Dunstan, monks may have undertaken teaching work, though to what extent it is not easy to determine; but that after this period the monk took any practical part in general education may be denied with complete confidence. Their rules forbade it. Even in the education of their own novices it became the custom to engage the services of a secular master. There is no instance of a monk pensioned at the Dissolution who was acting as a schoolmaster. In the case of nunneries it was perhaps different. Some nuns (to make ends meet) certainly did keep schools. For example, at the time of the Dissolution there were twenty-six girls receiving their education at St. Mary's, Winchester; but such teaching was, after all, only a side show, and was undertaken not out of zeal for education or from a desire to be useful, but from sheer necessity; just as many parochial clergy (of the Church of England) of the present day are compelled to take pupils, in order to eke out their miserable pittance, keep up their palatial rectories and enable them to pay their baker's bill—the Church of England not yet having risen to the simple but fundamental duty of paying its parochial clergy a living wage, an instance of a divorce between precept and practice which goes far to stultify its moral influence in the world.

Monastic schools.

But even allowing that the monks themselves took no part in teaching youth, did the Religious Houses maintain schools for the general public? Thorold Rogers was of opinion that grammar schools were attached to every monastery,[1] while a recent writer has declared that "there exists evidence that schools for the education of the laity existed in the neighbourhood of most if not of all the greater monasteries dependent upon the monastery."[2] This view is, however, against the weight of the evidence which we possess at present. To begin with, the maintenance of a grammar school for the benefit of the public was no part of the aim or ideal of monasticism. The only schools the monks professed to keep were for the instruction of their own novices, and even these were often

[1] *Six Centuries*, I, 165.
[2] Parry, *Educ. in Middle Ages*, pp. 105, 170–3.

in abeyance. There were also in certain monasteries almonry or choristers' schools which had their origin in the 14th century in the need of choir boys to sing the Offices of B.V.M. These boys attended the local grammar school as at York, but when no such school existed the Convent provided one, and hired a secular schoolmaster to teach.[1]

The monks as school founders.

There were, however, certain schools in connection with, or under the control of, monasteries, and this fact has led many into the error of attributing to the monk a zeal for education which he does not deserve. As the monks have often been unjustly attacked so they have been also unjustly praised. In the 12th century there was an extraordinary monastic revival. Abbeys sprang up in all directions and were liberally endowed by pious benefactors. They obtained lands, towns, churches, tithes; and when they settled in a place where a grammar school existed they naturally obtained control of the school, as they did of so much else. In places where no such school existed it is not improbable that some of the richer monasteries did found schools for the sons of their tenants, but they did this in their capacity not of monks, but of landowners.[2] In the case of cathedrals where monks ousted seculars the school was continued, but it was placed under the direct and exclusive control of the Bishop, who acted as trustee and appointed the master.[3]

The monks as trustees.

There were, it is true, a certain number of schools which had been placed by their founders under the management and trusteeship of monasteries. In such cases, while the monks were responsible for the school and appointed the master, they did not maintain it out of the general funds of the monastery, but only administered the special endowment which had been left for the school. This was the case at Bruton in Somersetshire, at Evesham, at Bridgwater and elsewhere. At York the wealthy Abbey of St. Mary "did not maintain a grammar

[1] For an almonry school see *Rites of Durham*, p. 91; and for the finances of an almonry school (Westminster), *Educ. Charters*, pp. 307–15.

[2] e.g. Bury St. Edmunds, founded by Abbot Sampson who bought a school house 1182. *Educ. Charters*, pp. 128–32.

[3] For Canterbury, *Educ. Ch.*, p. 239.

school of its own for outsiders, but only as part of its expenditure on alms maintained some poor scholars at St. Peter's School." Sherborne School was not maintained by the Abbey. "Out of an endowment of some £1200 a year the Abbey spent in 1535 just £5 2s. 8d. on education in exhibitions of three scholars at the Grammar School of Sherborne." Professor Savine states that in the *Valor Ecclesiasticus* there are very few entries of educational expenditure, most of them being crossed out and disallowed. There is no mention in the *Valor* of monastic schools for the general public.[1]

PART II

COLET AND ST. PAUL'S SCHOOL

ON February 6th, 1512, the Convocation of the Southern Province assembled at St. Paul's. It consisted of the most influential and most distinguished men in the Church—the Archbishop of Canterbury, the Bishops, Abbots, Deans, Archdeacons and Proctors of the parochial clergy. A meeting of Convocation was no unusual thing; and as this distinguished gathering assembled they were prepared for nothing more than the ordinary routine of business. Little did they anticipate the bombshell which was to be thrown into their midst by one of their own members. The Archbishop had invited John Colet, Dean of St. Paul's, to preach the opening sermon. The Dean had consented, but not without great misgiving; for he felt the responsibility too heavy for him. The sermon which he delivered is one of the most remarkable and most powerful that has ever been delivered from an Anglican pulpit. He took as his text the second verse of the second chapter of the Epistle to the Romans: "And be not conformed to this world, but be ye transformed by the renewing of your mind, that ye may prove what is that good and acceptable and perfect will of God." The Dean's subject was Church reform; and in dealing with it he exposed unmercifully the ecclesiastical abuses of the day, brought a

Colet's Convocation sermon, 1512.

[1] See *Early Yorks. Schools*, I, p. xxx; Savine, pp. 231–3.

most severe indictment against the rulers and dignitaries of the Church, and fearlessly denounced the worldliness, ambition, greed, selfishness and negligence which characterised so many of the upper ranks of the clergy. To these abuses he attributed the ills from which the Church was suffering. The sermon closed with the words : "Go ye now in the spirit that ye have called on, that by the help of it ye may in this your council find out, discern and ordain those things that may be profitable to the Church, praise unto you, and honour unto God, unto whom be all honour and glory for evermore. Amen."[1] The sermon created a profound impression. By the laity it was hailed with delight, and the preacher honoured as a prophet. By the rulers of the Church it was regarded with consternation. His Bishop, Fitz-James of London, was so enraged that he brought against him before the Primate the serious charges of having translated the *Paternoster* into English, of having expressed disapproval of written sermons ("a frigid custom in England"), of having attacked the worship of images, and (most heretical charge of all) of having denounced the swollen incomes of the prelates. The Archbishop was broad-minded enough to dismiss the case ; but the preacher's outspoken sermon had made him many enemies. The Dean was henceforth a marked man.

Early life of Colet.

John Colet was born in London in the year 1466, the eldest child and only survivor of a family of eleven sons and eleven daughters. His father, Sir Henry Colet, a wealthy merchant, was twice Lord Mayor of London and lived just long enough to see his son become Dean of St. Paul's. His mother, who was connected with the noble house of Clifton, outlived him.[2] After an education in London, Colet went up to Oxford in his eighteenth year and entered Wayneflete's new College of Magdalen. Here for some years he devoted himself to a course of severe study, reading widely in the Latin classics, scholastic philosophy, mathematics, law and poetry. In

[1] The sermon was delivered in Latin ; but a contemporary translation was published. The English version is reprinted by Lupton, pp. 293–304.

[2] In 1517 the Dean, writing to Erasmus, dates his letter : "From his mother's house in Stepney, who is a cheerful old lady." *L. and P.*, II, 2941.

1493 he left Oxford and travelled to Italy. Here he came under the influence of the Italian Renaissance and imbibed the philosophy of Plato in the academies of Ficino and Mirandola. But he was a deeply religious man, and learning only appealed to him as an aid to religion. He was repelled by the licence which marked Italian humanism, and he was disgusted at the state of the Church, then at its lowest ebb under the notorious Alexander VI. But he came into touch with higher influences as well. He visited Florence, where the great Savonarola was at this time preaching his famous sermons. There was much in common between the Englishman and the Italian. Both were deeply religious; both were filled with anger at the political and ecclesiastical conditions of the age; and both were eager reformers, who spoke with the courage and indignation of Hebrew prophets.

Return to Oxford and appointment to St. Paul's.

In 1496 Colet, who had been deeply impressed by his experiences in Italy, returned home and took up his abode at Oxford. He was ordained deacon in December, 1496, and priest in the spring of the following year; but, in accordance with the evil custom of the age, he had, ever since his nineteenth year, held several valuable benefices and prebends which the influence of his father had obtained for him, and in none of which does he ever seem to have resided. After eight years at Oxford, during which he delivered his famous lectures upon the New Testament, Henry VII appointed him to the Deanery of St. Paul's. Here he came into conflict both with his Bishop ("a superstitious and invincible Scotist") and with the Chapter, who distrusted the tendency of his teaching, resisted his attempts at reform and were put to shame by his ascetic and self-denying life. A year after his appointment his father died, leaving him a large fortune, which rendered him independent of ecclesiastical preferment and gave him the opportunity of carrying out his educational plans. In 1512 came his famous Convocation sermon which created so great a sensation; and in the following year, when Henry VIII was preparing a war against France, Colet denounced the war and argued that an unjust peace was preferable to the most just war. The rest may be told in the words of Erasmus: " After Easter, when the expedition was ready against France, Colet preached on Whit-Sunday before the King and the Court, exhorting men rather to follow the example of Christ, their prince, than that of Cæsar or Alexander. The King was afraid that this sermon would have an ill effect upon the soldiers, and sent for the Dean, who was dining at the Franciscan monastery near Greenwich. When the King heard of it, he entered the garden of the monastery, and on Colet's appearance dismissed his attendants; then discussed the matter with him, desiring him to explain himself, lest his audience should suppose that the Dean intended to insist that no war was ever justifiable. After the conversation was over, he dismissed him before them all, drinking to Colet's health, saying aloud: 'Let every man have his own doctor, this is mine.' "[1]

From this time no striking event marks the Dean's career. After the year 1516 his health, which had long been undermined by extreme asceticism, began visibly to fail. He had several attacks of the sweating sickness. In 1519 he was seized with a mortal illness, and passed away at the Deanery on September 16th. He was buried in the cathedral.

Death and character.

In appearance Colet was tall and, in his early days, handsome, but the austerity of his life made him old before his time. He was extremely neat in his person and apparel, and always wore black while his compeers wore purple. In character he was sincerely religious, though inclined to narrowness and even bigotry; generous on a large scale, though parsimonious in small things; like all ascetics somewhat hard, unsympathetic and lacking in the qualities which make for popularity; a man to command respect rather than affection; but a man who, by reason of his integrity, high ideals, munificence and moral earnestness, won for himself a high place both as a religious leader and as a pioneer of educational reform.

Colet was at Oxford at the very time when the influence of the Italian Renaissance was making itself felt in the Universities. During the 15th century the Universities had declined from their former prosperity. The blight of the Black Death had fallen upon them, as it had fallen upon the Church and upon the country generally. Many of the colleges were impoverished by falling rents and had got into financial

The Universities in the 15th century.

[1] *L. and P.*, III, 303.

difficulties; a feud sprang up between the Universities and the Friars; while the teaching of Wycliffe had caused great intellectual ferment and much religious unsettlement. Wars, foreign and domestic, and the general social and political conditions of the age had diverted the attention of the nation from literature and learning. Nor were the studies which then prevailed calculated to attract literary students. Erasmus, writing in 1516, speaks of them with scorn: "Thirty years ago nothing was taught at Cambridge except Alexander's *Parva Logicalia*, some scraps of Aristotle and the *Questiones* from Duns Scotus."[1] Scholasticism had long since seen its best days, and was ignobly expiring in a long drawn-out agony, fighting desperately for life and obstinately resisting all change. The abuses of ecclesiastical patronage were at this time so great that merit was rarely rewarded, and as students found so little encouragement in the pursuit of literature or theology they devoted their time to the civil and canon law, which alone seemed to offer any guarantee of a lucrative and successful career. It was not until the accession of the Tudors that the condition of the country became favourable to the Renaissance.[2]

Beginnings of the New Learning in England.

Greek.

The New Learning had, however, attracted a few select students earlier in the century. Humphrey, Duke of Gloucester, had founded the public library of the University of Oxford and had presented to it a large number of valuable classical manuscripts. John Tiptoft, Earl of Worcester, nicknamed for his cruelty the "butcher," was a munificent patron of learning. Towards the close of the 15th century several Englishmen made the Italian tour, came under the spell of the Italian Renaissance and returned with a passion for classical literature. The ambition of the humanist was the study of Greek, but outside Italy this was at that time by no means easy. Colet, with all his love of literature, did not learn Greek until his closing years. This is certainly surprising, but we know that it was so. More, writing to Erasmus in February, 1516, when Colet was fifty years of age and within three years of his death, says: "Colet is

[1] *L. and P.*, II, 2321.

[2] See the resolutions passed in Convocation in 1420 to meet the complaints of Oxford and Cambridge of their decreasing numbers owing to the abuses of ecclesiastical patronage. *Concilia*, III, 401.

earnestly studying Greek and has made use of my page"; Erasmus, writing to Fisher in the following year, says he is glad that Colet is studying Greek; and Colet himself, writing to congratulate Erasmus upon his edition of the Greek Testament, tells him he welcomes the new light, but bewails his ignorance of Greek "*sine cujus peritia nihil sumus.*"[1] His famous lectures upon St. Paul's Epistles were given from the Vulgate,[2] and it is not improbable that it was this fact which led Erasmus, who attended the lectures, to feel the need of studying the New Testament in the original language, and induced him to prepare his Greek edition. Colet felt so severely the handicap of his ignorance of Greek that he made careful provision for it in his school.

The great difficulty in the way of acquiring a knowledge of Greek was the scarcity both of books and of teachers. It was as difficult then to learn Greek as it would be to-day for a boy in a remote country grammar school to learn Chinese. There were so very few competent teachers. True, there were a few who had some knowledge of the language, but they had acquired this in Italy. William Selling, Prior of Christ Church (1472–95), had learnt Greek there, and on his return may have taught it. Thomas Chandler, Warden of New College (1454–75), knew it, and he brought an Italian, one Cornelio Vitelli, to Oxford to teach it. Grocyn certainly was a Greek scholar and lectured upon it at Oxford (1491–3). Linacre knew it and acted as instructor to More; but the number of Englishmen before 1540 who knew Greek was extremely limited. Erasmus left Oxford in 1499 because the University could not teach it, and went to Paris to learn it. For many years there was a strong theological prejudice against Greek, and it was very slow in gaining a footing in the Universities. Its study received a great impetus from Bishop Fox, who founded the College of Corpus Christi at Oxford "for the inculcation of theology, philosophy and the arts." The studies of the Renaissance, and particularly Greek, were to be carefully taught. Elaborate statutes were drawn up.[3]

Fox and Corpus Christi College.

[1] *L. and P.*, II, 1588, 2941, 3668; III, 303.

[2] Even so recent a writer as Prof. Cubberley has fallen into the error of thinking that Colet's lectures were given upon the *Greek* text. *Hist. Educ.* (1921), p. 288.

[3] "Scholastici, veluti ingeniosæ apes dies noctesque ceram ad Dei

The President was to be neither a monk nor a bishop. The College was to be a beehive, and its bees were to gather honey day and night. The discipline was severe, the study hard, the vacations short, the recreations mild. A challenge was flung down to the old learning. Scholasticism was banned; medieval Latinity was ousted for that of Cicero; and regular provision was made for the systematic teaching of Greek. The College attracted much attention, and Erasmus thought it would soon be one of England's chief ornaments; but though it played an important part in the English Renaissance, it was quickly overshadowed by its neighbour, the magnificent college planned by Wolsey.[1]

Greek at Cambridge.

At Cambridge the Renaissance was favoured by Fisher and his patroness, the Lady Margaret, who founded St. John's College and did so much for learning. Erasmus gave some elementary lessons on Greek in 1511, and the Regius Professorship was founded in 1540, Sir J. Cheke being the first Professor. But Greek was for many years a very rare accomplishment even among the best University scholars. Until 1540 there were in England few printed Greek books and Greek *Grammars* were practically inaccessible. The first of any circulation was one by Clenard, printed at Louvain in 1530; while the earliest one printed in England was David Tolley's in 1547. Schoolmasters who could teach Greek were extremely rare. Lily knew it and taught it at St. Paul's; but Wolsey did not include it in the Ipswich curriculum. At Eton it was not taught until 1560.[2] Certainly in 1541 Henry VIII's statutes for the Cathedral Grammar Schools stated that the master must be learned in Greek as well as in Latin, but it is doubtful how far this could be insisted upon. Until the accession of Elizabeth, Greek teaching in schools was the rare exception.[3]

honorem et dulciflua mella conficiant ad suam et universorum Christianorum commoditatem." Fowler, *Hist. C.C.C.*, p. 38.

[1] *L. and P.*, III, 333, 566; also II, 4042 for the opposition which the College and Greek aroused.

[2] See Watson, *Gr. Sch.*, pp. 488, 495. Sir Thomas Pope's statement seems to indicate Greek at Eton very much earlier than 1560. Greek *may* have been taught at Canterbury and at Winchester in the 15th century.

[3] For early Renaissance in England see Creighton, *Lectures*, pp. 188 *seq.*; Allen, *Age of Erasmus*, pp. 118–34; Taylor, *Thought and Expres-*

Colet occupies a very honourable place in the history of English education. Having inherited a considerable fortune from his father, he decided to devote it to the cause of learning; and with this end in view, desiring "the education and bringing up of children in good manners and literature," he founded in 1509 in St. Paul's Churchyard a school for 153 boys of all classes and nationalities, endowing it with an estate in Buckinghamshire and property in London, spending upon it, out of his own private means, a sum equal to about £50,000 to-day. Colet's plans for his school express in concrete form the aims of the new movement in educational reform, and a glance at his statutes will reveal the Dean's ideals. These were in the main fourfold—freedom from the trammels of medievalism, a higher class of teacher, new educational methods and a curriculum which might be summed up in the phrase, Christian humanism.

Colet founds St. Paul's School.

The religious and intellectual world of the Middle Ages was narrow and confined. It was dominated by authority; in religion by the authority of the Church; in thought by the authority of scholasticism. There was little freedom of thought or spirit. Differences of religious opinion were sternly repressed as heresy; while the spirit was cramped and the intellectual horizon limited by the formulæ and conceptions of the medieval mind. The acutest thinkers were confined to a narrow circle, and their thought was intensive rather than extensive. There was no liberty to expand, for conclusions must be in harmony with certain theological, scholastic, and even political ideas and preconceptions. The blight of a dominating authority lay upon everything, hampering the freedom of the spirit and the liberty of the individual. This narrow medievalism was broken down by many causes, by the growing sense of nationality, by the natural decay of scholasticism, by the growth of international commerce, by mechanical inventions and by the revival of classical letters. The latter opened up a new world, the world of Greece and Rome, very different from the medieval; an intellectual world untrammelled by

Colet's educational ideals: (1) Freedom from the trammels of medievalism and ecclesiastical control.

sion in 16th Century, II, c. 18; *Cambridge Mod. Hist.*, I, pp. 580–4; Seebohm, *Oxford Reformers*.

tyrannical authority; a world of free thought, of natural impulse, of wide outlook. Medievalism was shattered in this freer, wider, more natural outlook of the classical world. The medieval man walked in a narrow groove carefully prescribed for him by authority. He was a unit rather than an individual. Liberty of thought and action were impossible in a world dominated by authority, the authority of a gild, a society, a corporate organisation. The Renaissance gave him back his individuality, and exalted freedom and responsibility over the obligations of membership of an organisation.[1] It led to a reaction against authority, and this reaction showed itself not least in education. The educationalists of the Renaissance wished to be free from ecclesiastical authority and scholastic formulæ.

There was already a Cathedral Grammar School at St. Paul's of great antiquity, but it had fallen into decay, and was so entirely under the control of inert and reactionary clerical influences that Colet had little hope of its future progress and usefulness. The Chancellor, Dr. William Lichfield, was quite unfit to have the oversight of what should have been an important school; while the Bishop of London, Richard Fitz-James, was a type of ecclesiastic whose presence in the Church was a valuable asset to the enemies of religion and progress. Colet distrusted the ecclesiastical authorities of the day, and felt that it would be useless to re-endow the old school, if it were to remain under the same management. But he seems to have succeeded by some means or another in persuading the Chapter to hand over the old Cathedral school with its buildings and rights to the trustees of his own school, which, though it thus incorporated the old school, was for all practical purposes an entirely new foundation, with new statutes, new methods and complete freedom from clerical control. It was to secure this latter object that Colet placed the school under the trusteeship of the Mercers' Company, who were to control the endowments,

[1] The Reformation checked this liberty of thought. Protestantism tied down the human spirit in fetters as galling as medievalism, and the shibboleths of Luther and Calvin were as cramping to the human spirit as the formulæ of medieval theology. See an interesting study by Murray, *Erasmus and Luther; their attitude to Toleration*, esp. cc. 3, 5, 6 and pp. 88, 89. The exact relation of the Renaissance to the Reformation is a problem which needs further treatment.

enforce the statutes, appoint the master and have the general oversight of the school.[1]

Knowing how much depends upon the character and ability of the masters, Colet was careful to ensure that only the best men should be appointed. The position of a medieval schoolmaster was one of considerable importance. He was as a rule well educated, being a University graduate in grammar.[2] The profession was privileged, as no one could teach without a licence from the Church, and masters were intensely jealous of their monopoly.[3] In the 15th century, however, the supply of properly qualified masters (as of clergy) seems to have diminished. In the absence of good men the standard had become lower, and many men, untrained, ill-educated and distinguished rather by the brutality of their discipline than by the excellence of their teaching, had for a mere livelihood found their way into schools, to the great detriment of education generally. Colet, warned by such instances, took the greatest pains to obtain the right men for his school. The Headmaster was to be a man "whole in body, honest and virtuous, and learned in the good and clean Latin literature, and also in Greek (if such may be obtained)," married or single, layman or priest, it mattered not, provided only he were thoroughly suitable, and were willing to devote his whole time and energies to the work of the school. He is to teach good manners as well as good literature, and is to hold his post only so long as he adequately fulfils his duties. His stipend was generous. The Headmaster of Eton only received £16 a year, but the Headmaster of St. Paul's was to receive a mark a week, or £34 13s. 4d. a year, besides a livery gown of four nobles and a free house. For this post he was fortunate enough to secure the services of his friend William Lily, who had been his contemporary at Magdalen, had afterwards travelled in Italy, and was one of the most accomplished classical scholars

Colet's aims: (2) To secure good masters.

[1] *L. and P.*, I, 1076.

[2] Plainsong and grammar were essential for a master. For degrees in grammar see Rashdall, II, 599; Watson, *Gr. Sch.*, pp. 225–6. Medieval schoolmasters possessed few books; *ibid.*, pp. 229–30 for list of books. For tenure and pay of masters, Parry, *Educ. Middle Ages*, pp. 110–14.

[3] Unlicensed teachers were liable to excommunication. *Liber Albus*, p. 175; *Early Yorks. Schools*, p. 81; *Educ. Charters*, p. 91.

of the day. Colet had some difficulty in obtaining a suitable undermaster. Erasmus tried to obtain an assistant for St. Paul's; but he did not receive much encouragement; for when he mentioned the matter in a company of Masters of Arts, one exclaimed, "Who would be a schoolmaster who could live in any other way?"[1] Perhaps an usher did not have a very good time of it, though the stipend was not bad, being usually about half that of the Head, while the modern disproportion is considerably greater.

Colet's aims: (3) Better methods and more humane discipline.

The third aim of Colet was to secure better methods of teaching and a milder discipline. The discipline in schools was at that time harsh in the extreme. "Schoolmaster" has in England generally been a term of reproach, and chiefly because of the inhumanity which was for so long associated with the profession. Up to the middle of the 19th century it was considered that discipline could only be maintained and learning encouraged by an unsparing use of the rod. The state of affairs at Eton in Keate's time (1809–34) is well known; and in the 15th and 16th centuries, when parental discipline was harsh, the age cruel and punishments brutal, we can easily believe that the rod was not spared or allowed to care for the crying of its victim. The lot of the schoolboy was certainly not an ideal one. The usual picture of a medieval school is that of a master seated at a desk, with rod or birch uplifted ready to strike, and a few miserable youths standing trembling and terrified round him. The picture is probably not far from the truth, and the rod was the great incentive to learning from the days of Orbilius, through a long succession of great schoolmasters and greater beaters, like Udall, Cox and Malim, down to Busby, Keate and Squeers. Parents were great believers in harshness, and gave ample encouragement to the natural propensities of the pedagogue. On January 28th, 1458, Dame Agnes Paston, in a letter with reference to the education of her son Clement, a boy about sixteen, asked after his progress and sent a message to his master, begging that if he found the boy idle or backward he would "trewly belassch him, tyl he wyll amend," as did his last master, the best (she adds) the boy ever had. She promises the master ten marks if her son makes progress, for "she would rather see him fair

[1] *L. and P.*, I, 4448, 4528.

buried than lost through idleness." Children were notoriously ill-treated by their parents. Lady Jane Grey's account to Ascham of her ill-treatment and of her solace in Plato is well known. (I must behave myself perfectly) "or else I am so sharply taunted, so cruelly threatened, yea presently sometimes with pinches, nips and bobs and other ways (which I will not name for the honour I bear them) so without measure misordered."[1] When the Bachelor's degree in Grammar was conferred upon the future pedagogue he received the symbol of his office, not a book but a birch, and then and there proceeded to give an exhibition of his skill in the most important part of his duties by flogging a boy "openlye in the scholys, having first paid a groat for the birch and a similar sum to the boy."[2]

That the greatest beaters made the best schoolmasters was a commonly received opinion both in that age and for some centuries after. Cox, Headmaster of Eton and afterwards Dean of Christ Church and Bishop of Ely, had a great reputation as a schoolmaster and a still greater as a wielder of the birch. In this latter art, however, he was easily surpassed by his successor, Nicholas Udall (1534–43), of whom it was said, "The best schoolmaster of our time was the greatest beater," and whose name and deeds have been immortalised by one of his pupils in the well-known lines :—

"From Powles I went to Aeton sent
To learn straightwayes the Latin phraise,
Where fiftie three stripes given to me
At once I had.

For fault but small or none at all
It came to pass thus beat I was ;
See, Udall, see the mercy of thee
To me, poore lad."[3]

Erasmus tells of a schoolmaster, a foreign divine, who took delight in beating his pupils in order to tame their spirit. On one occasion he ordered his underling to beat a small boy of ten until he swooned, artlessly adding, "The lad, of

[1] *Scolemaster*, p. 118 (ed. Giles). [2] Rashdall, II, 599.

[3] Udall was described as 'Elegantissimus omnium bonarum literarum magister, et earum felicissimus interpres.' See *Scolemaster* (ed. Giles), p. 80.

course, has done nothing to deserve all this, but it is necessary to curb his spirit by wholesome discipline."[1] Such scenes were at one time common; and yet when we think of the barbarous punishments of our ancestors, of the public flogging of men and women for trivial offences, of the brutal flogging in the Army and Navy in the days of Wellington and Nelson, of the whipping-post set up in every parish, the castigations of pedagogues seem in comparison innocuous and almost humane.[2]

More enlightened views.

There were, it is true, a few wiser and more enlightened men who saw the folly and uselessness of brutality as a means of education. Sir Robert Cecil expressed the wish that there was "some more discretion in many schoolmasters in using correction than commonly there is; who many times punish rather the weakness of nature than the fault of the scholar; whereby many scholars that might else prove well be driven to hate learning." Ascham strongly condemned the use of the rod as the best incentive to learning and was all in favour of gentler methods. On one occasion he expressed the heterodox sentiment that a famous pupil of a brutal master had got on rather by the great towardness of the scholar than by the great beating of the master, a wise and enlightened sentiment not at all to the taste of the typical pedagogue, who treated the advice with the contempt it obviously deserved.[3]

[1] *De pueris instituendis* (ed. Woodward), p. 206.

[2] In Saxon days schoolboys were brutally flogged with knotted scourges of bull's hide, Woodruff and Cape, *Hist. King's School*, pp. 13, 14. Medieval schoolmasters sometimes punished peccant schoolboys with excommunication, *ibid.*, pp. 23 f. For later instances of brutality in schools take the following. John James, Headmaster of Basingstoke Grammar School (1673–1717) was indicted by the mother of a boy who died as the result of a brutal flogging. Another ran away and died, *V.C.H.*, *Hants.*, II, 381. For the cruelty of Rev. Thomas Griffith, Headmaster of Andover Grammar School (1776–98), see *Memoirs of Orator Hunt*, I, 57–80. Whipping posts in schools were not unknown. An 18th-century German pedagogue boasted that during his 51 years as a schoolmaster he had given no less than 2,349,944 blows with various instruments, besides other barbarous punishments, Cubberley, *Hist. Educ.*, pp. 455–6. For Eton under Keate, Wilkinson, *Reminiscences*, c. 3. See also Lecky, *England in 18th Century*, II, 134–7; Masefield, *Sea Life in Nelson's Time*, c. 6.

[3] *Scolemaster* (ed. Giles), Preface and pp. 88–106. Erasmus wrote tracts *De Ratione Studii* (1511) and *De pueris instituendis* (1529) advocating good masters, interesting teachers, persuasive methods and a more humane discipline.

Sherborne, Bishop of Chichester, issued enlightened rules for his school at Rolleston in 1520. The master was to use persuasion and encouragement in teaching, and tact and judgment with the boys. He must cultivate self-restraint, and must learn to avoid the not uncommon habit of schoolmasters (then and since) of behaving and teaching "like maniacs." And Wolsey cautions his masters at Ipswich against severity "even in looks" as apt to discourage the learner.[1] Colet was strongly opposed to the brutality which disgraced education, and did his best to ensure that the life of the schoolboy should be robbed of some of its worst terrors. But such enlightened views were centuries before their time; a brutal age thought them foolish and sentimental; and the rod and the birch (appropriate only to disciplinary offences) continued to descend with unabated vigour in the firm belief that it was the only way of instilling into youth a love of learning, an appreciation of literature and a zeal for that dullest of all human studies, the grammar of the ancient languages of Greece and Rome.[2]

Colet's aims: (4) Christian humanism.

Colet's fourth aim was a school devoted to the ideals of Christian humanism. The movement for a reformed curriculum had begun, naturally enough, in Italy. The discovery in 1416 of a complete copy of Quintilian's *Institutio Oratoria* and the study of Plutarch's work on education (περὶ παιδῶν ἀγωγῆς), both of which insisted upon the need of training all the faculties, mental, moral and physical, together with the new passion for the classical writers of Greece and Rome, led to a transformation of educational methods. Greek was taught; the authors of the golden age superseded the inferior writers of later date; Ciceronian prose was held up as the supreme model and the mark of true culture; and careful attention was paid to physical training, the medieval idea of the body

[1] *L. and P.*, IV., 4691.

[2] "Among the personification of the seven arts which adorn the front of Chartres Cathedral, Grammar alone carried a rod. There has always been considered to be some peculiar and mysterious connection between the rod and classical scholarship." Rashdall, II, 610. In the statutes of Queens and B.N.C. the birch was enjoined. At C.C.C. Fox ordered corporal punishment. In the reign of Mary, Edward Anne, a scholar of C.C.C., was publicly flogged by the Dean for a poem against the Mass, a stripe for every line—a useful warning against prolixity. *Hist. C.C.C.*, pp. 54, 96–7.

as one to be mortified rather than trained being rightly abandoned. The whole object was the development of the child's moral, intellectual and physical nature, in order to fit him to play his part as a citizen and do his work in life. In the schools of Vittorino da Feltre at Mantua (1425–46) and of Guarino du Verona at Ferrara (1429–60) these aims were carried out and Christian humanism established as the true ideal of education.[1]

The medieval curriculum.

A consideration of the medieval curriculum will show the superiority of the Renaissance ideal. The medieval grammar school taught the trivium, i.e. rhetoric, grammar (≡Latin) and dialectic,[2] the first and last subjects being essential in an age when, in the absence of newspapers, public opinion was influenced by the spoken rather than by the written word. A good knowledge of Latin was indispensable for the professional, governing and even commercial classes, for Latin was the language of the Church services, of the Vulgate, of lectures, accounts, registers, official documents, international correspondence, philosophical and theological works. Medieval Latin was a language of its own, living, loose, free and easy, very useful and expressive; and it was this language, superseded at the Renaissance by the more formal and somewhat stilted Latin of the classical writers, which the medieval grammar school taught. It did so by means chiefly of three books, the *Grammar* of Donatus, the tutor of St. Jerome; the *Institutiones Grammaticæ* of Priscian, a Constantinople schoolmaster of the 6th century; and the works of Alexander de Villa Dei, a friar who *c.* 1200 wrote a prolix *Grammar* in rhyming Latin hexameters. Towards the close of the 15th century two other *Latin Grammars* were published, both by

[1] See Jebb's Romanes Lecture (1899), *Humanism in Education*, pp. 16–21; Woodward, *Studies in Education*, pp. 1–47.

[2] The higher education consisted of the *Quadrivium*, i.e. Arithmetic, Geometry, Astronomy, Music. These subjects were as a rule reserved for the Universities. The question of *Elementary Education* in the Middle Ages is a difficult one. Grammar schools were secondary and did not profess to teach reading and writing in the Vernacular, nor (probably) did the Song schools. Yet these acquirements, in the 15th century, as we see from the *Paston Letters*, were not uncommon, and arose from the needs of an industrial community. They may have been taught privately, or in certain of the Chantry, Gild, Song and Grammar schools. See Adamson, *Short Hist. of Educ.*, pp. 73–88.

masters of Magdalen College, Oxford—Holt and Stanbridge, and these quickly superseded the older *Grammars*. Colet, however, was not satisfied with them, and asked Linacre to compose a *Latin Grammar* for St. Paul's School. But the result did not satisfy the Dean, who set to work upon one of his own, "trustynge of this begynnynge that ye shal procede and grow to parfyt lyterature and come at last to be great clarkes." Lily and Erasmus also tried their hands, with the result that *Lily's Grammar*, which embodied the ideas of Colet and Erasmus as well as his own, became the standard *Latin Grammar* until the middle of the 19th century. Colet held very enlightened views upon grammar as a *means* rather than as an end, and in this opinion was followed by Sir Thomas Elyot in *The Boke called the Governour*, 1531, and by Ascham in the *Scholemaster*; but these enlightened views received scanty support, and for more than three centuries formalistic grammar of the most mind-killing type, taught parrot-wise, ousted literature, neutralised the Renaissance and became, with only an occasional protest, enthroned as the idol of pedants and pedagogues.[1]

In the Middle Ages the Latin authors studied in schools were later writers such as Sedulius with his Paschal hymn, Juvencus with his *Gospels* in verse, and others. Some of the best authors, such as Virgil, Ovid, Terence and Cicero, were also used, but they were read neither as literature nor from a classical or humanistic standpoint. Until the invention of printing there were few books, as manuscripts were too costly for schoolboys. Teaching was, therefore, oral. Grammar was learnt by heart in rhyming couplets to fix it in the memory. But learning without books was an exceedingly slow and tedious process. The pupils had tablets on which they wrote at the dictation of a master; but only the more striking phrases could be dictated and progress was necessarily slow. Knowledge of texts was impossible. It was the invention of printing which rendered possible both the Renaissance and the Reformation, for without printing it is improbable that either the Renaissance or the Reforma-

[1] For Colet's views, Lupton, Appendix B. For other *Grammars*, e.g. Horman's *Vulgaria*, see Maxwell Lyte, *Hist. Eton College*, pp. 110–13; and for an exhaustive account of early English printed *Grammars*, Watson, *Gr. Schools*, cc. xiv, xv. For Elyot see Woodward, *Studies in Education*, pp. 268–95; and the *Governour*, I, 28–170.

tion could ever have been more than local movements. After the invention of printing educational textbooks were published in large numbers and education and learning received a great impetus.[1]

Colet's curriculum.

With reference to the subjects which were to be taught at St. Paul's, Colet frankly confessed that "it passeth my wit to devise and to determine in particular; but in general I would they were taught in good literature both Latin and Greek, and good authors such as have the very Roman eloquence joined with wisdom, especially Christian authors that wrote their wisdom with clean and chaste Latin either in verse or in prose." They are to learn Colet's *Latin Accidence* (or some other if there are others better to the purpose), certain books of Erasmus, and other Christian authors, such as Lactantius, Prudentius, Proba, Sedulius, Juvencus, Baptista Mantuanus and such other "as shall be thought convenient and most to the purpose of the true Latin speech, all barbary, all corruption, all Latin adulterate which ignorant blind fools brought into this world, and with the same hath distained and poisoned the old Latin speech and very Roman tongue. I say that filthiness and all such abusion which the latter blind world brought in, which more rather may be called blotterature than literature, I utterly banish and exclude out of this school, and charge the masters that they teach always what is best, and instruct the children in Greek and Latin, in reading unto them such authors as hath with wisdom joined the pure chaste eloquence." Colet had undoubtedly a somewhat narrow and unreasonable prejudice against the classical writers, and in this respect contrasts unfavourably with Wolsey, who was in some ways a more enlightened educational reformer, being a more typical product of the Renaissance than Colet.[2]

[1] For school books in use in 15th century see Allen, *Age of Erasmus*, p. 41; Leach, *Winchester College*, p. 157.

[2] Wolsey desired literature, not formalistic grammar. He included précis and essay writing in his curriculum, gave advice against overwork, and urged interest as the best incentive to learning. Greek is not mentioned. See *Venetian Cal.*, III, 1188; *L. and P.*, IV, 4691. See also *Educ. Charters*, pp. 451–69, for curriculum and time table at Eton (1530), Canterbury (1541), Westminster (1560). At Canterbury it is laid down for the boys, "Whatever they are doing in earnest or in play they shall never use any language but Latin and Greek."

Mr. Leach, who has done scant justice to Colet and his munificence, finds fault with his curriculum.[1] This, he says, was not progress but reaction; it was not promoting humanism, but reverting to theological prepossessions. But Colet was more than a humanist. He was a Christian first. Well he might be. He had been in Italy, and he had seen the disastrous results of the humanism of the Italian Renaissance when divorced from religion and morality; and in his revolt from the licence, the paganism, the moral corruption into which Italian humanism at length sank, he had acquired an unreasonable prejudice against the classics as the sole means of education. His aim was to found a Christian school free from the trammels of medieval and scholastic methods and reactionary clerical control, where a good education might be given, where the cultivation of character might occupy the chief place, where true religion might be taught and where humanism might assume its right proportion in the scheme of Christian life and education. "My intent," he declared, "is by this school specially to increase knowledge and worshipping of God and our Lord Jesu Christ, and good Christian life and manners in the children." In his zeal for religious education he drew up a book containing the rudiments of religious instruction, in which he expresses his ideal of education. "Wherefore, I pray you, lerne gladly this lytel treatyse, and commende it dylygently unto your memoryes. Trustynge of this begynnynge that ye shal procede and growe to parfyt lyterature and come at the last to be great clarkes. And lyfte up your lytel whyte handes for me, whiche prayeth for you to God, to whom be al honour and imperyal majestie and glory. Amen." As he wrote in noble words to Erasmus in 1517 at the close of his life: "Of reading books there is no end, but for this life there is nothing like living holy and purely, *meo judicio nulla via assequemur quam ardenti amore et imitatione Jesu*" (which in my opinion we can only gain by fervent love of Jesus and imitation of his life).[2]

Colet's ideal of education.

[1] *Med. Schools*, pp. 280–1; *Educ. Charters*, p. xlii.

[2] *L. and P.*, II, 3361. Colet directed that the *Institutum Christiani hominis* of Erasmus should be used as a textbook at St. Paul's. He made careful provision for religious instruction, as did also the Eton statutes. In the Middle Ages two textbooks were used for religious

The foundation of St. Paul's a landmark in the history of education in England.

Such was Colet's School of St. Paul's. Certainly it was no original idea, for in founding a school he was but following a practice which had been in vogue for many years, and which had been increasing as the Middle Ages drew to their close. St. Paul's was probably not the first school where Greek was taught, or where the Headmaster was not required to be in Holy Orders, or where the trustees were a City Company of laymen. St. Paul's, too, is less famous and less magnificent than the Colleges of Winchester and Eton, but it was for all that a very notable achievement, and, like the foundation of Winchester, a landmark in the history of English education. The number of boys, greater than at Winchester or Eton or any other English school; the munificence of the endowments, which came out of Colet's patrimony and not, as in the case of so many other schools and colleges, from the diversion of funds from other foundations; the position of the school in the very centre of English life; the elasticity of the statutes, which made for progress and did not hamper the future development of the school; the rigorous insistence upon complete freedom from reactionary ecclesiastical control; the generous provision for the masters; the encouragement of more humane methods of teaching; above all, the combination of a high Christian ideal with the enlightened studies of the Renaissance—all this has given Colet a high place among the pioneers of education in England. The very fact that a reactionary Bishop, "who pretended to be a very wise man," spoke against the school and said that it was "a pestiferous and useless thing and a home of idolatry," is in itself sufficient testimony to the high ideals of progress, religion and education which the school was carrying out.[1]

instruction: (1) *Expositio sequentiarum;* (2) *Expositio hymnorum.* Much of the Primer was learnt by heart. For medieval instruction of youth in good manners see *The Babee's Book* (E.E.T.S.), where much curious information is given.

[1] *L. and P.*, II, 3190.

CHAPTER VII

SIDELIGHTS, MAINLY FROM THE VISITATION DOCUMENTS, UPON CERTAIN OF THE ENGLISH RELIGIOUS HOUSES AFTER THE BLACK DEATH

PART I

FEW institutions have attracted so much attention or exerted so great a fascination as the religious houses of medieval England. The glory of their architecture, the exquisite beauty of their ruins, the romance of their foundation, the religious ideals which inspired their origin, the asceticism, piety, learning and good works attributed to their early inmates exercise a perennial charm over the minds of all who are interested in the past and have a feeling for art and an eye for beauty. But if few institutions have exerted greater fascination, certainly few have aroused more controversy. On the one hand they have been held up to admiration as homes of piety and learning; on the other they have been denounced as sinks of iniquity and dens of infamy. The evidence used by Henry VIII in their suppression is rightly regarded with suspicion; for, indeed, it is obvious that in the short time in which Cromwell's Visitors performed their task it was impossible to make an exhaustive inquiry or ascertain the true facts. The Visitors were given instructions to get up a case against the monasteries; it is always possible to see in life (as in history) what one sets out to seek; and by consistent suppression of the truth, considerable exaggeration of faults and a delicate manipulation of evidence it was not difficult to frame a successful indictment against the monks and nuns. For more than three centuries this black record was firmly believed, but its obvious bias has in recent years provoked a reaction which threatens to be as inimicable to truth as the calumniations of Henry and his satellites. Fortunately we have sufficient evidence of a thoroughly impartial and trust worthy type, quite apart from the revelations of 1536, to enable us to form some idea of the internal condition of certain religious houses during the century and a half preceding their dissolution. That evidence consists in the main of three series of valuable episcopal Visitations, which have in recent years been discovered and published. These are *The Visitations of the Diocese of Norwich*, 1492–1532, edited by the late Dr. Jessopp; *Bishop Redman's Visitations of the English Premonstratensian Houses*, covering the last quarter of the 15th century, edited by Cardinal Gasquet[1]; and the very exhaustive and illuminating *Visitations* of three Bishops of Lincoln—Fleming (1420–31), Gray (1431–36) and Alnwick (1436–50), recently edited with great care, learning and impartiality by Mr. Hamilton Thompson.[2] Of these the *Lincoln Visitations* are by far the most exhaustive and illuminating, for they throw a powerful searchlight upon the internal life and economy of the houses with which they deal, and are, indeed, among the most valuable of all the documents yet discovered dealing with the medieval religious houses. It is upon these series of episcopal Visitations that this chapter is mainly based.

Fresh light upon the English religious houses.

Before, however, proceeding to an examination of these records it may be advisable to give a brief account of the relationship which existed between a bishop and the religious houses in his diocese. A bishop was supposed to make every three or four years a formal visitation, either in person or by a duly authorised deputy, of those religious houses in his diocese which were not exempt from episcopal control. Conscientious bishops like Alnwick and Gray carried out their duties with great thoroughness, examining each member of the house,

Relation between bishops and religious houses.

[1] It should be added, to avoid confusion, that Bishop Redman did not visit in his episcopal and diocesan capacity, since the Premonstratensian houses were exempt, but as the appointed official Visitor of the Order in England.

[2] There are, in addition, a few stray Visitations to be found in the published episcopal registers; in the *Yorks. Arch. Journal*, Vol. XVI, and in *Archæologia*, Vol. XLVII. There are others in MS., but most of these are very brief and sketchy, and none approach the fullness and value of the Lincoln Visitations which Mr. Thompson has edited. The Norwich Visitations will be designated as *N.V.*, the Lincoln as *L.V.*, the Premonstratensian as *Coll.*

going into the minutest details, and taking great pains to arrive at the truth. This, however, was not always easy, for an abbot could make things very unpleasant for those who revealed the true state of the house. The Prior of Walsingham warned his canons just before Bishop Nicke's visitation in 1514 to be very careful what they told the Bishop, reminding them that *he* would be master when the Bishop had departed, and would not hesitate to visit his displeasure upon offenders. The Prioress of the Cistercian nunnery of Legbourne in 1440 forbade the nuns to report anything amiss, well knowing that her own conduct would not bear scrutiny. The sisters of Flixton in 1514 declared that they dared not speak the truth because of the cruelty of the Prioress. In 1517 the nuns at Littlemore complained that the Prioress had punished them for speaking the truth at the last visitation, and that she had hit one of them on the head with her feet and fists. Occasionally there was a conspiracy on the part of the community to report nothing amiss, as with the Abbey of Holme in 1514, when the majority of monks dutifully exclaimed, "*Omnia bene.*" The Bishop found, however, on closer inspection, that this euphonious phrase covered a multitude of sins—suppression of accounts, neglect of the services, doubtful morals and even an amiable desire on the part of the sub-prior to poison the abbot.[1]

Methods of episcopal discipline.

How did a bishop deal with the moral delinquencies which he discovered? The first and obvious way was to punish the offender. Sometimes he does this through the Head of the house, by ordering him to maintain better discipline and to punish adequately but impartially the culprits. Sometimes he takes the matter into his own hands then and there. Thus at Bourne in 1422 Bishop Fleming ordered monks who were in the habit of going into Bourne for the purpose of feasting and drinking to fast for a month every Wednesday and Friday on bread, ale and vegetables. At Caldwell in the same year he ordered as a punishment for idle, disobedient and refractory monks, for the first offence, a period of bread and beer; for the second, bread and water; for the third, bread, water *and* imprisonment.[2] At the Cistercian Priory of Esholt Archbishop Lee found in 1535 an erring nun. He ordered her to

[1] *N.V.*, pp. 126–8.

[2] *L.V.*, I, pp. 9, 26.

be kept in prison for two years and to fast twice a week on bread and ale. Bishop Nicke took a more lenient view of a similar offence, for upon an erring nun of Crabhouse he imposed a much lighter penalty: "She, Agnes Smyth, is to sit at the bottom of the table and say in the cloister the Psalter seven times."[1] There are several instances of bishops suspending, superseding or depriving Heads who were obviously impossible. Spofford in 1423 suspends the Prior of Chirbury for maladministration, and takes the temporalities into his own hands; Alnwick in 1442 suspended the Prioress of St. Michael's, Stamford, for laxity and bad example; Bubwith relieved the Prior of Bruton of his duties on account of his evil life; and Mayew in 1513 deprived the Prior of Flanesford for the same reason.[2] Sometimes bishops ordered erring monks to be expelled for a season to another monastery. In 1460 a canon of the Premonstratensian Abbey of Blanchland, guilty of apostacy and misconduct, was ordered to be sent to Welbeck for ten years, and in 1489 two offending canons at Cockersand were to be expelled, the one for three, the other for seven years. More often, however, the offender was allowed the privilege of compurgation. This was generally admitted in the case of moral charges, and the worst offenders were by this means enabled to escape scot-free. At Alnwick in 1482 a canon, accused of perjury, theft and immorality, had no difficulty in clearing himself; while at Bardney in 1437 evildoers easily escaped punishment by getting their cronies to swear to their innocence.[3] Compurgation was, as a rule, a complete farce and a sure refuge in time of trouble for the worst offenders; but not always; for when the general tone of the house was high and the scandal great this was not the case. We have, at any rate, two instances of failure. At Hales Owen in Shropshire two canons in 1478 were charged with evil living. One was condemned; the other was allowed compurgation, but failed. At Cockersand in 1489 (also in 1494) an offending

[1] *Yorks. Arch.*, XVI, 451; *N.V.*, p. 108.

[2] *Reg. Spofford*, p. 39; *Reg. Bubwith*, pp. 438–9; *Reg. Mayew*, p. 166. There are several other instances.

[3] *L.V.*, II, p. 12; *Coll.*, II, 94, 116; cf. Barlings, p. 35; Beyham, p. 78. The punishment was not always carried out. The offending canon of Blanchland was allowed to return in hope of amendment. There was generally a "nisi" clause, allowing a loophole of escape. Occasionally, though rarely, an offender was excommunicated, *ibid.*, II, 5.

canon could not find anyone in the Abbey who was willing to come forward and swear to his innocence.[1]

Another method of dealing with disorder was moral suasion. Bishops in their relation to religious houses were often placed in a position of great difficulty and delicacy. It was easy enough to order punishment, but very difficult to enforce it. The larger monasteries were powerful corporations, intensely jealous of their rights and (though outwardly civil) bitterly resentful of episcopal control. With their wealth, their aristocratic patrons, their vested interests and their great territorial influence they could, if injudiciously handled, make things *very* unpleasant for a bishop, who had therefore to proceed with great circumspection. Arbitrary action might defeat its own ends, and in any case a great monastery could always render futile by a quiet passive resistance the most peremptory episcopal injunctions.[2] How, therefore, could a bishop enforce his punishments? In the case of large and powerful abbeys he was more or less helpless. The difficulty of travel and communication made it practically impossible, without a regular system of spies and informers, to keep in touch with distant houses, and there was no public Press or enlightened public opinion to strengthen his authority and intimidate a recalcitrant monastery into compliance. He might, it is true, bring offenders to book in the spiritual courts, but this involved both expense and delay; and even if he were successful the convent would only appeal to Rome, where, in a case against a diocesan, it was always sure of a respectful hearing. Besides this, a bishop had, as a rule, little chance in a conflict with a religious house. The monks were none too scrupulous in their ways, and by bribery, by forgery, by letters of absolution bought from a

Bishops relied largely on moral suasion to effect reforms.

[1] *Coll.*, II, 116, 120, 241. At Ashby in 1442 a canon was refused purgation, but this was clearly due to the Prior's spite rather than to his zeal for respectability. *L.V.*, II, p. 45.

[2] The personal relations between bishops and abbots were sometimes so severely strained that an episcopal visitation must have been a trying ordeal. For instances of bad feeling see the violent contests between the Bishop of Norwich and the Abbot of Bury St. Edmunds in 14th century, Arnold, *Memorials of St. Edmund's*, III, 56, ff., and the fight resulting in mutilation and bloodshed, between the party of the Bishop of Ely and the Abbot of Ramsey in 1400 about a manor, *Reg, Fordham*, f. 214.

papal emissary could generally outwit an objectionable Visitor. An instance will show a bishop's difficulties. In 1441 a paramour (a layman) of a nun of St. Michael's, Stamford, was brought before the Bishop of Lincoln for punishment. Alnwick imposed as a penance whipping round the church of St. Mary's, Stamford, and in other places. This punishment was easily commuted for a cash payment of twenty shillings, but even then the offender appealed to the Court of Arches. The proceedings were stayed and he probably got off.[1] Men with great nominal and even legal powers are not seldom the most impotent of mortals. Hence the wiser bishops forebore threatenings and relied upon moral suasion. The effect of this depended, of course, entirely upon the character of the bishop. It was no use unless there was respect, and the exhortations of men like Nicke were scarcely likely to bring about a reformation in a flood. But the exhortations of a good bishop would carry great weight, for character always commands respect, and, after all, persuasion is a more powerful factor than force in the moral regeneration of mankind.

Fatherly action of bishops.

There are many instances of bishops acting in a kind and fatherly way. In 1440 Alnwick, as a rule a stern judge, ordered the Abbey of Bourne to search for an apostate canon, bring him back and treat him not harshly, but as the prodigal in "fatherly wise and with brotherly love." At Coverham in 1478 Bishop Redman found a guilty canon, and (accepting his repentance) allowed him to remain, in the hope that clemency would be more effective than harshness. "If, however," he wisely added, "he doesn't keep his promises, or like a dog returning to his vomit renews his sins, the Abbot strictly enjoined under threat of deposition to carry out the punishment without hope of grace." Joan Fletcher, the late Prioress of the Benedictine nunnery of Basedale in Yorkshire, had deserted the religious life and was living a doubtful life in the world. Archbishop Lee had sent her, on professing repentance, to Rosedale, but soon found her repentance a mere sham. He decided, therefore, to send her back to Basedale, expressing the hope that she would amend. In fatherly wise he urges the convent to receive her kindly.[2]

[1] *L.V.*, II, p. lx.
[2] *Ibid.*, II, p. 38 ; *Coll.*, II, 130 ; cf. Beauchief, p. 66 ; Blanchland, p. 94 ; *Yorks. Arch.*, XVI, 424–58.

This treatment may be compared with the sterner methods of the 14th century. In 1321 Walter de Melton, Archbishop of York, imposed a severe penance upon an erring nun, Maude of Terrington, who had relinquished her habit and gone into the world. The Archbishop ordered that she should live apart, be spurned by the nuns, fast daily and be flogged every Wednesday and Friday for the rest of her life. Here are two methods of inculcating morality and persuading to holiness. Which is the better let moralists debate and experience decide.

Before dealing with the evidence afforded by the Visitation documents a word of caution is necessary. These documents cannot be neglected by writers who deal with English ecclesiastical institutions in the 15th century. Their evidence is of first-rate importance and simply cannot be brushed aside as negligible. The mere recital of the rules of an institution may show its aims and ideals, but are no proof of its internal life and real character. Were the monastic rules kept? That is the point. These Visitation documents show very clearly that in many cases and at certain periods they certainly were *not*. They prove that the mere possession of rules was no guarantee of their observance; that the state of many 15th century religious houses was not as rosy as has sometimes been depicted and assumed; that all monasteries were not necessarily abodes of sanctity; and that even the best houses were not immune from the intrusion of natural frailty. The evidence must be frankly faced.

Nature of the Visitation documents.

At the same time caution and common sense are needed to enable us to preserve a right perspective. Several considerations must be borne in mind. These documents deal with houses not at their best, but in their decline, with houses not in the golden age of the 12th and 13th centuries, but in a difficult and depressing age, the 15th. After the Black Death religious houses were faced with peculiar difficulties and dangers, so that much allowance must be made. Again, these Visitations deal with the faults and not with the virtues of the religious houses. They do not profess to describe—that is not their purpose—the internal life of good houses. Their object is not to give any general account of monastic life, but to investigate and reform abuses. Thus they pass over good houses either in complete silence or with the simple remark "*Omnia bene*." No news, therefore, about a house visited may be regarded as good news. This must be remembered, for otherwise there would be some danger of laying too much stress upon black spots, and perhaps of assuming that all the religious houses were equally unsatisfactory. It does not in the least follow, because Bardney and Wymondham and Peterborough and Norwich were in a bad way in the 15th century, that *therefore* other great Benedictine houses, for which we have no evidence, were equally unsatisfactory. They may or may not have been. In the absence of specific evidence it is impossible to say. It is a wise rule to assume innocence both in persons and institutions until positive proof of guilt has been established. They should be given the benefit of the doubt. Again, the history of monasticism in all ages and in all countries shows that it has always had its ups and downs, its periods of exalted fervour and times of spiritual inertia. The monk was only human, and human nature was as strong in the cloister (whether there was a vocation or not) as in the outer world, while the temptations were probably harder because they could not be stifled by resorting to distractions. As Mr. Hamilton Thompson so admirably puts it in his introduction to the *Lincoln Visitations*, "if the character of the disclosures in these documents occasionally repels sympathy, we can at least extend lenience to shortcomings which are inalienable from human nature." Moreover, to quote the same writer, "against the tendency to condemn the monastic system entirely upon the evidence of these documents must be set the fact that they concern only a certain number of individual houses. We may well believe that there were monasteries in the diocese which under the headship of capable men were still instant in the observance of their religious duties, and needed little correction and few injunctions from the visitor. Whether the standard of piety in such houses as Bourne were high it is impossible to say; but they maintained a standard at any rate of respectability. While on the one hand nothing can be more strongly deprecated than the partisan spirit which sees nothing but piety in the religious houses of medieval England and reads all the virtues into the bare details of the daily expenditure of a nunnery, it is as great a mistake from the other side to apply the moral and social standards of our own day to the religious life of that bygone age."[1]

Nor must it be forgotten that institutions, like individuals, should be judged at their best rather than at their worst, by their virtues rather than by their vices, by their positive achievements rather than by their deficiencies and failures. Nothing is easier than criticism. Defects and failures at once attract attention. They are indeed obvious, and it requires no ability to see and denounce them. Institutions, like men, have the defect of their qualities, and the higher the ideal the greater is the fall when the ideal is lost. *Corruptio optimi pessima.* To concentrate the whole attention upon defects is calculated to produce a misleading impression and to obscure the brighter side of human life. These considerations are in danger of being overlooked when we are dealing with institutions in their decadence, or with a difficult and disappointing period like the 15th century. And after all, that century is only an episode in monastic history. An impartial estimate of monasticism can only be obtained from a wide survey of its complete history at its best as well as at its worst. It is pleasanter to describe institutions in their zenith than in their decline. Instead of dealing with the sombre evidence revealed in the Visitation documents of the period succeeding the Black Death, it would be a far pleasanter task to describe the golden age of monasticism—the Cluniac revival in the 10th century, with its inspiring influence upon Church life; or the piety, zeal and asceticism of the great monks of the 11th and 12th centuries, such as St. Bruno, St. Bernard, Stephen Harding and their devoted followers; or the great outburst of monastic fervour in England when monasticism was at its zenith and beautiful abbeys were springing up in all directions; or the good lives and good works of the monks, and their permanent contribution to learning and civilisation. But history requires wide views, and has to deal with bad as well as good. Though it may not, indeed, be merely a record of the crimes and follies of mankind, it yet remains true, certainly of monastic history, that without the darker side of life there would be but little to chronicle.

Before proceeding to formulate any general conclusions

[1] *L.V.*, II, p. lxii; I, pp. xii, xiii.

it will be necessary to give briefly a few examples of the life and character of some of the religious houses dealt with in the Visitation documents. Fortunately it will neither be necessary nor possible to enter into much detail, for which the reader is referred to the documents themselves, more particularly to the *Lincoln Visitations.* Here only a general indication of the conditions of the houses can be attempted.

The Abbey of Bardney in 1432.

Bardney was a Benedictine Abbey nine miles south-east of Lincoln. The Visitations of Bishops Gray and Alnwick show the dangers and temptations which beset a 15th-century convent. Bishop Gray, aware no doubt of the ill repute of the house, made a thorough visitation in 1432 and found it necessary to issue some very stern injunctions. The abbot was strictly forbidden to sell timber or grant corrodies, liveries, pensions and annuities ; the meadows were to be enclosed to prevent the cattle straying ; haymaking and mowing were to be done at their proper seasons ; the monks were to receive without fail their annual wages of twenty shillings ; the property of the abbey was to be better administered, and as a precaution against its fraudulent use the convent seal was to be kept under three locks. The Bishop was at great pains to effect some improvement in the tone of the convent. The rules of the Order are to be read daily in the Chapter House, so that there can no longer be any excuse for not knowing what they are. Due times are to be set apart for study and meditation, and the rule of silence must be observed. The alms for the poor are *not* to be wasted, and the novices are to be carefully taught without favouritism by a competent instructor. Unlawful games, gadding about, frivolity and idleness must cease at once, and seculars and undesirable persons are not to visit the abbey. The monks must not sit up late at night drinking, but must go straight to bed after compline and sleep in the dormitories, and all must attend matins. Finally, to quell the internal strife which was so inimical to the religious life of the convent, the Bishop strictly enjoined that there be no more quarrelling, no " disdainful and despiteful words of insolence and reproach."

Three years later the abbot died and was succeeded by John Wainfleet (1435–47), who seems to have been a well-meaning man, but was weak and incapable and quite unfitted to cope with the difficulties which confronted him. He was well described as a "good priest towards God, but not wary in temporal matters."

The Visitation of 1438.

In 1438 Alnwick personally visited the abbey, examined the abbot and sub-prior, and then left his chancellor to complete the visitation. It was carefully conducted, all being examined, even the sick in the infirmary. It soon became evident that there was little improvement. The finances were now so badly administered that there was a debt of 300 marks; corrodies had been foolishly granted; while the church, the conventual buildings and the monastic property generally were in a serious state of dilapidation. The discipline was very lax. The younger brethren were "somewhat saucy and rebellious," while there was so much beer drinking both by day and by night that the abbey might just as well have been a public tavern. Three brethren were accused of misconduct, but obtained the privilege of compurgation, and came through the ordeal by bearing testimony to one another's innocence.

But what rendered the life of the convent so sordid was the faction and strife which prevailed. This was attributed to the conduct of Brother John Bartone, who had managed to gain complete ascendancy over the abbot. Bartone was one of those quarrelsome, overbearing men who are impossible to get on with. He drove away the abbey's guests, refused to buy grain or repair the barns, withheld the monks' wages, wasted the almonry food, and was accused of pocketing the common funds. "Never," said one monk, "did any office prosper in his hands." The last abbot on his death-bed said to him: "You have never been faithful in any office wherein you have stood; nay I, had I done as you, would have left in this monastery no monk young or old." But it was his quarrelsome nature which gave so much trouble. Brother John Hale said that Bartone was the cause of all the bickering in the convent, and would prove its ruin. Brother Langtoft said that all the mischief could be traced to him. Brother Richard Anderby said that he completely spoilt the services by rushing the psalms and singing out of tune; while Brother Thomas Southwell summed up the general opinion by remarking, "Bartone is past bearing among the brethren." He recklessly brought the wildest charges against others, and even on one occasion called the abbot a thief. Things at last came to such a pass that the convent expelled him, but the Bishop unwisely ordered an unwilling community to take him back. They did so, but things were soon as bad as ever; and even the abbot turned against him and put him in prison. Unfortunately the Bishop released him, thinking that an exhortation to live peaceably would meet the case—with what results the Visitation of 1444 clearly shows.[1]

Of the internal condition of the large Benedictine Priory of Norwich from 1492–1532 we have reliable knowledge from the records of five Visitations of the Bishops of Norwich. The first was that of Bishop Goldwell in 1492. There were forty-five monks, including the prior, who did not put in an appearance. The Bishop found that the services were neglected, the rule of silence not enforced, and the salaries of the chantry priests not paid. The infirmary was badly served and the sick neglected; no students were sent to the University; and several offices were in the hands of one man. Discipline was very slack. The gates were not closed at night, and the monks were in the habit of going beyond the close. The Bishop concluded his injunctions by ordering that his predecessor's rulings should be more carefully observed.

Norwich Priory in 1492.

Twenty-two years later Bishop Nicke paid the convent a visit. The finances were in great disorder. The debt according to some was £40, according to others £70; and as no accounts were ever rendered this discrepancy was not surprising. Dilapidations were serious, being especially marked in the dormitory, the chapter house, on the monastic estates and in the dependent cells of St. Leonard's and Alby. As in 1492 too many offices had accumulated in the hands of one man; the dues of the monks were very irregularly paid; while the prior was accused of using the common seal for his own ends. The services were poorly attended, the sub-prior and the third prior setting a bad example in this respect. The chantries were not properly served. There was no schoolmaster and study was neglected. There was little discipline.

In 1514.

[1] *L.V.*, I, i; II, ii. The numbers were: in 1432, 15; in 1438, 16; in 1440, 13.

Some of the monks were addicted to parties and dancing, and had recently taken to wearing up-to-date "frokkes of worstead." Quarrelling was not infrequent, Brother Winkfield being at times so disagreeable that the Bishop is told he "acts the fool and despises the brethren." The Bishop expressed his opinion of the convent very bluntly.

The Priory was again visited in 1520. The majority of the monks said that all was well, and it was evident that the state of the house had greatly improved. The improvement, however, was only temporary, for six years later the house was again in an unsatisfactory state. The finances were disordered and the estates mismanaged. The senior monks seldom rose for matins, one of them, indeed, not having done so more than once or twice in the last two years. Grave fault was found with the officers, especially with the prior, Robert Catton. The precentor was quarrelsome and at times unruly. The junior members would persist, to the intense annoyance of the others, in addressing the prior as "my lord." The morals, too, of certain of the community were not above suspicion.

In 1520.

We have one more glimpse into the state of the house. It is in 1532, on the eve of the Dissolution. The records are, however, incomplete and break off abruptly, but short as they are they reveal a very unsatisfactory state of affairs.[1]

In 1532.

It is not difficult to find in the Visitation documents several other instances of Benedictine houses which were far from satisfactory, and in some cases positively scandalous.[2] In the 16th century, before there was any thought of a general suppression, there is evidence of deterioration in certain quarters. In 1516 the Bishop of Ely told Wolsey that he had found such disorder at Ely that but for his visitation it could not have continued as a monastery, and that he had been obliged to appoint a new prior and new officials.[3] In 1527 attention was drawn to the state of things in the large and important Abbey of Malmesbury. A court of inquiry was

Other instances of unsatisfactory Benedictine houses.

[1] *N.V.*, pp. 1–8, 192–4, 196–206, 262–70.

[2] e.g. Humberstone in 1440, Daventry in 1442, Croyland in 1432, Ramsey in 1432 and 1439. See *L.V.*, I, *Introd.*, p. xii. and Nos. vii, xv, xliii; II, Nos. xiv, xxxvi. For the state of Winchester Priory in 1387, see Moberly, *Life of Wykeham*, pp. 237 f.

[3] *L. and P.*, II, 1733.

instituted, and this reported that the monks were disorderly, rebellious and contumacious; that the sub-prior was unfit for his office; that the prior was a mere sportsman; and that the Abbot, whose character did not stand high, was guilty of mismanagement and inefficiency in the conduct of the house.[1] In 1507 the Vicar-General of Bishop Fox visited the large and wealthy Abbey of Hyde in Winchester and found there internal dissensions and general demoralisation.[2] In 1521 the Bishop wrote to Wolsey that in the diocese of Winchester he found "the clergy and particularly (what he did not at first suspect) the monks so depraved, so licentious and so corrupt that he despaired of any reformation even in his own diocese."[3] This is perhaps mere rhetorical declamation, and neither this nor the instances adduced afford sufficient ground for a general condemnation of Benedictine houses on the eve of the Dissolution.[4]

The Abbey of Dorchester in 1441 and 1445.

Some of the Augustinian houses dealt with in the Visitation documents were at times in an equally unsatisfactory condition. One of the most conspicuous in this respect was the Abbey of Dorchester near Oxford. Though not poor the abbey was heavily in debt; the jewels, books and even the chalices were in pawn; no accounts were ever rendered and corrodies had been recklessly granted. "The said monastery through mismanagement and extravagance is in manifold wise brought so low by debt and by the ruinous condition of the houses and buildings that it is likely to go its way to naught." The internal life of the convent was far from happy. The abbot was not a man to inspire much respect or insure good discipline, with the consequence that many

[1] *L. and P.*, *IV*, 3678, cf. 4808. [2] *Reg. Fox*, II, f. 119.

[3] *L. and P.*, III, 1122. For a description of the buildings and arrangements of a Benedictine monastery, see maps and plans in *Rites of Durham;* also *ibid.*, pp. 85–9.

[4] The Great Abbey of Peterborough was in a very unsatisfactory state in the 15th century, especially under Abbot Assheton. See *L. V.*, I, xlii and the introduction to vol. II, pp. lii–lviii. See also p. xii for the editor's remarks upon the Abbey of Ramsey. Wymondham Abbey in Norfolk was in a scandalous state in 1514. "For ages," writes Dr. Jessop, the editor of the *Norwich Visitations*, "the Wymondham monks had been an unruly and insubordinate body of men. In all its history there was little to its credit." See *N. V.*, pp. 20–23, 95 f., 161 f., 247.

of the canons hawked, frequented taverns, sat up late and neglected the services. For the latter offence there was, perhaps, some excuse. The clock (it appeared) would not go; and as no one ever knew the time it seemed hopeless to have any fixed hours for services. The younger canons were naturally demoralised by the example of their elders, and (we are told) the "entire religious discipline is almost turned upside down." The next Visitation took place four years later in 1445. There was a new abbot and only seven canons, but among these was unfortunately the late abbot, whose presence did not make for harmony. There was another canon, Ralph Carnelle, surely a rare and exceptional type even in the 15th century, whose conduct was utterly impossible. Besides being insubordinate he was quarrelsome and, if provoked, did not hesitate to resort to violence. He struck and injured the prior, abused the abbot, and encouraged Oxford students to invade the abbey. He used to carry a long and formidable knife about with him, stuck in his belt, and when in a passion used to rush at his fellow-canons brandishing the knife. All were unanimous in saying that there would be no peace so long as he was allowed to remain. He evidently reflected the lawlessness of the 15th century, and his presence shows how difficult at times it must have been for abbots with the best intentions in the world to maintain discipline and religion.[1]

Walsingham Priory. 1512–32.

One of the most famous of English religious houses was the Priory of Walsingham in Norfolk. This was a wealthy house of Augustinian canons, rendered famous as the shrine of our Lady of Walsingham and as a very favoured resort of pilgrims.[2] "Her name," wrote Erasmus, "is very famous all over England, and you will scarce find anyone in that island who thinks his affairs can be prosperous unless he every year makes some present to that Lady." It was to this shrine that both Henry VIII and Catherine of Arragon (the former barefooted) on separate occasions made a pilgrimage; and Erasmus, somewhere about the year 1512, also paid

[1] *L.V.*, II, xv, xvi.

[2] The gifts and offerings in 1534 amounted to £260 12s. 4d. (×12), Savine, p. 103. The numbers were 17 in 1494; 32 in 1514; 19 in 1520; 22 in 1526; and 24 in 1532.

it a visit, an account of which he has left in his *Colloquies*.[1] The small chapel of our Lady he describes as dark, the only light coming from tapers, which showed up the wealth of the shrine which was "glittering with jewels, gold and silver." A verger showed them the joint of a man's finger. "I kissed it and asked whose relic it was. He told me it was St. Peter's. 'What,' said I, 'the Apostle?' He said it was. I then took notice of the bigness of the joint which was large enough to be taken for that of a giant. Upon which (said I) St. Peter must needs have been a very lusty man. At this one of the company fell a-laughing." The officer next proceeded to show them a relic of the B.V.M. Erasmus asked what evidence they had that this was genuine, in order to "stop the mouths of some impious persons who are used to scoff at all these things . . . but the officer, as if he had been inspired with some enthusiasm, looking upon us with astonished eyes and with a sort of horror, cursing our blasphemous expression, said, 'What need is there for putting your question when you have an authentic record'? and had turned us out of doors for heretics had not a few pence pacified his rage."[2]

Erasmus was asked by a friend with reference to the canons of Walsingham, "Are they men of good lives?" He replied, "Not much amiss. They are richer in piety than in revenue." It so happens that we have several Visitations of Bishops of Norwich extending over the years 1494–1532, and from these we get some idea of the internal life of one of the most famous of English religious houses at the height of its fame and prosperity. These documents do not lead us to think that the state of the house was very happy. In 1514, two years after the visit of Erasmus, Walsingham was visited by Bishop Nicke, who personally examined the prior and brethren. There were evidently two parties in the priory who caused great dissension. The picture revealed in the Visitation is not altogether edifying, and shows the dangers which beset religious houses.[3] The Bishop issued a set of fresh injunctions and exhorted the

[1] Printed in Coulton, *Social Life*, pp. 251–7.

[2] For a description of St. Cuthbert's shrine and high altar at Durham, see *Rites of Durham*, pp. 4, 7, 102. The visit of Colet to Canterbury is well known.

[3] The condition of the house is shown in the Bishop's Visitation documents, which are printed in *Norwich Visitations*.

brethren to live together more peacefully.[1] The prior had the good sense to send in his resignation, preferring obscurity and a pension to notoriety and office. His successor was Richard Vowell, who ruled the house until the Dissolution. He had no easy task, but later Visitations show how under a good man a house could recover. In 1526 the Bishop's suffragan visited the priory, and found that there was now quite a different tone in the house, and that things had greatly improved. The Bishop ordered such delinquents as there were to submit and left further reformation to time. He was right, for its state steadily improved as the years went on until in 1532 it could honestly be said that all was well—"*Omnia bene . . . omnia bene et laudabiliter fiunt et observantur.*"[2]

Nunneries.

Of the religious houses for women we know less than of those for men, partly because there is less evidence and partly because the subject has attracted less attention than it deserves. While we cannot doubt that many of them were well governed and in as satisfactory a condition as any institution can be in a difficult age, it yet remains true that the occasional glimpses which we get of them from the limited evidence at our disposal lead us to think that some of them, like the monasteries, were badly in need of reform. A study of the episcopal *Visitations* in the diocese of Lincoln will prove the truth of this statement. There is no need to go into elaborate detail, and one or two instances will suffice to show the dangers which beset the nunneries in the 15th century.

Elstow in 1422.

Elstow was a Benedictine nunnery in Bedfordshire with an abbess and about fifteen nuns. It was visited by Bishop Flemyng in 1422. He found fault with the financial management of the house, and told the nuns, who were too fond of fine clothes, that they must avoid extravagance. The sick were to be better looked

[1] The canons should be "amantes et concordes nec aliqua verba opprobriosa, vilipendiosa, contumeliosa, convitiosa seu diffamatoria inter se habent, emittant, dicant, vel proferant." *N.V.*, p. 147.

[2] *N.V.*, pp. 57–60, 113–22, 146–7, 170–2, 252–3, 314–15.

There are many other instances in the Visitation documents of Augustinian houses which had fallen upon evil times. The case of Huntingdon in 1432 was about the worst. "Religion is no more . . . utter collapse." *L.V.*, I, p. 76; also II, No. xxxiii. See also Caldwell in

after, transgressors adequately punished, the novices properly instructed and the services more reverently conducted and more regularly attended. More attention was to be paid to the menu, which seems to have been meagre, and every nun was to receive on Mondays, Wednesdays and Saturdays a dish of fish or meat to the value of one penny, and five measures of good beer every week. Strict precautions were to be taken to avoid scandals, and in order to raise the tone of the house the Bishop ordered that for the future only really good women were to be accepted as novices. Finally, let there be no more quarrels or cabals "whereby charity, unity or the comeliness of religion may be hindered."

Ten years later Bishop Gray visited the abbey. Finding that the numbers had so decreased that the services could not be chanted, he urged the abbess to get some more sisters, but only such as were duly qualified in reading and song. One sister who was leading an apostate life in secular habit was to be brought back. These injunctions had such good effect that in 1442 Bishop Alnwick found that all was well. Nearly one hundred years later, in 1530, we get a glimpse of the house from a Visitation of Bishop Longland. The buildings were then in a grave state of dilapidation. The internal life, though not really bad, was scarcely satisfactory, as the Bishop's injunctions prove. All were to attend matins and mass, and the abbess was to set a better example, and be more careful and strict in her life. Finally, they must wear the habit of their Order, keep themselves carefully veiled and abandon the practice of dressing like seculars.[1]

In 1432 and 1442.

In 1530.

The Benedictine nunnery of Godstow was exposed to danger by reason of its vicinity to the University of Oxford. So early as 1284 Archbishop Peckham had urged precautions and issued injunctions. In 1434 Bishop Gray found the discipline of the house very lax. His injunctions of 1432 had been

Godstow in 1434.

1421–2, *L.V.*, I, ix, x; Newnham in 1432, *L.V.*, I, xxxvii; Chirbury in 1423, *Reg. Spofford*, p. 39; also in 1482, *Reg. Mylling*, pp. 83, 123; St. Oswald's, Glouc., in 1514, *L. and P.*, I, 5355. See also *Yorks. Arch.*, XVI, 438.

[1] See *L.V.*, I, xx, xxi. For the Visitation of 1530 see *Arch.*, XLVII, pp. 51 f.

ignored, and the commission which he had appointed to reform the convent had been ridiculed and insulted. His wrath at the tone of the house was shown by the severity of his injunctions. After rebuking delinquents, he ordered the gatekeeper to take a solemn oath that for the future he will be more careful in guarding the gate. All the other doors are to be " barred up." The convent was undoubtedly at this date in a very unsatisfactory state. Indeed the bailiff declared with some acerbity (and doubtless exaggeration), " There is no good woman in the house."[1]

The history of the Benedictine Abbey of Romsey is well known to us through the admirable work of its historian.[2] It was a large and wealthy abbey founded by Edward the Elder in 907. Like the majority of religious houses it fell into decline in its latter days, the Black Death proving fatal to its prosperity. Its revenues and numbers steadily declined. In 1333 there were ninety nuns; in 1478 only eighteen, and the number never rose again above twenty-five. In the last quarter of the 15th century the abbey fell into disorder under Abbess Elizabeth Broke (1472–1502). So unworthy, indeed, did she prove that six years after her election the Bishop of Winchester brought pressure upon her to resign, but the nuns, preferring an easy-going Head, foolishly re-elected her. It was an evil day for the abbey. From that moment it rapidly went down hill.

Romsey Abbey.

In 1492 Archbishop Morton ordered a visitation of all religious houses in the diocese of Winchester. A distressing state of things was revealed at Romsey. The abbess seems to have possessed little or no moral authority. The nuns defied discipline and restraint, while there was heavy debt through financial mismanagement. Nine years later the abbey was again visited, this time by an agent of the Bishop, a Dr. Hede, who found the state of things far from well. The buildings were in a state of serious dilapidation; the mark of incompetence lay over the whole administration; while the abbess was accused of being, to the hurt of the house, completely under the influence of her chaplain.

[1] *L.V.*, I, xxviii. In 1445 Alnwick paid a visitation and did not find much improvement. He gave his injunctions in English. *L.V.*, II, xxv. At Atwater's visitation in 1517 the house was in good order.

[2] *Records of Romsey Abbey*, by Mr. Liveing.

Elizabeth Broke died in 1502 and was succeeded by Joyce Rowse (1502–15), who was elected by acclamation and proved an equally unfortunate choice. In 1507 Bishop Fox issued a series of injunctions which throw light upon the state of the abbey. The abbess was sternly rebuked for her manner of life, which was under grave suspicion. The sisters were enjoined to be more regular in their attendance at the services, to observe the rules of their Order, and not to sit up late or go into the town. The abbey never recovered its prestige.[1]

The Visitation documents show that some of the Augustinian nunneries were at certain times also equally in need of reform. At Burnham in 1432 Bishop Gray found much that was unedifying.[2] At Crabhouse in 1514 the juniors were disobedient, the prioress partial, the house in debt.[3] In 1521 Henry VIII wrote to the Bishop of Salisbury, thanking him for the care he had taken in suppressing the nunnery of Bromehall "for such enormities as by them used," and three years later this nunnery and that of Higham were suppressed by a Bull of Clement VII on account of the "demerit of the nuns," and the revenues given to St. John's College, Cambridge.[4]

Of the internal life and condition of the monasteries belonging to the Cistercian Order we know little, since they were exempt from episcopal visitation. It was otherwise with the nunneries. Of the state of some of them we get occasional glimpses in the Visitation documents, and while we cannot doubt (in the absence of evidence to the contrary) that many of them were keeping the Rule it is certainly true that dark spots existed. One of the worst was certainly the small Cistercian Priory of Catesby in Northants in the year 1442. There were only seven nuns beside the prioress, but the house was thoroughly demoralised. The prioress was extravagant, harsh and cruel to the nuns, and very far from correct in her life. Indeed, the collapse of the

Instances of Cistercian nunneries.

[1] There are other instances of Benedictine nunneries in an unsatisfactory state, e.g. Markyate and Flamstead in 1431, *L.V.*, I, xxxiv; Redlingfield in 1514, *N.V.*, pp. 138–40. Also Wherwell in 1368, *Reg. Wykeham*, II, 71.

[2] *L.V.*, I, viii.

[3] *N.V.*, p. 108; cf. Flixton, p. 142.

[4] *L. and P.*, III, 1863; IV, 686.

house was due largely to her bad example, and only proves what harm a bad Head could do.[1]

One more instance of an unhappy house may be given. In 1531 Bishop Longland visited the Cistercian Priory of Nun Coton in Lincolnshire.[2] The house was impoverished through extravagance. The buildings were dilapidated; plate and jewels had been sold; corrodies and leases had been recklessly granted with disastrous financial results. The services were conducted carelessly and irreverently and were badly attended. The prioress, who lived as though the priory were her own personal property, was exceedingly lax in discipline. The Bishop solemnly charged her to be more charitable and impartial, not to encourage tale-bearers, and not to favour her relations at the expense of the convent. Stringent precautions were taken to safeguard the morals of the community. Finally, the Bishop, who writes in a kindly fatherly style, urges the sisters to avoid idleness, keep the Rule and live at peace among themselves.[3]

[1] *L.V.*, II, xi.

[2] The Visitation is printed in *Arch.*, XLVII, 55–60.

[3] There are several other references to Cistercian nunneries. Sewardsley in 1434 was reported to be in a bad state. *L.V.*, I, xlvi. See also Gokewell in 1440; *L.V.*, II, xxvi; and Sinningthwaite in 1534, Nun Appleton in 1534, Esholt in 1435, all three in Lee's Visitations, *Yorks. Arch.*, XVI, pp. 400 f. A volume upon medieval nunneries is announced in the *Cambridge Series of Medieval Studies* (ed. Coulton), so that fresh light will soon be thrown upon an obscure subject. The instances of unsatisfactory nunneries given above are too few, in view of the large number of English nunneries, to enable us to draw general conclusions of the general state of English nunneries.

CHAPTER VII

(*continued*)

PART II

WHAT inference are we to draw from the state of these and similar religious houses, and from the sombre, at times very sombre, evidence of the Visitation documents? That the evidence of the Visitations, composed as they were with no thought of publication and no suspicion of malice, forms a decisive indictment of the English religious houses during the period of their decline? Such an inference would be very misleading. The evidence afforded by the Visitations is of the highest value and, so far as it goes, entirely trustworthy; but it has serious limitations, which forbid our making it the ground for a sweeping condemnation of English monasticism in its later phases. In the first place, the evidence is very incomplete. For an adequate knowledge of the condition of the monasteries we should require a complete series of Visitations of all the houses of all the Orders, carried out regularly at intervals of not less than ten years, and extending over several centuries. Such evidence does not exist. The series of episcopal Visitations which have come down to us deals with what are, at the best, only brief periods in the internal history of monasticism, and the information which they give us of any house is confined to the particular year in which the visitation actually took place. It is clear, therefore, that, in the absence of other evidence, we are left in respect to the inner life of that house in preceding and succeeding years in complete ignorance, or are reduced to idle surmise. Not only is this the case, but of the internal

Difficulty of arriving at the truth with respect to the religious houses.

(1) Incompleteness of the evidence.

condition of a large number of religious houses, and these among the greatest in the land, we can never have any detailed knowledge, for the very simple reason that they were exempt from episcopal control. The Cistercian monasteries (though not nunneries) were exempt; great Benedictine abbeys, like St. Albans, were exempt; the Cluniac, Carthusian, Gilbertine and Premonstratensian houses were all exempt[1]; and even in houses which were not exempt, either for long periods bishops were too careless to visit, or all records of their visitations have been lost. At any rate, we know nothing about them. There were in the diocese of Lincoln 136 religious houses. Of these, 38 were exempt from episcopal visitation; of the remaining 98 Alnwick visited 63; so that of more than half the total number of houses we know practically nothing at all; and that, too, in the episcopate of one of the most active and conscientious Visitors of the Middle Ages. The plain fact remains that the greater part of monastic history is simply a blank.

(2) Their character and condition were constantly changing.

Another fact which militates against general conclusions on the state of the religious houses is the constant change in their personnel and character. A few examples will show this. At the nunnery of Flixton there were in 1493 six nuns; in 1514 there were 8; and of these only one had been there in 1493. At Norwich Priory there were 46 monks in 1492, and 26 in 1514; and of these 26 there were only 8 of the 1492 monks left; and out of 32 monks in the house in 1532 there were only 6 who had been inmates in 1514, and (if we can trust to the reliability of the Christian names) not one who was there in 1492. At Walsingham, out of 27 canons in 1514, only 6 had been members of the house in 1494; and in 1532, out of 22 there were only 6 of the 1514 canons. Thus it will be seen that in twenty or twenty-five years a monastery underwent a complete change of personnel, so that a description of the character of any convent soon required revision. It is, indeed, extraordinary how the religious houses fluctuated. We may take as an example the Premonstratensian Abbey of Hales Owen in Shropshire. Six Visitations during

[1] In the case of the Premonstratensian houses we have the records of the visitations of Bp. Redman, the official Visitor of the Order. Other similar visitations of exempt houses have not come to light.

a period of twenty-two years have been preserved. In 1478 its condition, though not really bad, can scarcely be described as satisfactory. In 1482, beyond a few matters connected with the education of the novices, all seemed well. Six years later things were not so well. There was a debt of two hundred marks, no accounts were rendered, matins were badly attended, and there was an apostate canon. In 1491 many things were amiss. The services were neglected, the monks spent much time in feasting with their secular friends in the town and special injunctions were given for the expulsion of certain suspicious persons. Three years later there was nothing of any consequence amiss, but by 1497 a complete change in the character of the convent had taken place. Silence was not observed, matins were neglected, the buildings were dilapidated, there was a debt of £50. Two canons had been convicted of immorality, one of them also of insubordination and of conspiracy against the Abbot. Three years later there was a great improvement, and nothing serious was reported.[1]

Case of Hales Owen.

In 1492 the small Augustinian Priory of Bokenham was in a bad way. The Prior was partial, rendered no accounts and had even pawned the gold plate. The sick were neglected, the food was bad, the dilapidations serious, internal strife common. A grave picture. We have, however, four later Visitations to relieve the gloom; and in 1514, 1520, 1526 and 1532 the state of the priory may be described as satisfactory.[2] The state of the wealthy Benedictine Abbey of Croyland in 1432 was far from satisfactory—drinking, quarrelling, dilapidations and general misgovernment. But eight years later there was a great change. The house was so much improved that most of the monks said, "*Omnia bene*," and Bishop Alnwick did not discover any serious defects.[3]

Bokenham.

Croyland.

Now, if we only had the Visitations of 1492 for Bokenham, or of 1497 for Hales Owen, or of 1432 for Croyland, or of 1514 for Walsingham, or the report of St. Albans in 1492, or that of any other house at its worst, we should immediately

[1] *Coll.*, II, 241 f, cf. Cockersand, II, 107; Sulby, III, 6, 7.
[2] *N.V.*, pp. 24, 94, 160, 247, 307.
[3] *L.V.*, I, xv; II, xiii.

be forced to the conclusion that these houses were thoroughly bad, and should be inclined to condemn them offhand as very culpable. So perhaps they were at that particular date, but there is too great a tendency to condemn the religious houses upon the evidence of isolated Visitations, and to assume that *that must* have been their normal condition. The comparison of a series of Visitations, in the rare cases where such exist, shows how fallacious and misleading such a method of procedure is likely to be. So constantly, indeed, do monasteries change from good to bad, or from bad to good in a few years, that, in the absence of fuller evidence, final judgment must be held in suspense. It would be as unfair to frame a sweeping indictment against English monasticism because the evidence reveals some very black spots, as it would be to condemn the English Public School system because of unsavoury episodes in its history. The career of most institutions is a chequered one; and, indeed, when we consider the immense variety of the religious houses, the various Orders and Rules, and the striking difference in size, wealth and importance, it will be seen at once how impossible it is to form conclusions generally applicable to the monks and nuns of the later Middle Ages. Some monasteries were situated on the highways of civilisation; others were to be found in remote wilds, or in desolate fens. Some enjoyed princely revenues; others were reduced to an income of five or six pounds a year. Some were homes of religion and learning; others of ignorance and vice. The solidarity of the "religious" is a fiction of the imagination. A monk of the haughty and aristocratic foundations of Westminster, or St. Albans, or Glastonbury could hardly be expected (human nature being very much the same in all ages) to be on speaking terms (eager as the monks always were to break the rule of silence) with members of lesser foundations; and, indeed, between great, powerful and wealthy abbeys and small, unfashionable and poverty-stricken houses there must have been about as little in common as there is between an aristrocratic foundation like Eton and some obscure plebeian country grammar school.

Reserve of judgment necessary.

But though we must exercise a considerable reserve in forming a judgment upon the condition of the religious houses of England in the 15th century, it must certainly be admitted that it is peculiarly unfortunate for their reputation that, when we *do* get the searchlight of episcopal Visitations thrown upon them, many of them are found to be in a state which even their most enthusiastic apologists can scarcely regard as altogether satisfactory or edifying.[1] Indeed, it is obvious, even from the limited evidence at our disposal, that after the Black Death the religious houses entered upon a period of marked decline; and though we cannot go beyond the evidence and dogmatise about the unknown, we shall not be outraging historical probability in assuming that the causes of decline were at work in the great majority of the English religious houses. At the close of the 15th century monastic scandals were sufficiently frequent to attract the notice of Henry VII and Archbishop Morton, who applied to the Pope in 1490 for power to visit all religious houses, including those which had hitherto been exempt from episcopal control, in the Province of Canterbury. The Bull conferred large powers upon the Archbishop to correct abuses, by censure, suspension, excommunication and (if necessary) by calling in the secular arm. The Pope stated that in many monasteries the Rule was relaxed and zeal had grown cold; many, forgetting the fear of God, gave themselves up to a life of pleasure, and thereby brought religion into contempt and caused a grievous scandal.[2]

The religious houses after the Black Death.

[1] There are, however, many cases in the Visitations of "Omnia bene," which may mean either a model convent or bare respectability. See, for example, the following: In *L.V.*, Missenden, I, xxxvi; Fineshade, I, xxvii; Chacombe, II, xii; Elstow, II, xix; Fosse, II, xxi; Harrold, II, xxix; Kirby Bellars, II, xxxv. In *N.V.*, Blythburgh, p. 177; Ingham, pp. 27 f.; Ixworth, pp. 44, 83, 149, 302; Snape, pp. 37, 177. In *Coll.*, Hagnaby, II, 224 *seq.*; Croxton, II, 150; Leiston, III, 47 f.; Dereham, III, 212 f. This list is not exhaustive. If we are to accept the evidence for scandals as trustworthy, it is only reasonable to do the same with "*Omnia bene.*" The former is as likely to be due to malice as the latter to a conspiracy of silence. It must not be forgotten that the object of episcopal visitations was to hear complaints and note defects. Good houses have no history.

[2] *Concilia*, III, 630. Cf. the Papal Bulls given to Wolsey in 1518 and 1524 to visit and reform the monasteries, *L. and P.*, II, 4399; *Concilia*, III, 703. In sending the Bull of 1518 Silvester writes to Wolsey, "Has often been struck with the necessity of reforming the monasteries. Great care will be required in visiting the nunneries as many errors will be found in them."

The causes of the decline, into which some religious houses, by almost universal consent, fell in the later Middle Ages, were manifold. Some of these were inherent in the monastic system itself; and when the first enthusiasm wore off would have shown themselves even in the best houses and in the most devout ages. In the first place, the ideal of monasticism was pitched a little too high for the average man and woman. In an age of spiritual revival there were many who proved their vocation for the religious life, but with the average person, whose vocation was doubtful, what certainty was there that the early outburst of fervour would continue, when faced with the very severe test of the religious rule? Many entered in a moment of spiritual excitement, only to find, when the first enthusiasm had worn off, that they had no aptitude for the life of the cloister. The early rising, the incessant round of services, the strict fare, the unnatural life of celibacy, the lack of innocent recreations, the confinement within the convent precincts, the prohibition of social intercourse with members of the opposite sex, the dullness and monotony of the daily round, year in and year out, all these were too much for some of the brethren, especially in the case of the young, whose desire for female society, for converse with secular neighbours and even for frequenting taverns was by no means always a sign of an idle and vicious disposition, but rather the promptings of human nature which were too strong to be repressed. The monastic life was very suitable for those who had a real vocation, or for those who were getting on in years and had done their life's work and now wished to spend their closing years in prayer, meditation and the service of God. It was, except in rare cases, unsuitable for the young and vigorous, who craved for a more active, more useful and more natural life.

Causes of decline.

High ideals of monasticism.

Another inherent cause of decline was the growth of wealth and worldly power. The ideal of poverty was soon forgotten when, in an age of enthusiasm, pious donors (not, however, without an eye to their own salvation) heaped upon favourite religious houses lands, houses, manors, rectories, tithes and oblations. From this time the monks became landowners and men of this world, absorbed in business and in material pursuits. Their abbots

Wealth and worldliness.

were chosen for their business capacity, and the most popular were not those who insisted upon the religious ideal, but rather those who were able to further the material and financial interests of the house. Hence arose a worldly spirit; hence a gradual loss of religious enthusiasm; hence a worship of prosperity, which grew as the money flowed in. Their minds were now set not so much upon prayer as upon property; not upon God, but upon mammon; not upon increasing holiness, but upon increasing wealth. The house was in danger of ceasing to be a house of prayer and of becoming a house of business. The chief interests of the religious now lay in acquiring fresh lands, in maintaining their property rights, in expensive lawsuits with their neighbours, in their houses, their manors, their buildings, their tithes, their barns, their cattle, their sheep, their servants, their worldly prosperity, their well-being in this life, in the abundance of the things which they possessed. It was inevitable; for wealth and spiritual ideals go ill together.[1]

Quality of the religions.

To these causes, inherent in the system, there were added in the later Middle Ages special causes, due largely to the social, political and economic conditions of the times. The Black Death may be taken as the great dividing line in medieval history; for, though its effects can be exaggerated, it did create a revolution in the life of the nation, and, like the French Revolution or the Great War, marks the end of one epoch and the beginning of another. One special cause of decline due to the Black Death was, undoubtedly, the changed character of the inmates of the religious houses. There is evidence that, in the 13th and 14th centuries, much greater care was taken about the fitness and character of novices. Thus, for example, in 1328 Edward III wished the Prior of Worcester to receive as a monk "our well-beloved Henry de Lichfield." The Prior courteously refused, on the ground that, after

[1] Monastic decadence was not peculiar to the 15th century. It existed, though it was not so widespread, in the 14th, and even 13th, centuries. The wealthy Benedictine Abbeys of Selby and Bury St. Edmunds, and the Augustinian Priory of Bridlington were in a very bad condition in the early part of the 14th century before the Black Death; see *V.C.H.*, Yorks., III, 98; Arnold, *Memorials of St. Edmund's Abbey*, III, 56 f.; *Yorks. Arch.*, XVI, 424–58. See also Duckett, *Visitations of English Cluniacs*, for state of Cluniac foundations in 13th and 14th centuries.

inquiry, the man was found to be unfit for the religious life. In the next year a similar rejection occurred, a would-be monk failing in his entrance examination. "After examining him in literature and other things, as is our custom, we have found him incompetent to discharge the usual duties due to our Church in divine service."[1] All this was changed by the Black Death, which broke the continuity of custom and tradition. Numbers fell off with tragic suddenness. At the Cistercian house of Meaux, in Yorkshire, there were, on the first day of August, 1349, 42 monks and 7 lay brothers. On the last day of the same month there were only 19 monks and 1 lay brother, and a little later only 10 monks. All the rest had been carried off by the plague.[2] For years there was a paucity of inmates, and great difficulty was experienced in filling up the numbers; indeed, the monasteries never recovered their full complement, and some of the smaller houses were reduced almost to extinction. At the Benedictine Priory of Daventry in 1433 it was said that, owing to the paucity of inmates, the Offices could not be chanted; and the same was said of the nunnery of Elstow in the previous year.[3] At Humberstone Abbey there were only five monks in 1440. At Breedon Priory, in Leicester, only the Prior and one canon were in residence; the priory was in debt and its buildings were falling to pieces.[4] At the Augustinian Priory of Beeston, in Norfolk, there were, in 1494, only the Prior and one canon, and the latter was non-resident.[5] The same tale can be told of the larger houses. In 1387 Wykeham addressed a letter to the Prior and Convent of St. Swithin's, Winchester, about the serious falling off of their numbers. Seventy was the ideal for large Benedictine houses, but Winchester at this time fell far short. The number was only 46 in 1387; in 1404 it was 42; in 1495 it fell to 39; and in 1533, on the eve of the Dissolution, it was 43.[6] In 1492 there were only 17 canons at the wealthy and important Augustinian Priory of Walsingham. In the Premonstratensian abbeys, during the last quarter of the

Decline in numbers after the Black Death.

[1] *Liber Albus*, Nos. 1134, 1144.
[2] Fletcher, *Cistercians in Yorkshire*, p. 183
[3] *L.V.*, I, xvii, xxi. [4] *Ibid.*, II, ix, xxxii.
[5] *N.V.*, p. 55. Several other instances could be given.
[6] *V.C.H.*, Hants., II, 112, 113.

15th century, there were rarely more than 25 inmates. At the large Cistercian Abbey of Furness there were, at the Dissolution, only 30 monks ; and at Bury St. Edmunds, with its great wealth and enormous size, not more than 60. At St. Albans there were, in 1380, 58 monks ; in 1451, 46 ; in 1492, 54 ; and at the Dissolution, in 1539, only 39. Nunneries were in the same case. At Romsey there were 91 in 1333, and only 18 in 1478, and never again more than 25. The Black Death had proved disastrous to the religious houses.

Novices.

When it was possible, in some degree, to fill up the depleted ranks of the religious, the age of enthusiasm had passed, and a very inferior type took the vows. Little care was now exercised in filling up the numbers. Abbots were only too glad to get whom they could, especially as bishops expected to see a good number, and were always urging (not very wisely) that more inmates should be obtained. At the Premonstratensian Abbey of Sulby, at his visitation of 1491, Bishop Redman orders the Abbot to get two or three boys and clothe them in the habit, in order to increase the numbers.[1] Particular injunctions were given that the almonry schools should be kept up, in order to insure a constant supply of monks. What was the result ? Many, who had been educated in these schools, were professed young, without any special aptitude or vocation, some indeed against their will. Others entered because they had failed elsewhere, or for family reasons, or even for a mere livelihood ; while others still (but these of the baser sort) may have been attracted by the ill repute of a house, thus increasing the least desirable portion of 15th-century "religious." Hence we get a lower type of monk. Unless there is a real vocation, there can be nothing but failure and disappointment ; for, where religious zeal is lacking, the monastic life must have been intolerably irksome and its rules almost impossible to keep. Hence we find amongst the monks men with no special vocation, with strong human instincts, with little occupation, few healthy recreations, no interest in learning and a strong craving for the natural life of their secular neighbours. The result was what we should naturally expect. Many indulged in dice, gambling and other games unbecoming the gravity of the

[1] *Coll.*, III, 112.

cloth; some kept hounds and became, like Chaucer's monk, jovial huntsmen; many more in their boredom took to drinking in the houses of seculars, or in taverns, or even after compline in the abbey itself. Some few of these latter carried their habits to excess, for at Newbo we read of excessive drinkings, at Newnham of great drunkenness, while at the Abbey of Cockersand Bishop Redman in 1500 found the Abbot and many of the canons all seriously ill through their habit of late hours and deep potations.[1] The majority of such men as these were not necessarily vicious or corrupt, but only frail, average human beings, certainly no worse, if at times little better, than their brothers outside. At the best, they lived harmless, respectable lives; at the worst, they were a positive scandal to religion.

Case of the nunneries.

The case of the nunneries was similar. The class from which the nuns are generally supposed to have been taken were the gentry, but it is clear that they must often have consisted of the least desirable members of that class. At Ankerwyke in 1441 one of the sisters told Bishop Alnwick that the Prioress was in the habit of admitting as nuns some that are "almost witless and incapable";[2] and at Thetford in 1514 it was complained that the Prioress was about to receive persons untaught and deformed, especially Dorothy Sturges, a deaf and deformed lady.[3] These were, of course, exceptional cases, but only serve to prove the prevalence of a much lower standard than that of earlier and happier days. Many took the veil from purely secular motives, because they were lonely, or because they were disappointed in life, or because they were invalids and could no longer enjoy the world, or because they were unmarriageable, or because their home life was miserable beyond further endurance. The Paston Letters show us the unhappy lot of the 15th-century spinster. Elizabeth Clere, writing to her cousin John Paston in the year 1449, urges him to get a husband for his sister, in order to save her from her home and parents. "For," she continues, "she was never in so great sorrow as she is nowadays, for she may not speak with no man nor with servants of her mother but that she beareth her an hand otherwise than she

[1] *L.V.*, I, xxxvii; *Coll.*, III, 58; II, 126. There are many references to dice, gambling, unlawful games, hounds, hunting, and excursions.
[2] *L.V.*, II, i.
[3] *N.V.*, p. 90.

meaneth (=but her action is liable to misconstruction). And she hath since Easter the most part been beaten once in the week or twice, and sometimes twice in one day, and her head broken in two or three places."[1] Little wonder that such women, if they were unable to find a husband (and the civil wars had killed off a good number of bachelors), were only too glad to exchange the miseries of home and the brutality of parents for the lighter severities of the cloister and the veil.

Heads of religious houses.

And this decline in the general standard of the religious not seldom extended to the heads and rulers of houses, who, being elected by the convent, naturally reflected the prevailing sentiments. It must be obvious, from the instances which have come before us, that the prosperity and moral well-being of a religious house depended very largely upon the capacity and character of its head. The power and influence of the abbot of a large and wealthy foundation were certainly very great. He had a seat in the House of Lords, held a great social position among the surrounding gentry, enjoyed a princely income, had his own separate household with a large staff of servants and officials, held supreme sway over both the abbey and its dependent cells, and exercised jurisdiction over the numerous manors, churches and villages which comprised the monastic property, as well as over the town which had sprung up at the abbey gates. When he set forth on his journeys, he did so in great state, accompanied by his servants, chaplain, secretary and other officials; his revenues enabled him to dispense a profuse and splendid hospitality; and he was brought into constant touch with the highest in the land, not seldom entertaining royalty, and even at times furnishing to the King loans and supplying his necessities.[2] The Italian traveller in 1500 speaks of great Benedictine and Cistercian abbeys, which were "more like baronial palaces than religious houses"; and he singles out the Abbeys of Glastonbury and Shaftesbury, the heads of which enjoyed enormous revenues. "The Abbot of the former has an annual income of more than 25,000 crowns, and the Abbess of the other above 10,000; and the English say among themselves that the finest match that could be

[1] *Paston Letters*, I, No. 71.

[2] In 1400 the income of St. Albans was £1053 6s. 6d. (×15), of which the abbot took as his personal share £465 5s. 8d.

made in all England would be between the abbot and the abbess."[1]

It is obvious that with so much material power in his hands the head of a religious house could exercise very great influence (for even in small and poor foundations the power and privileges of the Prior was very great), and could make or mar the happiness and well-being of the convent. Compared with the proportion of good, or at any rate respectable, heads, the proportion of really bad ones was probably small; but that the latter were by no means a rarity in later days is proved by the evidence of the episcopal Visitations. Sometimes they were harsh, capricious and partial, and gave their monks a very bad time. At Croyland in 1432 the Bishop enjoins the Prior to be courteous, temperate, discreet, kind to young monks and impartial in punishments.[2] The Prior of Ashby in 1432 was told to be more just and kind, "not enjoining out of spite for a slight fault a heavy penalty, nor out of carnal affection a light penalty for a grievous fault." At Leicester in 1440 the Abbot was accused of harshness; "he looks on the brethren very despitefully and with a sour visage and will only speak to guests."[3] Prioresses were notorious offenders in this respect, and there are many complaints of their capricious punishments and cruelty. Thus (besides instances already recorded) at Redlingfield in 1514 the Sub-prioress was found to be very cruel and unfair in punishing; at Campsey in 1532 great complaints were made about the meanness, harshness and unfairness of the Prioress; while at Flixton in 1514 the Prioress was so harsh, partial, incapable and unpopular (her morals, too, not being above suspicion) that the convent was reduced to a miserable state of dissension, strife and want.[4] Nunneries cannot, indeed, have been at times very pleasant places to live in.

Instances of unsatisfactory Heads.

Not seldom we find charges brought against the moral character of the head. There are many instances in addition to those already given. Thus at the Premonstratensian Abbey of Langley, in Norfolk, in 1482, the house was going all to pieces through the influence of a bad Abbot, who was both inefficient and immoral. The only thing to do was to

[1] *Italian Relation*, pp. 29, 40. See also Dugdale, I, 443.
[2] *L.V.*, I, xv.
[3] *Ibid.*, I, xii; II, xli.
[4] *N.V.*, pp. 138–40, 142, 290–2. See also pp. 47, 185, 190, 261, 318.

pension him off. At Bradsole, in Kent, in 1500 the Abbot was setting the house by the ears and causing discord and scandal. He was accused of extravagance, bad conversation, drinking and immorality.[1] The moral character of the Abbot of the great, wealthy and all-powerful Abbey of St. Mary's, York, was, at the visitation of Archbishop Lee in 1535, gravely suspect[2]; while the case of the notorious Abbot Wallingford of St. Albans in 1492 is so well known (and so controversial) that no details need be given.[3]

Of unsatisfactory abbesses we have already had a few examples, and more can be found in the Visitations. What could be expected of such people? Nothing can be more certain than that a convent whose head bore a doubtful character would quickly degenerate, for a ruler's spiritual influence depends upon his character, and an abbot or abbess who failed to win the respect of the convent would lack the moral authority necessary for the maintenance of discipline and the preservation of a high religious and spiritual tone. There was much to be said for the young monk of Walsingham who, when reproved for some fault, calmly replied, "As long as I do no worse than our father prior doeth, he cannot rebuke me."

Results of misrule.

But though, undoubtedly, the 15th-century abbot was inferior to his predecessor of the 13th, there were, nevertheless, as the evidence of the Visitations proves, many striking exceptions. The difficulties of a good abbot in the troubled period succeeding the Black Death must indeed have been great. He had to contend with serious financial anxieties, with the growing spirit of insubordination and with the general decline of religious enthusiasm. Discipline was relaxed, and

Difficulties of good rulers after the Black Death.

[1] *Coll.*, III, 18; I, 103. See also Ashby, *L.V.*, I, xii, II, x,; Caldwell, I, x; and Bruton, *Reg. Bubwith*, pp. 438–9. In 1534 Bp. Bothe deprived the Prior of Monmouth for neglect and debt, *Reg. Bothe*, p. 287.

[2] *Yorks Arch. Journal*, XVI, p. 446.

[3] See Rushbrook Williams, *Hist. of Abbey of St. Albans*, p. 223. He thinks the charges incredible, and says that the Abbey was too near London for the abuses to have reached such a pitch "without some fierce outbreak of popular horror." On this it is sufficient to remark that the 15th-century populace was not distinguished by outbreaks of moral indignation; that tyranny and oppression, rather than moral delinquencies, are the occasion of popular fury; and that the Archbishop of Canterbury would scarcely have brought such a charge without some solid foundation.

amid all the confusion of the time it was not easy, even in the best houses, to preserve a high moral tone. A strict abbot, whose predecessor had been weak, lax or worse, would have, as we saw in the case of Walsingham, no easy time in reforming the house. Such an abbot in a lax age would certainly incur much opposition and unpopularity, however kindly or tactful he might be. An upright and conscientious ruler can never be generally popular, for he is compelled in the performance of his duties to make things unpleasant for the lawless, and to offend the susceptibilities of the erring. Popularity is one of the very worst and most misleading tests either of efficiency or of moral worth. What the average 15th-century monk wanted was an easy-going ruler who would let him do as he liked, and close his eyes to breaches of the Rule. If the Abbot was too strict, insisted upon too high a standard of discipline and did not allow the lawless element to go their own way, he would at once run the risk of incurring their wrath. Cliques would be formed against him, charges might be trumped up, and the Bishop at his next visitation regaled with a fine tale of the misdoings of the Abbot.[1]

Instances of good rulers.

It was, therefore, all the more to their credit that good men were able to steer their house through a period of difficulty, or raise it from a bad condition to a position of respectability. Abbot Thomas I (1349–96) maintained the morale of St. Albans at a time of peculiar difficulty. The Abbot of the great house of Bury St. Edmunds, which had been in a very evil state in the 14th century through the influence of a bad head, raised it by his piety and ability to a high level in the 15th century.[2] At Eye a new Prior so greatly reformed a house characterised by strife, moral scandals and general mismanagement, that six years after his appointment it could be reported that all was well.[3] At Coverham in Yorks there was in 1478 a heavy debt; and drinking, slackness and misconduct were quite common. In 1489 John Askew was elected Abbot and at once inaugurated a thorough reformation of the convent. He was so successful that at the

[1] In 1494 a false accusation was brought against the Abbot of Langley and disproved, *Coll.*, III, 25.

[2] Arnold, *Memorials of St. Edmund's Abbey*, III, 56 f.

[3] *N.V.*, pp. 140, 185, 221.

visitation of 1491 the Visitor said he was doing so well that he might almost be called a new founder; and at subsequent visitations he is praised as an excellent abbot.[1] These are a few typical instances which serve to show that, amid the general decline of the later Middle Ages, there were many abbots and priors keenly alive to their responsibilities and doing their best under difficult conditions to further the best interests of the communities under their charge.

The spirit of the 15th century reflected in the religious houses.

Another cause of the decline of monasticism in the 15th century was the spirit of the age, which, in spite of their traditions, was mirrored in the religious houses as clearly as in any other institution. For some callings in life there is an hereditary aptitude, which preserves continuity and guarantees efficiency. The son, bred in its atmosphere and educated in its schools, follows naturally the profession of his fathers. This could not be so in the case of celibate monks and nuns, each generation of whom was recruited from fresh ground, and thus brought into the convent the spirit, tastes, feelings and outlook of the world outside.[2] The whole spirit and tone of the 15th century was incompatible with the monastic ideal, and rendered difficult any general revival of the religious life. The age of enthusiasm had passed, and the Rule of asceticism and prayer which had been so great an inspiration in happier days was now found to be intolerably irksome and difficult. Instead of inspiring, it merely bored; and there was a general revolt against the strictness of religious ideals. Chaucer's monk openly derided the rule of St. Benedict:—

> "The rule of seint Maure or of seint Beneit,
> Because that it was old and somdel streit,
> This ilke monk leet olde things pace,
> And held after the newe world the space."[3]

This was the prevailing spirit. The rule was out of date. The ideal was too high. The point was put clearly and bluntly to Wolsey, who was trying to enforce monastic disci-

[1] *Coll.*, II, 130, 140, cf. 72; III, 219.

[2] We do not know what proportion of the religious had been educated in the almonry schools, but with them there was no hereditary aptitude and even less guarantee of vocation.

[3] *Prologue*, ll. 173–6.

pline, by the Order of the Black Monks: "The rule of St. Benedict is too severe and cannot be enforced without rebellion. In the present times, now the world is drawing to its end, very few desire to lead an austere life."[1]

The 15th century was an age of lawlessness, and this spirit reacted upon the monasteries, leading to insubordination and rendering very difficult the enforcement of discipline. Even powerful abbeys were not immune from external attack, and were compelled in self-defence to place themselves by heavy financial sacrifices under the protection of powerful lords. They adopted the wise advice of an anonymous correspondent of John Paston, who wrote: "Spende sum what of your good now, and gette you lordshep and frendshep there, *quia ibi pendet tota lex et prophetæ*."[2] This spirit of lawlessness found expression in many ways. Occasionally, though not very often, it took the form of actual violence. At West Dereham in 1491 one canon struck another and threw him into a pond. The offender is punished by a diet of bread and water for forty days.[3] From the Augustinian Priory of Newnham Bishop Gray demanded in 1435 one hundred shillings for the reconciliation of the cloisters, which had been defiled by the forcible shedding of blood by two of the canons.[4] In some places the monks were, it appears, in the habit of carrying about with them long knives which, when occasion offered, the holy men had no scruple in using; for at the Abbey of Eggleston in Yorkshire one of the canons was stabbed to death by a fellow-canon,[5] and we have already had occasion to notice the violent conduct of Brother Ralph Carnelle of Dorchester, who, when roused, brandished his long knife, terrorising the abbot and brethren.

Occasional outbursts of violence.

But more often the lawless spirit of the age found vent in insubordination and quarrels. The younger members of convents often proved very intractable; abbots had the greatest difficulty in maintaining discipline and keeping the peace; and quarrels, faction and strife characterised the internal life of many houses.

Quarrelling.

[1] *L. and P.*, IV, 953.

[2] Oct., 1450. *Paston Letters*, I, No. 116. For an armed attack upon a nunnery, resulting in rape and murder, see *L. V.*, I, xliv.

[3] *Coll.*, III, 219.

[4] *L. V.*, I, xxxvii (b).

[5] *Coll.*, II, 217; cf. the injunctions for Tupholme, III, 161.

After a disputed election to the headship of the abbey, or after a visit of the Bishop, feeling generally ran very high. At episcopal visitations the brethren were encouraged in the very un-English practice of telling tales of one another, a practice which presented a grand opportunity of venting one's spite upon one's enemies, or of paying out a disagreeable brother. Accusers of their brethren could hardly escape detection, and their presence would scarcely make for peace. Hence the earnest exhortations of the Visitor to live in amity and the solemn warnings against making the visitorial comments an occasion of mutual recrimination, strife and disorder.

It often happened that one or two violent and quarrelsome men set the whole convent by the ears. Brother Bartone of Bardney has already come before us, and his case is by no means exceptional. At Coxford the canons were disobedient, quarrelsome and refractory. At Herringfleet in 1492 it was reported: "One brother is very quarrelsome and disagreeable."[1] At the Augustinian Priory of Elsham in 1440 Bishop Alnwick received a complaint of a particular canon, one Yorke, who "gets drunk so easily, and is then so quarrelsome and cross that to live with him is irksome to all. He is very puffed up and arrogant." The Bishop enjoins: "No one of you do vex another with chidings, taunts, upraidings or cursings."[2] At Westacre Priory in 1494 there were dissensions and quarrels among the canons, and the Sub-prior was so violent, quarrelsome, overbearing and disagreeable that some actually left the abbey because they could put up with him no longer; and at Wendling (also in 1491) the language and conduct of one of the canons were so disgraceful and violent that some of the novices had left in disgust.[3]

Nunneries.

It cannot, unfortunately, be denied that this love of quarrelling and strife reached its height in houses of religious ladies, which must indeed have been at times veritable little bedlams. One or two examples will suffice. The Prioress of the Benedictine convent of Carrow used to listen to tale-bearing favourites, with the natural result that the convent was torn by dis-

[1] *N.V.*, pp. 38, 111. [2] *L.V.*, II, 88.

[3] *N.V.*, pp. 49–51; *Coll.*, III, 204; cf. similar cases at Alnwick and Langdon, II, 22; II, 5.

sensions.[1] Minchin Barrow in Somersetshire was a house for well-born ladies who, we are told in 1410, were always quarrelling among themselves. It was because of her quarrelsome disposition that the late Prioress had been removed. Though pensioned off she was still living in the priory, not a particularly happy arrangement for her successor, one would have thought.[2] But the worst instance is probably that of the Augustinian Priory of Gracedieu, near Leicester. It was in 1440 heavily in debt through mismanagement, but its chief fault was quarrelling and backbiting. The Bishop had to issue some very scathing injunctions. " Charity and lovingkindness were," he wrote, " utterly banished, and strivings, hatreds, backbitings and quarrellings have ever flourished in that place." The Prioress had two particular favourites who toadied, sneaked and retailed the gossip ; and she was singled out for a very severe rebuke because she was mainly responsible for the miserable state to which the convent was reduced. " We found that love, charity, peace and concord are utterly excluded and exiled from you, and nothing among you but envy, hate, simulations, discords, upraidings and rebukes."[3]

Growing revolt against the ascetic ideal.

The spirit of the age showed itself, too, in a growing revolt against monastic austerity with respect both to food and dress. There are frequent complaints about the insufficiency and bad quality of the food. At Welbeck on one occasion the Visitor ordered " better food " ; the canons of the small Augustinian Priory of Hempton complained of shortness of commons ; at Trinity Priory, Ipswich, in 1532 the canons told the Bishop of Norwich that the cook was dirty and the cooking bad ; while at Thetford Priory in 1526 one of the canons grumbled at the beer which, he said, was not fit to drink, being both sweet and small (*dulcis et tenuis*).[4] The nuns, however, seem to have kept the poorest table, for it is from them that we hear the loudest complaints. At Flixton in 1514 Sister

[1] 1492, *N.V.*, p. 15.
[2] *Reg. Bubwith*, pp. 84, 115.
[3] *L.V.*, II, p. 124. This spirit of lawlessness extended even to the servants, of whose insolence mention is frequently made. At Dunstable Priory in 1442 it was reported : " The cook of the house is overmuch puffed up and surly," *L.V.*, II, p. 85. At Ixworth Priory in 1526 it was complained that the butler was " insolent," *N.V.*, p. 240, cf. p. 135.
[4] *Coll.*, III, 180 ; *N.V.*, pp. 112, 293, 242.

Isabella Ashe said that twice a week there was only bread, butter and cheese with occasionally a little milk ; and six years later the commons were found to be distinctly short. At Carrow Priory, so said the nuns, the food was scanty and the beer distinctly thin.[1] Sometimes, certainly, there was good cause to grumble, as the food was really bad. Thus at the Priory of Campsey in Norfolk the nuns complained bitterly in 1532 about the menu. The cook was negligent, the food was bad and insufficient, and on one occasion the meal consisted of a "sick bullock."[2]

Now, these complaints were perfectly natural and no doubt fully deserved, and as meals were the chief excitement in the dull monotony of the day it must have been peculiarly disappointing to be set down to so poor a diet as bread and cheese and to so thin a potation as small beer, the potentialities of which (even at a gallon a day), whether for cheering or inebriating, were so painfully limited. The grumblers will secure the ready sympathy of all epicures ; they were, without doubt, hardly treated ; the only point that might be raised by cavillers is whether such particularity about creature comforts is quite in accordance with the ascetic ideal which, professing indifference to the delights of the flesh, extols the virtue of self-denial and regards pulse and water as dainty fare.

Dress.

It was the same with dress. The religious as well as the secular clergy were continually being warned against luxury and extravagance in dress, and Visitors found it needful to make careful regulations with respect to tonsures, cloaks and personal adornment. In 1488 Bishop Redman legislates for the canons of Maldon about the size of the tonsure, the length of the hair and the luxury of their cloaks. At Barlings on three separate occasions he warned them against new and extravagant fashions in dress, especially the luxurious imitation of the laity and the wearing of wide shoes.[3] Archbishop Lee in 1534 made some nasty remarks to the canons of Warter with reference to their objectionable habit of using belts adorned with silver

[1] *N.V.*, pp. 142, 145, 190, 209. Beer was liberally supplied in nunneries. At Elstow in 1442 we are informed : "Every nun has for her maintenance at the beginning of every week seven convent loaves and six gallons of beer or more," *L.V.*, II, p. 89.

[2] *N.V.*, pp. 290–2.

[3] *Coll.*, III, 85 ; II, 33.

and gold and of wearing gold rings.[1] Chaucer's monk, we know, did not disdain personal adornments :—

> " And for to festne his hood under his chin
> He hadde of gold y-wrought a curious pin."

Abbots and priors were often very luxurious and rode abroad in great state, clad in the height of fashion and extravagance. The Abbot of St. Mary's, York, had his hood and sleeves made of velvet, and went forth riding with gilt spurs and bridles. In 1432 Bishop Gray informed the Prior of Ashby that when he rode abroad on business he was *not* to do so in a showy and gaudy habit, nor with a haughty or fastidious, but with a devout gait, in order that spectators might not be led astray by such an example of pride, loftiness and arrogance. He must put on a humble and suitable dress, " so that the comeliness of your habit may declare your cleanness of thought and modesty of heart."[2]

Nuns naturally fell easier victims to such temptations than monks. The small Benedictine Priory of Langley was poor and heavily in debt, largely because the nuns neglected religion for dress. In future they are *not* to wear silk veils or flowing robes.[3] Flemyng in 1422 strictly exhorted the sisters of Elstow against luxury and extravagance. No nun is to presume to wear silver pins in her hair or silken gowns or several rings on her fingers ; and Bishop Longland more than one hundred years later ordered the nuns to wear the correct dress, keep veiled and cease to imitate their lay sisters.[4] But perhaps the climax of extravagance was reached in the Prioress of Ankerwyke, of whom in 1441 Bishop Alnwick was told : " The Prioress wears golden rings exceeding costly with divers precious stones, and also girdles silvered and gilded over, and silken veils, and she carries her veil too high above her forehead, so that her forehead being entirely uncovered can be seen of all ; and she wears furs of squirrel. Also she wears kirtles laced with silk, and tiring pins of silver. Also she wears above her veil a cap of estate furred with wool of lambs."[5]

One great reason, undoubtedly, for the decline of the religious houses was the financial difficulties into which most

[1] *Yorks. Arch.*, XVI, 445. [2] *L.V.*, I, p. 32. [3] *Ibid.*, II, xxxvii.
[4] *Ibid.*, I, p. 52 ; *Arch.*, XLVII, 51 f. [5] *L.V.*, II, p. 3.

of them fell after the Black Death. This diminished their resources and blighted their prospects. A very large number of manorial tenants died; in some places the entire population was swept away; and the lord (if he himself survived) was left with no one to cultivate the land. Hence customary services could not be rendered, and rents, whether in money or in kind, could not be paid. This meant a dead loss to the religious houses, some of which suffered severely. St. Albans at one stroke lost a quarter of its annual revenue. The smaller houses were still more acutely affected, for they were less able to endure financial loss. Much of the land went out of cultivation altogether through lack of cheap labour, and the monks being so reduced in numbers could not till the land themselves. The corn lay rotting on the ground; the countryside was desolate; and both man and beast perished. The wealthy Priory of Christ Church, Canterbury, complained that it had lost 257 oxen, 4585 sheep, and 511 cows with calves, the whole estimated to be worth £792 12s. 6d. (×15).[1] At the beginning of the 15th century the Abbey of Chertsey petitioned for the appropriation of the rectory of Stanwell, assigning as a reason for its poverty the fact that its arable land could not be cultivated through lack of labour following on epidemics and pestilences; and nearly a century after the Black Death the Priory of Bernewell complained to the Bishop of Ely of its serious financial position. The revenues had greatly fallen off in consequence of pestilences, sterility of the soil and scarcity of farm hands and servants; expenses had been increased by unusually heavy taxation, and by the burden of maintaining the poor and infirm, who flocked to the priory in very great numbers; the services and customary dues had been so depauperated that they no longer sufficed for the full number of the canons.[2] The result was that the manorial system, which had long been tottering, began to break up completely, and gave place to new methods in agriculture and land tenure. The monasteries, like other landowners, were compelled to adopt the practice of letting or leasing their lands at a rent, instead of cultivating them by means of manorial labour, a policy which, while it saved trouble and responsibility, detached the monks

Financial difficulties of the religious houses.

Enclosures by the monks.

[1] Gasquet, *Monasteries*, I, 5. [2] *Reg. Bourchier*, f. 9.

from the soil and proved a fruitful source of financial difficulty. A few turned their arable into pasture, became sheep farmers and as such shared in the general unpopularity which then attached to this mode of farming. More refers to this in the *Utopia*. "Certeyn Abbottes, holy men no doubt, not contenting them selfes with the yearely revenues and profytes . . . leave no grounde for tillage ; they inclose all into pastures ; they throw doune houses ; they plucke downe townes, and leave nothing standynge, but only the churche to be made a shepehouse."[1] Robert Kirton, Abbot of Peterborough (1496–1528), was a notorious offender in the matter of enclosures and must have been one of the abbots whom More had in his mind. He had enclosed nearly a thousand acres, having at the same time evicted a hundred people, who had thereby been brought to the greatest misery. He had even committed the sacrilege of emparking a churchyard, to the horror and indignation of the inhabitants, who declared that "the place where the bodies of the faithful lay is now simply a pasture for wild beasts," "an eloquent commentary," writes Mr. Leadam, "on the humane administration of their estates currently assumed in favour of monastic landlords."[2]

But the monasteries themselves were at times hardly hit by this system of enclosures. The Priory of Bradenstoke in Wilts held land in the manor of Northaston, Oxfordshire, where a wealthy landowner "inclosed, ditched and converted to pasture" 700 acres of arable, which included, scattered about amongst it, 142 acres belonging to the priory. The Council of Henry VII gave the Prior redress, but the offender refused to either pay or to give up the land which he had illegally enclosed. The

Case of the Priory of Bradenstoke.

[1] *Utopia*, p. 18 (Temple Classics). See the letter of the Vicar of Quinton in Gloucestershire to the President of Magdalen College, Oxford (the lord of the manor), at the close of the 15th century. "I pray you in God tenderly to remember the welfare of our church of Quinton and the supportacion of our poor village which falls fast in decay and is near to the point of destruction . . . for the houses go down, fallen within this four year." Denton, *England in 15th Century*, p. 318.

[2] Leadam, *Select Cases*, II, 123–42 ; Introd. pp. xci–xciii. Against the above, however, may be set the case of John Mulso *v.* the Abbot of Croxton, *ibid.*, II, 49 f., where the Abbot took the part of the villagers of Thingden against illegal and oppressive enclosures.

Prior then sued him in the local courts, but an Oxfordshire jury, preferring the claims of an Oxfordshire man to those of an ecclesiastical outsider, refused to give him justice. Whereupon he appealed to the King, and sued the offender, one William Anne by name, in the Star Chamber. He complained that Anne "so kepeth and holdeth all the seyde grounde inclosed and diched, whereby foure howses and twoo plowes of the seyde Prior be decayed and fallen down to the disherison of the seyde Prior and his monastere, and also eyght howses fyve plowes be decayed fallen and pulled downe to the minisshyng of Goddes Churche there and services :—the seyde Priore hath susteyned greate losses damages costes and charges."[1]

Heavy expenses of the religious houses.

Another cause of financial decline was the heavy and constantly increasing expenses of the religious houses. If their income was often large, their expenses were correspondingly great. They were liable to heavy taxation in the shape of tenths and subsidies, to exacting papal demands both ordinary and extraordinary, to the various ecclesiastical dues which were an annual charge upon the income of the house, and to the large outgoings in the way of fees and hospitality which must have detracted somewhat from the pleasures of an episcopal visitation.

Dilapidations.

The upkeep of the monastic buildings also involved a heavy outlay. After the middle of the 14th century donations and endowments ceased, being given to colleges and schools instead. Abbots had lived and built, and the expenses had been calculated on the basis of a ceaseless flow of fresh money. When this began to fall off the monasteries were faced with a difficult situation, the ordinary income, diminished as it was by the economic and agricultural conditions of the period, proving insufficient to maintain the buildings and even to meet current expenses. Many monasteries, especially the poorer ones, were suffering from overbuilding ; and even in the case of the wealthier foundations great building abbots, like Abbot John Moot (1396–1401), who built the beautiful cloisters of St. Albans at a time of bad harvests, often brought their convents into financial straits. During the 15th century many of the buildings were showing signs of

[1] Leadam, *Select Cases*, II, 1–4 ; Introd., p. cxiii.

age, and just at the very time when dilapidations were becoming acute, the revenues were rapidly falling. Many houses were reduced to poverty through overbuilding, and we hear constant complaints, increasing as the 15th century advanced, of dilapidation, decay and ruin.

Hospitality and charity, too, were often a great drain upon the resources of the monks. Some houses were famous for their hospitality, entertaining daily large numbers of guests; while at monasteries situated near the high roads the cost of hospitality must have been very considerable. Hospitality was, indeed, one of the most useful functions of the monasteries, for which they were always gratefully remembered in later times, the loss of which was much felt after the Dissolution. The case of alms to the poor stands on a different footing. Much of this was compulsory, the monks being simply trustees under the wills of donors, or, as in the case of appropriated churches, legally liable by the terms of endowment. This was no charity at all; and it is not going too far to say that the voluntary alms of the monks were, at any rate in their later days, a very precarious and uncertain item in the monastic budget. The income of Salley was £347 14s. 7½d., but in the year 1381 only 5s. 8d. was distributed in charity.[1] We have the balance-sheet of the Priory of Huntingdon for nine months from Michaelmas, 1517. There were a Prior, eleven canons and thirty-four servants. The income was £220, but there is no mention of alms to the poor.[2] In the account roll of the Abbey of Romsey for 1412 the total receipts were £404 6s. 1d. Alms for the poor amounted to £8 19s. 4d., which is not very much more than the bill of £6 13s. 4d. for "wine for nobles visiting the Abbess; and less than a gift of £10 to Lord Henry, Bishop of Winchester, on his return from the Holy Land, but perhaps this latter item was a necessary charge upon the Abbey.[3] The number of poor living on the liberality of the monasteries was certainly much smaller than the number of monks. Professor

Hospitality.

[1] Fletcher, *Cistercians in Yorks.*, pp. 119–20.

[2] Gasquet, *Monasteries*, II, 507–8. Gasquet thinks alms are included under "expenses of Household, as appereth by ye kechyn boke," but this is very doubtful as alms are generally given as a separate item.

[3] Liveing, *Records of Romsey Abbey*, pp. 194–5.

Savine, the great authority on the subject, says: "The tax free alms constituted less than three per cent of the monastic budget, and most of these represented food for the poor on certain holidays or commemoration days; it is very difficult to believe that the taxed alms greatly exceeded the amount of the alms which were tax free." "We shall have to admit that in their latter days the monasteries did very little (in the way of corrodies) to alleviate the acute distress of their times."[1]

Another cause of financial difficulty lay in the misfortunes which often overtook the monasteries. The ordinary revenue left no margin for bad harvests, fires, floods, pestilence and other misfortunes. The income of a religious house was dependent upon land, there being no comfortable dividends coming in every half year from gilt-edged securities. A fire might break out and destroy their buildings, and there were no Insurance Companies to make good the loss. A flood might do enormous damage to crops, and this meant a dead loss. Plague might carry off useful tenants, and dead men can't pay rent. A series of bad harvests would embarrass even the wealthiest houses. In 1432 the Hospital of St. John at Northampton was released from certain obligations on account of poverty, due to land which had gone out of cultivation through "pestilences and mortalities and epidemic disorders of mankind and disasters of different sorts."[2] In 1440 the Cistercian nunnery of Heynings was seriously in debt, and the reason given was scarcity of corn and bad harvests for a succession of years.[3] In 1513 the Bishop of Ely granted an appropriation of a rectory to the Abbess and Convent of Denny because of the great falling off of the revenues occasioned by "repeated deadly epidemics, paucity of tillers and servants, sterility of soil, immoderate expenses therefrom, sudden and frequent murrain among the cattle, extraordinary floods and the general ruinous condition of most of the houses."[4]

Natural misfortunes.

In addition to all these liabilities, the immense property of the religious Orders, while it was a source of revenue, was also a source of very heavy expense. Their land was generally widely scattered, and even when it lay in the same county

[1] Savine, pp. 241, 265. See the whole of c. iv, Bk. II.
[2] *L.V.*, I, p. 95.
[3] *Ibid.*, II, p. 133.
[4] *Reg. West*, ff. 61–8.

it was rarely contiguous. "Large monasteries possessed manors in many counties. St. Peter's, Westminster, had manors in Glouc., Worc., Midd., Surrey, Bucks., Oxon., Essex, Notts. Even a monastery of moderate size, W. Dereham in Norfolk, had manors in five counties, viz., Norf., Camb., Suff., Yorks., Lincoln."[1]

Expenses as land-owners.

Very great must have been the expenses of travelling, of the collection of distant rents and tithes, and of the horde of officials—bailiffs, stewards, auditors, agents and receivers whom they had to employ, and upon whose help, fidelity and honesty they were so largely dependent. Besides this, their position as great landowners involved the monasteries in constant litigation, which in bribery and legal costs entailed an enormous expenditure. The monks were often reproached with greed, and held up in contemporary ballads as hard and unscrupulous landlords ; the charge is to some extent true ; it must not, however, be forgotten that neighbours and tenants, as in the case of William Anne, often sought to invade the legal rights of the religious houses, rob them of their land, deprive them of their rents and take the first opportunity of resorting to threats and violence. Lords and knights looked with jealous eyes upon fair lands which would admirably round off their own estates ; and the wealth of the monasteries proved a sore stumbling-block to lay proprietors, whose piety took other forms than that of paying their debts, respecting their neighbours' property, and observing the tenth commandment.[2]

The monks as land-lords.

Indeed, with respect to the character of monks as landlords there is a considerable difference of opinion and the question is not easy to decide, for a few instances of friction or oppression prove little. The truth is that the character of the religious houses varied so greatly in different places and at different times that it would be rash to jump to general conclusions. Monks were landowners, and landowners are generally regarded by tenants and by the landless as grasping capitalists, ever

[1] Savine, p. 152.

[2] For instances of such lawlessness see the brutal way in which Lord Molynes in 1448 stormed the manor of Gresham, drove out Margaret Paston, and sacked the mansion ; or the siege of Caistor Castle in 1469 by the Duke of Norfolk. *Paston Letters*, I, Nos. 77, 107 ; II, Nos. 616–22.

ready to trample upon the weak, and in the furtherance of their own interests strain to the uttermost the letter of the law. This, no doubt, was often the case; but as a rule monks were kinder and more indulgent than other landowners, and after the Dissolution their comparative leniency was favourably remembered by tenants, who found in the favourites of Henry VIII hard taskmasters, whose harsh business methods served to throw into relief the more easy-going ways of the monks.

It is not always easy in the case of disputes between the monks and their tenants, or the towns which had grown up round their gates, to discover the truth or fix the blame. It is certain, however, that, if many houses were rich, powerful and grasping, their tenants and neighbours were not seldom violent, quarrelsome and unreasonable. The records of proceedings in the law courts and Star Chamber remain to show that in such disputes the monks were by no means always in the wrong. In 1504 the Abbot of Shrewsbury brought an action in the Star Chamber to establish his claim to local jurisdiction in a part of the city of Shrewsbury. The Abbot claimed that from time immemorial the part in dispute had been under the jurisdiction of the abbey and not of the town. The bailiffs of Shrewsbury denied this, and asserted that the Abbot was usurping their privileges, invading their rights and illegally claiming jurisdiction over what was clearly within the liberty and franchise of the town. They also complained bitterly of his "uncharitable and unlawful vexations," especially in having arrested a citizen and reduced him to ruin by extorting the large sum of £38. All this sounds very dreadful, and if we only had the bailiffs' view of the question, it would go hardly with the Abbot. But we have his reply, in which he presented a strong case. He said that, if the town was "greatly in decay and so daily groweth," as the citizens assert, the cause lay not in his actions, but "by their misrule and in default of good order and for lack of due ministration of justice." The case was tried, witnesses were examined, and in the end judgment was pronounced in favour of the Abbot.[1] In 1518 the Abbot of Peterborough

The Abbot of Shrewsbury.

[1] Leadam, *Select Cases*, I, 178–88, *The Abbot of Shrewsbury v. the Bailiffs of Shrewsbury*. For monks as landowners *ibid.*, *Carter v. A. of Malmesbury; P. of Bath v. A. of Aug., Cant.;* also p. xiii.

brought an action against Power and others for violence. The Abbot held in possession some waste ground called the Borough Fen, upon which the inhabitants of Peterborough had admittedly the right of pasture. The dispute arose as to whether they could pasture any number of cattle there, or only a limited quantity. The citizens maintained the former position ; the Abbot the latter. Hence inevitable friction. In June, 1517, the Abbot gave orders that as the citizens defied his ruling their cattle were to be driven away or impounded, and the fen enclosed. Thereupon a violent quarrel arose. The citizens resorted to violence, broke down the fences, drove in their cattle and (glad of the opportunity) broke open the head of one of the Abbot's servants. This was more than any self-respecting Abbot could possibly stand, so he decided to arraign the citizens before the Star Chamber on a charge of conspiracy, riot and forcible trespass.

The Abbot of Peterborough.

"Among the causes of the unpopularity of the religious houses with the commercial classes," writes Mr. Leadam, "was their rivalry in trade." Of this a striking example is to be seen in a case brought before the Star Chamber in 1510 by the Mayor of Newcastle against the Prior of Tynemouth.[1] The Prior of Tynemouth, a keen man of business, was in the habit, it was stated, of engaging in trade, and had gone so far as to build houses and wharves in order to obtain the coastal trade to the ruin of the town of Newcastle. When the merchants of Newcastle made a protest the Prior replied by throwing some of them into prison. They now appealed to the Star Chamber for protection, at the same time charging the Prior with riot and false imprisonment. "Thus, most gracious sovereign lord, the said Priour of his great myght maliciouse mynde and extort power riottously dayly taketh encrocheth and converteth to his own propre use your ground and enheritance, and by subtill and crafty meanes by his Fisshegarthes so ebbeth and shalloweth the same port and by means of chargyng and discharchyng of shippes att Sheeles, so that if it continue your seid poore Towne of Newcastle shall be utterly decayed." The Prior was befriended by Wolsey, but in 1529 Parliament passed an Act, protecting Newcastle and practically destroying the rival port.

Rivalry in trade.

[1] Leadam, *Select Cases*, II, 68 ; Introd. p. xciii, f.

Large monasteries which were situated in towns, or round which towns had sprung up, exercised an enormous power upon the town and its inhabitants. Though the town often owed its prosperity to the patronage and proximity of the abbey, yet as time went on and the town grew in size, wealth and importance, the relations between monk and citizen became so strained that serious friction often arose. Then it felt its position of dependence upon the Abbot to be an exceedingly galling yoke and devoted its energies to shaking it off. In some places there was a fierce struggle extending over centuries between the monastery and the town. At Reading, for example, there was a struggle of 250 years between the Abbot and the Merchant Gild. The monks were all powerful over the trade of the town, and being a very powerful ecclesiastical corporation they could retard the growth of civic liberty and the right of self-government. It was only gradually that the towns gained their liberty. Their opportunity came when in the 15th century wealthy abbeys fell into financial difficulties and were only too ready to sell liberties, rights and exemptions to the towns. The necessities of the monks were the opportunity of the citizens.[1]

Monks and citizens.

But perhaps the chief cause of financial difficulties lay in the maladministration of a house on the part of an unscrupulous or incompetent ruler. Instances of this have already been given; a few more will suffice to show how widespread was the evil. Thus at the nunnery of Aconbury in 1406 the Bishop of Hereford sequestrated the revenues and placed them in the hands of trustees, because the nuns had so greatly mismanaged their property.[2] Abbots often provided for their relations and friends out of the common funds and so helped

Financial maladministration.

[1] See Hurry, *Reading Abbey*, c. v. For earlier instances of friction see the case of Norwich in 1271, where the citizens set fire to the Priory, Coulton, *Social Life*, p. 237; the grave friction between the city of York and the Abbey of St. Mary's in the 13th and 14th centuries; the strained relations at Daventry in the 14th century, where the townsfolk conspired to deprive the Priory of tithes and maliciously rang a bell to deceive the monks. See also *Reg. Spofford*, p. 110. In 1428 the Bishop is asked to suppress the Priory of Kilpeck because the Rule could not be observed "propter loci ipsius inquietacionem populique solitam infestacionem." But such cases were exceptional.

[2] *Reg. Mascall*, p. 27.

to impoverish the house. Gray ordered the Prior of Ashby to banish his secular relations, whose presence had caused unpleasantness, bitterness and expense.[1] Abbot Anglie of Malmesbury provided for his natural son from the revenues, and was guilty of gross oppression.[2] There are continual injunctions to abbots not to cut down trees, or sell timber, or grant leases, or bestow corrodies without the consent of the whole convent ; and particular precautions are taken that the common seal should be kept under three keys to prevent its fraudulent use. The extravagance and incapacity of abbots often brought their houses to the verge of ruin. Thus in 1482 the Priory of Chirbury was in decay and ruin through the maladministration, waste and luxury of its prior.[3] In 1482 the Abbot of Welbeck was found to have wasted the goods of the house, allowed the buildings to get into a ruinous state, pledged jewels, sold cattle, alienated lands, woods and tithes by the illegal use of the seal, to the great detriment of the monastery. By his utter mismanagement he had brought the house into the greatest misery.[4] At Hickling in 1492 the same cause was responsible for the evil state into which the house had fallen. The servants were badly paid and no accounts ever rendered.[5] At Cokesford Priory in 1514 the buildings were dilapidated ; there were no accounts, no infirmary and no schoolmaster ; while the canons were disobedient, quarrelsome and refractory. It was all due to maladministration.[6] In 1531 Bishop Longland found a very bad state of things at the Augustinian Abbey of Missenden in Bucks. The house had fallen into great decay through the Abbot's negligence, extravagance and maladministration. His kinsfolk lived at the convent's expense ; the church, cloisters, dormitory and infirmary were all badly in need of repair ; no accounts were kept, no audits held and corrodies were recklessly granted ; the abbey was burdened with a heavy debt, and the whole place was in a state of decay, neglect and filth ("every place to be more

[1] *L.V.*, I, xii.

[2] Leadam, *Select Cases, Calford v. Wotton*, I, p. 47.

[3] *Reg. Mylling*, p. 83 ; cf. Wigmore, *Reg. Spofford*, pp. 64–76 ; *Reg. Bothe*, p. 232.

[4] Magna ruina, maxima miseria, *Coll.*, III, 184.

[5] *N.V.*, p. 25.

[6] *Ibid.*, pp. 28, 111, 313 ; cf. Thetford in 1514, p. 88 ; Woodbridge, p. 292.

honestly kept from filth and stench "). What was the result? Exactly what might be expected amid such squalor and misery. The monks were idle and ignorant; the services were neglected; the Prior was so utterly slack about discipline that the canons did just what they liked; the moral tone was low, and strict orders had to be given that the doors were to be kept locked, and that no undesirables were to enter the cloister or visit the cells of the canons. One monk, indeed, was so bad that he was to be put in prison and *kept* there. Finally, the Bishop ordered that " every canon be occupied either at his study in grammar or in writing, painting, carving or some other honest study and craft so as to avoid idleness.[1]

Even when there was no actual maladministration there was often very bad finance, and the financial expedients employed only led the monasteries deeper into the mire. Monks were, as a rule, bad business men and did not always get the best value out of their property. At the Abbey of Peterborough, Bishop Gray in 1432 found that farms had been badly let to unreliable tenants, who gave no good security. The financial officers of monasteries often proved highly incompetent, and (spurning all principles of sound finance) sought to obtain ready money by reckless borrowing, or by selling crops in advance, or by imprudent leases, or by other unwise and shortsighted measures. Houses in financial difficulties often granted leases of their land for a long number of years on the easiest terms, on condition that the whole of the money should be paid down on the spot; and as they generally spent this in the relief of immediate necessities, it is obvious that they were only mortgaging the future prosperity of their house. The Prior of Ashby in 1442 leased out the tithes of Murleigh for five years at £10 per annum and received the whole then and there[2]; and at St. Albans the large cash payments for leases were generally spent at once.[3]

Bad Finance.

[1] *Arch.*, XLVII, 60–64. In 1534, on the very eve of the Dissolution, the Bishop of Hereford had to deprive the Prior of Monmouth for neglect, absenteeism, dilapidations, and debt, *Reg. Bothe*, p. 287.

[2] *L.V.*, II, x.

[3] These bad financial methods had been employed before the Black Death. See how Worcester Priory raised ready money to pay off its large debt in 1301, *Liber Albus*, No. 29. The Cistercians borrowed

But perhaps the most usual method of raising ready money was by the sale of corrodies. A corrody was the grant to a person of free food and lodging in the monastery for life, or for a number of years, either for a lump sum down, or more rarely for a weekly or annual payment. In the former case it was a speculation both for the monastery and for the corrodian, and was similar to the present custom of sinking capital in an annuity. Large sums were frequently raised by the sale of corrodies. In 1321 the Prior of Worcester raised twenty marks, and in the following year £40. The monastery certainly obtained ready money for its present needs, but only at the cost of draining the future resources of the convent. Besides this, corrodies were granted with reckless profusion and utterly unbusinesslike methods. "Alnwick's visitations contain many specific examples of corrodies sold for comparatively small sums which eventually proved a dead loss to the monastery."[1] A great many instances of corrodies are to be found. Take one at Worcester in 1308. Richard de Lynde obtained a corrody, and the terms of his agreement with the priory were that he was to have for the remainder of his life a private room in the priory, straw and firewood, six pounds of candles of Paris tallow and pocket money to the value of twenty shillings a year. Every day he was to receive a monk's loaf and one for his attendant, two gallons of superior beer and an ordinary monk's rations (but double for supper). For his horse he was to have the use of the stable with hay and oats.[2]

Corrodies.

Corrodians were often very bad for discipline, setting a bad example and offering great temptations. Nunneries, especially, suffered. Many of them being extremely poor took in corrodians as boarders or paying guests as a means of helping out their slender resources. At Littlemore in 1445 there were three boarders,

Corrodians.

freely from the Jews. Chartulary of Rievaulx (Sur. Soc.), LXXXIII, 348 f.

[1] *L.V.*, I, 229.

[2] For corrodies see *Liber Albus*, Nos. 411, 714, 940. Some corrodies were freely granted by the monastery as a reward for service. Others were claimed as a right by the King, by founder's kin, or by patrons who by this means pensioned off their friends and dependents. Thus, "for Richard Stok, M.A., student at Oxford, to have a corrody in the Monastery of St. Frideswide of 50s. per an." *L. and P.*, I, 1235.

one of whom paid eightpence a week and the other two fourpence each. Bishops greatly disliked the practice, being of opinion that it was detrimental to religion and morality. At Elstow Nunnery Bishop Gynwell in 1359 found lady boarders, and forbade the unlicensed practice of taking paying guests, " because by the living together of secular women and nuns the contemplation of religion is withdrawn and scandal engendered."[1] Flemyng was of the same opinion in 1422, for he ordered, " No boarders or visitors over twelve, especially married people (without permission), as they are detrimental to true religion " ; and ten years later Gray ordered their removal in the interests of morality. They were right. Corrodians brought the world into the cloister. And not only were they a danger to the religious life, but they were often a great nuisance to the nuns, who resented their presence. At Langley in 1440 the Bishop received a complaint about Lady Audeley, a boarder, who " has a great abundance of dogs. Twelve follow her to church, and make a great uproar and terrify the nuns " ; while at the Cistercian Priory of Legbourne " Margaret Ingoldesby a secular woman lies in the dormitory, bringing with her birds, by whose jargoning silence is broken and the rest of the nuns disturbed."[2]

The result of this financial depression was inevitable—debt, dilapidations, sordid anxieties, decline in morale, in ideals, in religion. Even the wealthiest abbeys felt the strain. The debt upon St. Albans in 1519 was about £2666, while its income was about £2100 ; while four years later the abbey, owing to its debts, was unable to pay its full quota of the subsidy to the Crown.[3] If this was the case with some of the largest and wealthiest abbeys, what was the condition of the smaller ones ? To them the financial strain was crushing and fatal. The debt at Bourne in 1440 was £75 with an income of £167.[4] At Easby in Yorkshire the debt in 1478 was £100 ; in 1482, £130 ; reduced, however, to £16 in 1491. At Alnwick with an income of £189 the debt in 1482 was £70, and £86 four years later. At Bileigh in Essex with an income of £157

Debt.

[1] *V.C.H.*, Beds., I, 355

[2] *L.V.*, I, xx, xxi ; II, xxxvii, xxxix.

[3] *L. and P.*, III, 3239.

[4] *L.V.*, II, p. 37. The incomes are taken from Savine.

the debt in 1482 was £100, reduced to £76 in 1488. At Beyham, a small Premonstratensian abbey in Kent, the debt in 1472 amounted to the huge and overwhelming total of £600.[1]

The nunneries were in even worse straits. They were, to begin with, much less richly endowed. The richest monastery in England, Westminster, had in 1535 a gross income of £3912 ; the richest nunnery, Shaftesbury, not more than £1324. In the *Valor Ecclesiasticus* there are 14 nunneries with a gross income of less than £20 a year ; 39 with less than £50 ; 69 under £100 ; 97 between £100 and £200 ; and only 6 over £500 (as compared with 73 monasteries).

The result of this extreme poverty was deplorable. The Priory of Ankerwyke is a case in point. Its debt in 1441 exceeded its income, and it was ill-governed and demoralised. The Sub-prioress said, indeed, "*Omnia bene*" ; but she received no support from the rest of the community. Sister Agnes Dychere said she had insufficient clothing for her bed and for herself, and that she suffered intensely from the cold. She wanted better food as well. Sister Margaret Smythe said the Prioress was harsh and excessive in her corrections. Sister Thomasine Talbot said that the Prioress did not provide her with bedclothes, insomuch that she had to lie upon straw. The Bishop had ordered her to lie in the dormitory, and when she asked the Prioress for bedclothes, she replied, " Let him who gave you leave to lie in the dorter supply you with raiment." The Prioress, she said (with, doubtless, a slight touch of envy), wears a golden ring with a diamond in it. Dame Juliane Messengere deposed that hay was stored up in the church ; that no repairs were ever carried out ; that the Prioress was in the habit of bringing in strangers at the cost of the house, and of admitting very undesirable inmates. She treats the nuns very harshly, and rarely comes to matins or to mass. The younger nuns have no one to instruct them in reading and song. Dame Margery Kyrkeby said that the buildings were in a state of dilapidation ; that the Prioress keeps the common seal in her own possession ; that the vest-

Case of the Priory of Ankerwyke.

[1] *Coll.*, II, pp. 4, 18, 83, 72. Sometimes a good Abbot cleared off the debt, e.g. Titchfield, III, pp. 129, 135. For sequestration of the incomes of Wigmore Abbey in 1530, and Monmouth Priory in 1533 see *Reg. Bothe*, II, 232, 284.

ments and psalters have disappeared; that one chalice is in pawn and others broken up; that no accounts were ever rendered, and that six nuns are apostates at the present time. She brought a serious indictment against the luxury and extravagance of the Prioress. No wonder the house was in debt; no wonder the food was bad; no wonder the nuns went about in clothes patched and threadbare, when the Prioress squandered the income upon her own finery!

The Prioress was compelled to admit that many of these charges were true, but she also said that the nuns were in the habit of sitting up late to drink, that they moved against her on slight occasions, and that Margaret Kyrkeby had called her a thief. The good Bishop was somewhat nonplussed when confronted with religious ladies of this description. He contented himself (what else could he do?) with the usual injunctions, which he took care to send in English.[1]

Results of poverty.

It is clear that a great deal of the sordidness, internal strife and lack of a high religious ideal which have been already touched upon in the religious houses were undoubtedly due to poverty. Poverty is all very well as an ideal; but when it means inability to pay one's way, hopeless debt and constant anxiety as to ways and means, it is as inimicable to the religious life as prosperity and wealth. How could any community preserve its religious fervour, or carry out its spiritual duties while engaged in a desperate struggle against financial ruin, and when the chief thought that occupied the mind is not the worship of God, but the best way of finding the cash for daily bread? Unless those who minister in spiritual things are placed above the sordid cases and harassing anxieties of grinding poverty, they are scarcely likely to preserve intact that spirit of inward calm, without which no true work can be accomplished either for God or man.

Decline in learning.

Such were among the chief causes which led to the decline of English monasticism. Nowhere is that decline more visible than in the decay of learning, which is so marked in the Religious Orders in the period succeeding the Black Death. The monks have often been regarded as men of learning, but it was only the Benedictines and perhaps a few of the Augustinians who

[1] *L.V.*, II, i. If the Prioress came late to church she was not to order the service to begin all over again. Cf. Langley, II, xxxvii.

devoted much attention to letters. The Cistercians professed to despise study, and refused to allow their *conversi* or lay brethren to be taught to read and write. The famous monastic chronicles came from the Benedictines, but even these ceased in the 15th century.[1] St. Albans was, certainly, an honourable exception and never lost its interest in learning, Abbot Wallingford (the "wicked" abbot) doing his best to encourage printing. Benedictine houses were supposed by an order of Benedict XII in 1335 to send a proportion of their members to the University, where colleges had been founded for their use[2]; and it is a sign of the times that this duty was often neglected. The truth is that by the 15th century the monastic Orders had lost interest in theology and in learning, having been easily surpassed in these by their rivals, the Mendicants. The result was natural. As the monk lost his intellectual interests he was in danger of deterioration.

Neglect of the novices.

We have already seen that the educational activities formerly attributed to the monks have turned out to be very doubtful, and that even their own almonry schools were rapidly falling into decay. And not only so, but there was an increasing neglect in providing instruction for the novices and juniors. In earlier days great care had been taken with the novices. At Durham, we are told, there were always six novices who went daily to school in the house for the space of seven years, and one of the elder monks who was learned was appointed to be their tutor. The said novices had no wages, but only meat and clothing. If they were apt, they were sent to Oxford.[3] It was very different in the 15th century. At the Priory of Dunstable in 1442 there was no teacher to instruct the younger canons in grammar, "therefore they do not understand what they read." At Ashby in 1432 Gray ordered the Prior to procure someone to instruct in the

[1] See Rashdall, II, 481, where in a footnote he quotes a saying of Richard de Bury in 1345: "calicibus epotandis non codicibus emendandis indulget hodie studium monachorum."

[2] Durham College (Trinity) in 1289; Gloucester Hall (Worcester), 1293; Canterbury, 1331; St. Mary's College (Augustinian), 1435, all at Oxford. At Cambridge, Magdalen.

[3] *Rites of Durham*, p. 96. For regulations for the care of the novices at Canterbury c. 1075, see Lanfranc's Constitutions, *Educ. Charters*, pp. 61–7.

elementary branches of knowledge, but his advice was unheeded, for in 1440 we find Brother John Bartone praying Bishop Alnwick for an instructor in grammar. At Elsham in the same year one of the canons said that when he entered religion his purpose was to make progress in letters and religious discipline, and this the Prior promised him, and yet he has made progress in none of these things, seeing there is no one to teach him.[1]

All these were Augustinian houses, and perhaps things were better in those of the Benedictine Order. They may have been; yet it is notorious how indignant Bishop Gray was to find that in a large and wealthy Benedictine foundation like Peterborough there was no instruction for the novices and younger monks. So slack, indeed, did the monasteries become, so indifferent to the claims of learning, that several of the monks, more especially in the smaller houses, were often very illiterate, at the best only partially educated, at the worst hopelessly ignorant. If the majority of them knew sufficient Latin to understand the mass and muddle through the psalter, they were therewith content. Testimony to the ignorance of monks abounds. In 1387 Wykeham enjoins the Prior of St. Swithin's, Winchester, to see that the monks are taught, since some are "almost wholly ignorant of letters."[2] Owing to the general decay of learning in the religious houses, and the consequent difficulty of finding learned men as abbots, Henry VII in 1504 provided for the education at Oxford of three monks from Westminster. In 1511 Warham made a visitation of the important and wealthy cathedral Priory of Canterbury, and was so scandalised at the ignorance of the inmates, especially the younger ones, that he ordered immediate provision for their instruction. "For in default of such instruction it happens that most of the monks celebrating mass and performing other divine services are wholly ignorant of what they read, to the great scandal and disgrace both of religion in general and the monastery in particular." Indeed, it became so unwise to trust to the chance of a knowledge of

The 15th-century monk.

[1] *L.V.*, II, p. 83; I, p, 32; II, pp. 45, 87. At Ipswich there was no schoolmaster for the novices either in 1514 or 1526, *N.V.*, p. 137.
[2] *Educ. Charters*, p. 444.

Latin that bishops sometimes took the wise precaution of issuing their injunctions in English to make sure that they were understood. Thus to the Abbey of Missenden in 1531 Bishop Longland wrote in " oure vulgare Englishe tong," so that the whole convent might be able to understand.[1] Bishops had, long before the 16th century, used English when writing to nuns, for they knew no Latin, read no books and were in the habit of using English versions of the Bible.

Monasticism after the Black Death.

The truth is that by the end of the 14th century decline had evidently set in. The 12th and 13th centuries were the golden age of monasticism, and its subsequent decline must not lead us to underrate the high ideal which it set before the world in its earlier days, nor allow us to forget the good work which it accomplished before prosperity had lowered its standards and the Black Death had thinned its ranks. Monasticism has played a great part in the history of European civilisation. The Benedictines kept the lamp of learning burning in Europe during ages of ignorance and darkness. The monks were, indeed, at one time most useful members of society. They provided hospitality for the traveller and alms for the poor ; were good agriculturists, who made roads and bridges, cleared forests, and drained marsh and fen ; proved themselves to be great architects and builders, the glory of whose churches are still the wonder of the world ; and produced scholars and writers to whose labours we are indebted for much of our knowledge of medieval history. But by the opening of the 15th century their work was done. The conventual church had been built, and they no longer had the bracing tonic of great things yet to be accomplished. They had long since ceased to produce scholars and writers, and even the copying and illustration of manuscripts, for which they had been famous, was now done by professional scribes. The ideal of asceticism had for several lost its attraction in the general decline of the 15th century. What further good purpose could the monks serve without a radical change in their work and methods ? The men of the New Learning looked with contempt upon their ignorance ; agriculturists found fault with the management of their estates ; the attacks of Wycliffe and the Lollards, the satires of Chaucer, Erasmus and Simon Fish undermined

[1] *Arch.*, XLVII, pp. 60–4.

their authority; and the nation was losing respect for the monastic ideal as they saw it in practice in its later history. "In England no ecclesiastic, no statesman, no scholar of any eminence had of late years sprung from the Religious Orders. Their influence had collapsed. The general complaint against them is ignorance, bigotry and idleness."[1]

Conclusion.

And this incapacity of the monastic Orders to mend their ways, or make their institutions subserve the needs of the new age was being recognised by some of the best men in the Church. Erasmus is constantly poking fun at the monks. Rich men no longer founded or endowed monasteries. There was, indeed, a tendency the other way. Wykeham so disliked and distrusted the monks that he founded Winchester College as a nursery for the secular clergy. Many alien priories were suppressed by Henry V; Wayneflete endowed Magdalen with the property of the Abbey of Selborne; out of monastic lands Eton and King's were founded by Henry VI, and the college of All Souls by Archbishop Chichele. When at the beginning of the 16th century Bishop Fox was thinking of founding a monastery, he was dissuaded by Bishop Oldham of Exeter: "What, my lord," he said, "shall we build houses and provide livelihoods for a company of bussing monks, whose end and fall we may live to see? No! No! It is more meet a great deal that we should have care to provide for the increase of learning, and for such as by their learning shall do good to the Church and the Commonwealth."

Yet in spite of all that can legitimately be urged against some of the religious houses in their latter days, their treatment by Henry VIII can never fail to evoke both pity and indignation; the decline of monasticism in a difficult age must not blind us to its high ideals and its permanent contributions to religion and civilisation; nor must the failings of the few be allowed to obscure the virtues of the many.

[1] Brewer, *L. and P.*, Introd., p. lxxvii.

CHAPTER VIII

CONCLUSION

SUCH was the Church in England on the eve of the Reformation. What was the life of the people to whom it ministered? Then, as now, there was a sharp division between the life of the townsman and that of the country-man. Few sights can have been more picturesque than a large medieval city, with its walls and gates, its beautiful Gildhall and churches, its narrow streets and quaint houses, its hostelries, lazar house and friary. Nor were the inhabitants less picturesque than their buildings. Here is a wealthy merchant in his rich robes hurrying to a meeting in the Gildhall; here a knight riding upon his charger through the streets, reckless of the lives of others; here a friar or monk in cloak and hood; here a burgher's wife in her best attire; here the armed retainers of some powerful nobleman, making themselves a nuisance and a terror. Along the principal streets are the shops with the apprentices at the door inviting customers to come inside and buy. A walk through a medieval town would have been most interesting, but we should have had to be careful where and how we trod. The streets were narrow, ill-paved and filthy. The upper storeys of the houses overhung the streets, and from their windows the refuse of the house was emptied promiscuously into the road. There was no attempt at sanitation, and the streets were rarely cleaned. "Godly" our medieval ancestors may have been; "cleanly" they certainly were not; and the disgusting state of the streets, with their heaps of putrid and decaying refuse, their undrained gutters, their narrow lanes and ill-ventilated houses, afforded a sure breeding ground for pestilence, fever and disease.[1]

A medieval town.

[1] An Act of 1383 attempted to enforce cleanliness, but to no purpose. See Erasmus' description of English houses, *L. and P.*, II, pp. ccix, x. See also *The Babee's Book* (E.E.T.S.), *Introd.*, pp. lxii–lxvii, for medieval love of dirt in house and person.

The life of a townsman was more interesting and exciting than that of a countryman. He took a great pride in the welfare of his town, for there was little flitting about, and his family had probably been settled there for centuries. He was a soldier, for all citizens had to defend their city and bear arms according to their rank, from the dagger of the prentice to the mail, bucklers, swords, bows and arrows of the richer citizens. If he lived by the sea he had to keep a sharp outlook for pirates, and in time of war for hostile ships, the crews of which often made sudden attacks upon the seaports, stormed the walls, burnt the houses, slew the inhabitants and inflicted injury from which the town took long in recovering. At any moment the church bell might ring out its summons to the citizens to hurry on their arms and rush to the defence of hearth and home. Nor were domestic brawls infrequent. The weapons which the citizen carried for defence would prove equally useful when he himself wished to break the peace and, taking advantage of the unlit and unguarded streets, to disturb the night with violence and robbery. The inefficient police arrangements were powerless to guarantee peace and safety to the citizens. Broken heads and bleeding wounds were frequent sights, for life and limb were cheaply held in medieval times. On Gild or Festal Days the townsman would array himself in the striking and picturesque robes of his gild, and after attending a solemn service in his parish church would proceed to the Gildhall, where he would partake of one of those Gargantuan feasts which delighted his heart and shortened his life. He might then witness those remarkable miracle plays which depicted in rude gesture and homely language some scene, tragic or humorous, from the Bible story; or he would proceed to the recreation fields, where he would witness or take part in the games of old England, and he would share in that rough merriment and boisterous good humour which made medieval England, rough and brutal as it was, still on holy day and holiday "Merrie England."

Life of a medieval townsman.

Judged, indeed, by modern ideas of comfort, the lot of the medieval countryman, whether peasant or smallholder, seems miserable in the extreme. He lived in a wretched house built of mud and rubble, containing but a single room which served the family, and often the family pig, for all domestic purposes. There were no windows, no ceiling and no chimney, the smoke escaping when it would (it generally wouldn't) by a hole in the roof. For a floor there was only the bare ground, covered over with straw or bracken; and upon this were thrown promiscuously bones, scraps and the refuse of all sorts which now finds its way into the ash-pit or the pig-pail, and only when the odour of this decaying vegetable and animal matter became too powerful even for the hardened nostrils of our medieval ancestors was this mass of filth swept away and fresh straw laid down.

The countryman at the close of the Middle Ages.

His food, though in ordinary seasons it was both cheap and abundant, was monotonous, coarse and unwholesome. Quantities of badly salted meat were consumed, and this led to those terrible skin diseases which disfigured and tortured poor and rich alike in medieval England. Indeed, pestilence and disease hovered like birds of prey over a medieval village or town, ready to swoop down upon victims whose unwholesome food, whose neglect of all sanitary precautions, whose ignorance of medicine and of the laws of health simply invited sickness and death. We have no details, but when parish registers were kept after 1540 there is much evidence of the visitation of plague and disease to our villages and cities.[1] Nor, again, was the danger of famine by any means an imaginary one. A couple of bad seasons reduced the peasant to real want, for villages were self-contained and food could not readily be imported. If the countryman lived near the seat of war, on the Scottish borders, or on the scenes of civil strife, he would be in danger of having his roof burned over his head, his cattle driven off and all his foodstuff commandeered. Or he might be a victim of the greed and violence of "great" men, who often made armed attack upon manors and lands which they coveted for themselves.

The countryman lived in almost complete isolation from the outer world. He was cut off from surrounding villages

[1] There is a dramatic entry in the *Burial Register* of Hurstbourne Tarrant, Hants, for the year 1593. A list of nearly fifty names is given of those who were buried within a few weeks of one another. One large family was almost entirely swept away. The Vicar and his family died. The entry concludes, "All these died of ye visitacion of ye plague."

and towns by bad and at times impassable roads, by dense forests, by marsh or fen or flood. He was without newspapers, without books, without society, without those comforts which to-day are regarded as so essential to the happiness even of the very poorest. And even if he were fortunate enough to escape plague, pestilence and famine, the fire and the sword, his life at the best was hard, dull and monotonous. He worked long hours for small pay; he was forbidden by law from seeking to improve his lot by learning a trade, or removing into a town; and if he became sick or poor his master was forbidden to give him alms, since that might be regarded as an infringement of the Statute of Labourers. Under the Tudors his lot in many places altered appreciably for the worse. The close of the 15th century was a period of great agricultural depression; the increase of sheep farming deprived the smallholder of his lands, and the peasant of his Common rights; at last, his services being no longer required, he was turned adrift to make a precarious livelihood as best he could. He took to begging, and experienced the tender mercies of the Tudor Poor Law, which put him in the village stocks and whipped him as a sturdy beggar. Or he took to stealing, became a highwayman and, after revenging himself on society for his wrongs, was captured and ended his miserable existence on the gallows.

His isolation and hard lot.

And yet even this hard lot had its compensations, and we should be left with a very misleading picture of medieval country life if we omitted the other side. There was the parish church in which the villagers took great interest. It was the one beautiful house in the parish, and all took delight in helping to maintain the fabric and to increase the beauty of the interior. There were the Church Ales, which provided funds for the Church and amusement for the people. There were visits from the friars, who, if they came to sponge, came also with news and gossip of the outer world; or from pilgrims, who possibly passed that way; or from the wandering minstrel, or quack, or mountebank, or cheapjack. Above all, there was the village inn, which then, as now, played so important a part in the social life of the village. Many of our present village inns, with their quaint names and still quainter signs, are very old and date back to the Middle Ages. Their hosts had

The brighter side of his life.

a bad reputation with travellers, as they were often in league with the highwaymen who infested the country roads and lurked in the dense forests. Round the inn fire, blazing with logs, there gathered in the evening the village folk, and sometimes even the village parson, whose lonely life led him to share in the social life of his humbler neighbours. Nor did the ladies of the parish disdain at times to leave their filthy hovels and join in the festive gathering. And so with gossip and song, cards and dice, beer and ale, the long winter evenings were whiled away. Occasionally the sitting was prolonged to midnight, until empty pockets and aching heads recalled the company to the hard realities of daily life.

Influence of medieval religion.

Religion in the Middle Ages had a far greater hold over men that it has to-day. It was in many ways a more living reality, for it was more vitally bound up as an indispensable part with the habits, customs and work of daily life. The Church was a very real force in every man's life. People believed in its teaching, in its power, in its claim to possess the passport to Heaven. The world of spirit was a very real world indeed to the medieval mind. Men believed not merely in the existence of good and evil spirits, angels and devils; but they believed that such spirits concerned themselves with the affairs of men and had great influence over their lives. Man was surrounded by spiritual powers; there were angels to bless and protect; there were devils to tempt and to injure, to smite the cattle with disease, to spoil the harvest, to bring pestilence and famine and the sword. Religious fear was a great power in the Middle Ages, fear of the power of evil spirits, fear of witchcraft, fear of the pains of Purgatory, fear of the power of the Church to condemn to the fires of hell. In the Middle Ages the Church dominated over men; in this age men dominate over the Church.

Examples of this influence.

The 15th century, corrupt, vicious, decadent as it was, was neither an age of unbelief nor an age of religious indifference. It is interesting to note what the Italian who visited England at the close of the 15th century has to say about the religious habits of the people. " Although they all attend Mass every day, and say many *Paternosters* in public (the women carrying long rosaries in their hands, and any who can read taking the Office of Our Lady with them), they always hear Mass on Sunday in their parish church, and give liberal alms because they may not offer less than a piece of money, of which fourteen are equal to a golden ducat, nor do they omit any form incumbent on good Christians. There are, however, many who have various opinions concerning religion."[1] The *Paston Letters* (1422–1509) are a mine of information for the habits and customs of the English during this period; and they give us a good idea of the influence which religion exerted over men's lives. Some of these letters are very beautiful, both in language and in sentiment; and as they were not written for effect or for publication they give a good picture of their age. Religious expressions and religious sentiments continually appear even in the most businesslike letters, and, though customary and stereotyped, certainly *seem* to be sincere. "I grete you well, and sende you Godde's blessing and mine." "The blyssed Trinitye have you in His kepying." Very touching is the account of the death of Sir John Henyngham; or the religious advice which is often given by parents to their children; or the firm belief, everywhere displayed, in religion, in the Church, in prayer, in the protection of the saints. Take as an example that remarkable and beautiful letter sent by the Duke of Suffolk to his son in 1450 (just before his murder): "My dere and only well-beloved sone, I beseche our Lord in Heven, the Maker of alle the world, to blesse you, and to sende you ever grace to love Hym, and to drede Hym. . . . And last of alle, as hertily and as lovingly as ever father blessed his child on earth, I give you the blessyng of oure Lord and of me, which of His infynite mercy increase you in alle vertu and good lyving."[2]

Church building an evidence of the goodwill of the laity.

In spite of the ecclesiastical abuses of the age there was more goodwill on the part of the laity towards the Church than might have been expected. Indeed, complaints are not seldom a sign of zeal and an evidence of a very real desire to obtain reform; for when men are indifferent they do not take the trouble even to complain. There was often an intense local patriotism and devotion to their own particular parish church. Many of our existing churches afford striking

[1] *Italian Relation*, p. 23. His opinions must be taken for what they are worth. He was a credulous person.
[2] *P.L.*, No. 91.

evidence of this. In the 15th century a very large number of beautiful and splendid parish churches were built by laymen at their own expense. In Bristol, in Norwich, in the Eastern counties there are many magnificent churches built at this time by pious laymen or by the united efforts of the parishioners, who certainly would not have given their money for the purpose if the Church had been generally unpopular. The 15th century was a great age of church building, though the Perpendicular style of architecture, impressive and beautiful as it often is, was far inferior to the dignity of the Norman, or the delicate grace of the Early English, or the gorgeous beauty of the Decorated.

The medieval parish church.

The parish church was the centre of parish life. There it stood (much as it stands to-day), towering over the medieval village. It was the one beautiful building in the place, for the cottages and houses were but miserable hovels. The people took great delight and pride in their parish church, for parishes were as a rule worked upon a democratic basis, and the parishioners had a considerable voice in the management of the church and its affairs. They regarded it as their own, and took deep interest in its welfare. They gave valuable gifts ; left money or goods in their wills ; made themselves responsible for Church finance ; and undertook the collection of funds for the restoration of the fabric or for the beautifying of the interior.[1] The interior was, indeed, often very striking and beautiful. The walls were decorated with frescoes or hung with pictures ; the windows were filled with coloured glass ; the altar was a mass of rich colour and ornament, with its beautiful frontals, hangings and candlesticks. " There was not a parish church in the kingdom so mean as not to possess crucifixes, candlesticks, censers, patens and cups of silver."[2] Everywhere there was striking evidence of the affection of the people for their church.

It must, however, be added that, like everything else in the Middle Ages, churches were exceedingly dirty. The floor of the church was covered with straw or rushes which

[1] See Gasquet, *Parish Life in Medieval England* ; Weaver, *Somerset Medieval Wills* ; Hobhouse, *Somersetshire Churchwardens' Accounts.* The remarks on p. 58 must be borne in mind. The generosity was not *always* quite voluntary.

[2] *Italian Relation*, p. 29.

were only changed three or four times a year, and were generally swarming with vermin. In the churchwardens' accounts of the period there are frequent payments to the ratcatcher, who was a regular village institution. Pews were not introduced until the middle of the 15th century, and were then simply plain benches to which were added later, as the age became more luxurious and worshippers more particular, backs and an extra width to make them more comfortable.

Church life in medieval England.

In parishes where the parson was resident and performed his duties there was a vigorous Church life. The church and its services played an important part in the life both of villager and townsman, and added much interest to an existence which was often dull and monotonous. There were the ordinary Sunday services, High Mass, preceded by a procession round the church; the special services on Holy Days and Gild Days; the solemn and beautiful services on the great Festivals of the Christian year, those at Candlemas with processions of lighted candles; those of penitence on Ash Wednesday; the solemn *Creeping to the Cross* on Good Friday[1]; the blessing of the palms on Palm Sunday; the ritual of the Easter Sepulchre; the beautiful services at Easter, Rogationtide and Whitsuntide; the many special processions which were so often made for special objects. There were also the mummery of the "Boy Bishop" on the Feast of the Holy Innocents, and the women's feast at Hocktyde. The conclusion left upon the mind is that, wherever the Church was doing its duty, it was, in spite of grave defects, popular and influential with the people.

The later medieval Church.

Such was the Church in England at the close of the Middle Ages. It was immensely rich and immensely powerful; it had vested interests of enormous value; its prelates still occupied the highest positions in the State; its clergy formed a large, powerful and almost independent caste; its bishops and abbots dominated the House of Lords. In spite of flagrant abuses it was in many ways doing much good work, was possessed of considerable vitality, and still played a great part in the life of the nation. Money was still given with all the

[1] For a description of the service of Creeping to the Cross, and for those of Easter, see *Rights of Durham*, pp. 11, 12.

generosity of a former age for school or college or gild or parish church. Religious books were being multiplied. Heresy, though alive, was quiescent. Nor were the more highminded churchmen altogether blind to the signs of the times. Reform was in the air. Synod after synod condemned the ecclesiastical abuses of the age and suggested remedies. The best churchmen tried hard to make things better, but the evil was too deep-seated to be remedied in a day, being the result of a long period of demoralisation and decline. The truth is that the Church of the 15th century had been thoroughly corrupted by the degeneracy of the times, and that it had not risen superior to its surroundings. The history of the later Middle Ages in England is the history of decline—decline in literature, in learning, in architecture; decline in chivalry, in morals, in ideals; decline in all that was noblest and most inspiring in the best period of the Middle Ages. The ideals of the 13th century had long since vanished. The charm and the romance had departed, and war and pestilence had done their fatal work. England had been brutalised and demoralised by a long period of civil strife; by contending factions butchering and proscribing their opponents; by the fierce strife of rival claimants contending for the throne; by the failure of constitutional government; by the lawlessness which, as the *Paston Letters* show us, often made life intolerable for the poor and weak; and unfortunately the Church, instead of trying to correct the evil tendencies of the times, degenerated under the influence of the demoralisation of the age. Indeed, the Church had some responsibility for these troubles. It had been foolish enough to encourage the military ambition of Henry V, and to give its blessing to his unholy war with France. A terrible nemesis overtook it. When the Church allies with the world it may achieve a momentary success, but it cannot in the long run escape divine retribution; and in its loss of spiritual influence and its growing unpopularity the Church was rightly punished for its support of a war which brought untold miseries both to France and to England. It spoke with diminished force; it acted with a lowered prestige; and in spite of much energy and zeal, in spite of its highly organised system, in spite of its good works, it failed—failed to use its great opportunities, failed to correct its own abuses, failed to hold up to society a high standard of spiritual life. And for this failure how can it evade responsibility ?

Prospects of Christianity on the eve of the Reformation.

Christianity has rarely been at a lower ebb than during the latter half of the 15th century. It suffered both from internal weakness and external attack, and the prospect seemed even to the most hopeful dark indeed. The best churchmen were deeply depressed, for the end of Christianity itself seemed to be in sight. But just when things were at their worst the dawn began to break, and brighter prospects came in view. The borders of Christendom were being enlarged. The Moors were conquered in Spain, and the Peninsula became entirely Christian. Vast new continents were being discovered by Christians and claimed for their own religion. At the very time when the Mohammedans were pressing into Eastern Europe, Europeans were sailing westward. The darkest hour is always before the dawn ; and just when Christendom was being threatened by the Turk, just when its boundaries were being narrowed in Eastern Europe, just when humanism was breeding a spirit of infidelity which seemed likely to be fatal to religion, the New World was discovered, new possibilities and new opportunities were being presented, and the religion of Christ again found itself in a position to become world wide. The conditions of the new age, though they broke up the old ecclesiastical system, led to reform and brought fresh vitality to religion. Men became less tolerant of ecclesiastical abuses ; the unedifying lives of unworthy ecclesiastics began to provoke general disgust and open condemnation ; and a desire for reform animated the best men in the Church. Savonarola in Italy and Colet in England fearlessly attacked the evils of the day ; and when evils cease to be silently acquiesced in brighter days are at hand. The great work of Thomas à Kempis, *The Imitation of Christ*, was eagerly read, and over seventy editions were printed during the last thirty years of the 15th century. A new generation was growing up which was to bring a new spirit into the Church. Learning was becoming more widely diffused, and laymen were now taking that position in the State which had formerly belonged exclusively to the higher ecclesiastics. The abuses of the Church pressed heavily upon the laity, and it was these practical abuses which in the end made reformation inevitable. Dogma was attacked because it was believed that dogma formed the basis of the corruption and tyranny of the ecclesiastical system, and that until the dogmas upon which these rested were abolished no relief could be obtained. Luther in his attack upon the Papacy and all that it stood for was but voicing the general discontent and, more fortunate than Wycliffe or Huss, was aided by the conditions of the age—the printing press, the rise of nationalism, the disrepute into which the Renaissance Popes had brought the Papacy, the critical and disruptive tendencies of Italian humanism, the writings of Erasmus, of Brandt, of the author of the *Epistolæ obscurorum virorum*, which, now easily disseminated, employed the effective weapons of ridicule and satire to weaken and discredit the medieval ecclesiastical system. But though there were other contributory causes, it was practical abuses which lay at the root of the Reformation. Had the Pope left off pillaging Germany, the doctrine of justification by faith would have excited but a languid interest, and Luther's revolt, if it had not voiced widespread discontent, might have been local and temporary. Had the worst evils been voluntarily removed, had the Church effected a thorough reform in morals and insisted upon a higher standard of clerical life and duty, it is certain that the Reformation would have taken a very different form. But it did not. Institutions which are in need of reform must (like minorities) expect to suffer; but they would be wise to reform themselves from within; or they will certainly be violently revolutionised from without.[1]

[1] Though the Reformation would probably have taken a different course without the incentive of practical abuses, this must not blind us to the existence and influence of a deep vein of popular Protestantism. The connection between Lollardy and the Reformation has not yet been adequately or satisfactorily worked out and demands a separate monograph. There can be little doubt that, though repressed, Lollardy survived here and there all through the 15th century, and that the Protestant doctrines of the early part of the 16th century found in many places a soil very favourable for their growth. It is, however, very improbable that either Lollardy in England or the evangelical piety of German burghers, that either the personality of Luther or the power of Henry VIII could by themselves, unaided by deep-rooted popular grievances, have split Christendom and broken with the Papacy. For the survival and influence of Lollardy see the Episcopal Registers, e.g. *Reg. Stanbury*, p. 118 *seq.*; *Reg. Mylling*, pp. 65 *seq.*, 109; *Reg. Bubwith*, pp. lxiii–lxxi; Summers, *The Lollards of the Chiltern*

Hills; Deanesley, *The Lollard Bible*; Rashdall, *Universities*, II, 542; Gairdner, *Lollardy and the Reformation*, and the *Victoria County Histories*. Heresy is constantly mentioned in episcopal exhortations in the 15th century. Bishop Pecocke thought that it was due to a dearth of learned clergy able to expound and teach. For heresy in the reign of Henry VII see the extracts collected by Pollard, *Henry VII*, III, 234 *seq.*

APPENDIX

EPISCOPAL INCOMES FROM THE "VALOR ECCLESIASTICUS" IN THE ORDER OF VALUE

Winchester,	MMMDCCCiiij^{xx},	iij,	iij	(II, p. 2)
Canterbury,	MMMCCXXiij,	xviij,	viij	(I, pp. 1–7)
Durham,	MMDCCCXXj,	— ,	xvij	(V, pp. 299–300)
Ely,	MMCXXXiiij,	xviij,	v	(III, p. 499)
Lincoln,	MDCCCCLXij,	xvij,	iiij	(IV, pp. 1–7)
Bath and Wells,	MDCCCXLiij,	xiiij,	v	(I, pp. 121–3)
York,	MVj^{c}ix,	xix,	ij	(V, p. 1)
Exeter,	MDLXvj,	xiiij,	vj	(II, pp. 289–91)
Salisbury,	MCCCLXvij,	xij,	viij	(II, pp. 69–72)
London,	MCxix,	viij,	—	(I, pp. 356–7)
Worcester,	MXLix,	xvij,	iij	(III, pp. 217–20)
Norwich,	DCCCCLXXviiij,	xix,	iiij	(III, pp. 281–2)
Hereford,	DCCLXviiij,	x,	x	(III, pp. 1–4)
Coventry and Lichfield,	vii^{c}iij,	v,	ij	(III, pp. 128–30)
Chichester,	vi^{c}iii^{xx}jxvij,	— ,	xv	(I, pp. 293–4)
Carlisle,	DXXXXj,	iiij,	xj	(V, pp. 273–4)
Rochester,	CCCCXj,	— ,	xj	(I, pp. 99–100)
St. Asaph,	ciiij^{xx}vij,	vj,	vj	(IV, pp. 433–4)
Llandaff,	CLiiij,	xiiij,	j	(IV, p. 345)
Bangor,	CXXXj,	xvj,	iij	(IV, pp. 415–16)

INDEX

A. = Archbishop. B. = Bishop. n. = note. dio. = diocese.

Printed in Great Britain at
The Mayflower Press, Plymouth. William Brendon & Son, Ltd.

ADENEY, Rev. J. H., M.A., Missionary to the Jews in Roumania.

THE JEWS OF EASTERN EUROPE. With four Illustrations. 3s. 6d.

ARNOLD-FORSTER, FRANCES, S.Th.

THE HYMN-BOOK OF THE CHURCH; or, THE GROWTH OF THE PSALTER. 8s.

BARRY, G. D., B.D.

THE INSPIRATION AND AUTHORITY OF HOLY SCRIPTURE. A Study in the literature of the first five centuries. 4s. 6d.

BELL, Rev. G. K. A., M.A. (Editor).

THE MEANING OF THE CREED. Papers on the Apostles' Creed. 7s. 6d.

BENSON, Edwin, B.A.

LIFE IN A MEDIÆVAL CITY ILLUSTRATED BY YORK IN THE FIFTEENTH CENTURY. With eight Illustrations. Paper, 4s.; cloth, 5s.

BIRKBECK, W. J., M.A., F.S.A.

BIRKBECK AND THE RUSSIAN CHURCH. Essays and Articles collected and edited by his friend, ATHELSTAN RILEY, M.A. With Portrait. 8s. 6d.

BROWNE, The Right Rev. G. F., D.D., formerly Bishop of Stepney and of Bristol.

THE VENERABLE BEDE. His Life and Writings. With Illustrations. 10s.

KING ALFRED'S BOOKS. Cloth boards. 30s.

THE IMPORTANCE OF WOMEN IN ANGLO-SAXON TIMES; THE CULTUS OF ST. PETER AND ST. PAUL, and other addresses. With two Illustrations. 7s. 6d.

CARPENTER, S. C., M.A., Fellow and Tutor of Selwyn College, Cambridge.

CHRISTIANITY ACCORDING TO ST. LUKE. 10s. 6d.

CARRINGTON, Philip, B.A.

CHRISTIAN APOLOGETICS OF THE SECOND CENTURY. 7s. 6d.

CUTTS, The late Rev. E. L., D.D.

TURNING POINTS OF ENGLISH CHURCH HISTORY. 3s. 6d.

TURNING POINTS OF GENERAL CHURCH HISTORY. 3s. 6d.

PARISH PRIESTS AND THEIR PEOPLE IN THE MIDDLE AGES IN ENGLAND. With numerous Illustrations. 7s. 6d.

DARRAGH, Rev. John T., D.D.

THE RESURRECTION OF THE FLESH. 18s.

DUCHESNE, Monsignore L.

CHRISTIAN WORSHIP. ITS ORIGIN AND EVOLUTION. A Study of the Latin Liturgy up to the Time of Charlemagne. Translated by M. L. McClure. Fifth Edition. 15s.

ELLIS, Harold, B.A.

CONFIRMATION INTERVIEWS. 7s. 6d.

FERRAR, W. John, M.A.

THE EARLY CHRISTIAN BOOKS. A short introduction to Christian Literature to the middle of the second century. 3s. 6d.

THE UNCANONICAL JEWISH BOOKS. A short Introduction to the Apocrypha and the Jewish Writings 200 B.C. to A.D. 100. 3s. 6d.

FIELD, John Edward, M.A.

THE ENGLISH LITURGIES OF 1549 AND 1661 COMPARED WITH EACH OTHER AND WITH THE ANCIENT LITURGIES. 12s. 6d.

FLETCHER, J. S., Member of the Yorkshire Archæological Society.

THE CISTERCIANS IN YORKSHIRE. With Seven Illustrations by Warwick Goble, and a facsimile from the Chronicles of Meaux. 17s. 6d.

FOXELL, W. J., M.A.

THE TEMPTATION OF JESUS. A Study. 6s. 6d.

GEDEN, Rev. A. S., D.D.

COMPARATIVE RELIGION. 3s. 6d.

GOUDGE, H. L., D.D.

THREE LECTURES ON THE EPISTLE TO THE EPHESIANS. 3s. 6d

GREENWOOD, Alice Drayton, F.R.Hist.Soc.

HISTORY OF THE PEOPLE OF ENGLAND. The BEDE HISTORIES. Edited by Miss H. L. POWELL, St. Mary's College, Lancaster Gate.
Vol. I.—55 B.C. to A.D. 1485. With 27 Illustrations and 15 Maps. 8s. 6d.
Vol. II.—1485-1689. 7s. 6d.

HANDCOCK, P. S. P., M.A., Lecturer of the Palestine Exploration Fund.

THE LATEST LIGHT ON BIBLE LANDS. Second Edition, revised. With numerous Illustrations. 6s.

HARDEN, J. M., B.D., LL.D.

DICTIONARY OF THE VULGATE NEW TESTAMENT. 4s.

HARDWICK, John Charlton.

RELIGION AND SCIENCE. From Galileo to Bergson. 8s.

HARDY, Rev. T. J., M.A.

SPIRITISM IN THE LIGHT OF THE FAITH. A Comparison and a Contrast. 3s.

HASLEHURST, R. S. T., B.D.

THE PENITENTIAL DISCIPLINE OF THE EARLY CHURCH IN THE FIRST FOUR CENTURIES. 5s.

HIGGINBOTTOM, Sam, M.A.

THE GOSPEL AND THE PLOW; or, The Old Gospel and Modern Farming in Ancient India. 5s.

HOLLOWAY, Henry, M.A., B.D.

THE REFORMATION IN IRELAND. A Study of Ecclesiastical Legislation. 7s. 6d.

HOPE, The late Sir William St. John, Litt.D., Hon. D.C.L., Durham, and ATCHLEY, E. G. Cuthbert, F., L.R.C.P. Lond.

ENGLISH LITURGICAL COLOURS. With a Coloured Frontispiece. 25s.

ENGLISH LITURGICAL COLOURS, An Introduction to. 3s. 6d.

HUMPHREYS, Arthur James, B.A., D.D.

CHRISTIAN MORALS. Cloth boards. 4s.

JENKINSON, Wilberforce.

LONDON CHURCHES BEFORE THE GREAT FIRE. Illustrated by twenty reproductions in collotype, from old prints and drawings, by Mr. EMERY WALKER. 15s.

KELLY, The Rev. Alfred Davenport, M.A., Society of the Sacred Mission.

VALUES OF THE CHRISTIAN LIFE. With a Preface by the Right Rev. WILLIAM TEMPLE. 7s. 6d.

KIDD, B. J., D.D. (Editor).

DOCUMENTS ILLUSTRATIVE OF THE HISTORY OF THE CHURCH. Vol. I. To A.D. 313. 7s. 6d.

LUCE, A. A., M.C., B.D.

MONOPHYSITISM PAST AND PRESENT. 7s. 6d.

MACKEAN, W. H., D.D.

CHRISTIAN MONASTICISM IN EGYPT TO THE CLOSE OF THE FOURTH CENTURY. 8s.

MACLEAN, The Right Rev. Arthur J., D.D., Bishop of Moray, Ross, and Caithness.

RECENT DISCOVERIES ILLUSTRATING EARLY CHRISTIAN LIFE AND WORSHIP. Second Edition, revised. 2s. 6d.

MARTIN, Edward J., B.D., formerly Scholar of Oriel College, Oxford.

THE EMPEROR JULIAN. An Essay on his relations with the Christian Religion. 3s. 6d.

MAY, G. Lacey, M.A.

SOME EIGHTEENTH-CENTURY CHURCHMEN. Glimpses of English Church Life in the Eighteenth Century. With several Illustrations. 9s.

MERCER, The Right Rev. J. E., D.D.

THE PROBLEM OF CREATION. An attempt to define the Character and Trend of the Cosmic Process. 7s. 6d.

MINISTRY OF WOMEN, THE. A Report by a Committee appointed by the LORD ARCHBISHOP OF CANTERBURY. With Appendices and fifteen Collotype Illustrations. 12s. 6d.

MORISON, The Rev. E. F., D.D.

THE LORD'S PRAYER AND THE PRAYERS OF OUR LORD. A Scriptural Exposition. 3s. 6d.

MOZLEY, The Rev. J. K., B.D.

THE ACHIEVEMENTS OF CHRISTIANITY. 2s. 6d.

OESTERLEY, W. O. E., M.A., D.D.

IMMORTALITY AND THE UNSEEN WORLD. A study in Old Testament religion. 12s. 6d.

OESTERLEY, W. O. E., D.D., and BOX, G. H., D.D.

A SHORT SURVEY OF THE LITERATURE OF RABBINICAL AND MEDIÆVAL JUDAISM. 12s. 6d.

TRANSLATIONS OF EARLY DOCUMENTS. A Series of texts important for the study of Christian origins.

Twenty-four volumes of this series have now appeared. The *Book of Enoch* is the best known of the documents, but all deserve the attention of students.

PAGE, Jesse, F.R.G.S.

SCHWARTZ OF TANJORE. With Photogravure Frontispiece, Map, and six Illustrations. 7s. 6d.

PAKENHAM-WALSH, Herbert, D.D., Bishop in Assam.

DIVINE HEALING. Paper, 1s. 3d. ; cloth, 2s. 6d.

PARRY, The Right Rev. O. H., D.D., Bishop of Guiana.

THE PILGRIM IN JERUSALEM. With numerous Illustrations. 10s.

PEACOCK, Alice Evelyn, M.B.E.

THE DELIGHTFUL JOYS OF HEAVEN. 6s. 6d.

PEARCE, Ernest Harold, Litt.D., F.S.A., Bishop of Worcester.

WALTER DE WENLOK, Abbot of Westminster. With a Frontispiece. 12s

POOLE, Reginald Lane.

ILLUSTRATIONS OF THE HISTORY OF MEDIÆVAL THOUGHT AND LEARNING. Second Edition, revised. 17s. 6d.

REICHEL, The Rev. O. J.

THE CANON LAW OF CHURCH INSTITUTIONS. Vol. I. 10s. 6d.

STOKES, The Rev. H. P., LL.D., Litt.D., F.S.A.

A SHORT HISTORY OF THE JEWS IN ENGLAND. With eight Illustrations. 5s. 6d.

STURGE, M. Carta, Moral Sciences Tripos, Cambridge.

THEOSOPHY AND CHRISTIANITY. A Comparison. Second Edition. 2s.

SWEET, Charles F.

NEW LIFE IN THE OLDEST EMPIRE. [Japan.] 6s.

SWETE, The late Rev. Henry Barclay, D.D., D.Litt.

THE LIFE OF THE WORLD TO COME. With a Portrait. 3s.

SWINSTEAD, The Rev. J. Howard, D.D.

THE SWEDISH CHURCH AND OURS. With two Illustrations. 6s. 6d.

WATSON, Herbert A., D.D.

THE INCARNATION AND PERSONALITY. 9s.

WESTLAKE, H. F., M.A., F.S.A.

THE PARISH GILDS OF MEDIÆVAL ENGLAND. With six Illustrations. 15s.

WILLIAMS, The Rev. N. P.

THE FIRST EASTER MORNING. Paper, 2s. 6d.; Cloth, 3s. 6d.

WILSON, The Rev. James M., D.D., Canon and Vice-Dean.

THE WORCESTER LIBER ALBUS. Glimpses of Life in a Great Benedictine Monastery in the Fourteenth Century. With a collotype facsimile. 15s.

WOOD, Percival, M.R.C.S., L.R.C.P.

MOSES: THE FOUNDER OF PREVENTIVE MEDICINE. 4s.

WRIGHT, The Rev. Leslie, M.A., B.D.

THE EUCHARISTIC OFFICE OF THE BOOK OF COMMON PRAYER. 3s. 6d.

YOUNG, The Rev. P. N. F., M.A., and FERRERS, Agnes.

INDIA IN CONFLICT. 3s. 6d.

ZWEMER, Samuel M., F.R.G.S.

THE INFLUENCE OF ANIMISM ON ISLAM. An account of popular superstition. With twelve Illustrations. 10s.

JOHN COLET, DEAN OF ST. PAUL'S

To face p. 112